AMERICAN
X&Y PLANES
Volume I: Experimental Aircraft to 1945

Other titles in the Crowood Aviation Series

AMERICAN
X&Y PLANES

Volume I: Experimental Aircraft to 1945

Kev Darling

The Crowood Press

First published in 2009 by
The Crowood Press Ltd
Ramsbury, Marlborough
Wiltshire SN8 2HR

www.crowood.com

© Kev Darling 2009

British Library Cataloguing-in-Publication Data
A catalogue record for this book is available from the British
Library.

ISBN 978 1 84797 141 8

Typeset by Servis Filmsetting Ltd, Stockport, Cheshire
Printed and bound in India by Replika Press

Contents

Introduction

No matter where you look in the annals of aviation history, it is littered with strange and wonderful aircraft, many of which were evolutionary dead ends. The American aircraft industry was no exception as it first attempted to catch up and then overtook the rest of the world in aircraft development. Along the way, problems were encountered; many were circumvented successfully, but there were some bloopers along the way that resulted in some exceptionally dangerous machines being constructed.

When swept wings and jet engines became available the armed forces of the USA appeared to go mad as contracts were issued for aircraft that in reality had no chance of entering service. However, many of these aircraft led to the development of useful aircraft types – one of Convair's many elegant experimental aircraft was the XF-92A that finally led to the F-102. In competition with Convair, the Glenn L. Martin Company were definitely in the 'losers can be winners' category. Their XB-51 bomber for the USAF was rejected in favour of the English Electric Canberra, but by way of compensation Martin was awarded a contract to build the USAF's Canberras, as the Martin B-57.

Not all of the American manufacturers could be winners, as the demise of Curtiss shows. One of the pioneers of aviation in the USA, Curtiss did not survive long after 1945, as they seemed unable to compete in any field of aviation and were forced to close. Subsequently the American aviation industry has shrunk to a handful of aviation conglomerates. They now use extensive computer modelling to develop their new products: although this helps in reducing development costs, it does mean that the chances of strange aeronautical creations appearing in the skies today are remote.

This book could not have been written without the help of others, including my good friend Dennis R. Jenkins who put me in contact with many of the organizations mentioned and also did much research on my behalf. As ever, Air Britain played its part in filling in those small but vital pieces.

Kev Darling
Wales, 2009

CHAPTER ONE

The Aviation Roots of America

When the US Navy and the US Army returned home from Europe at the end of the Great War in November 1918 they were fully confident in the design and production of ships for the navy and the equipment for the army. One area, however, in which the USA was sadly lacking was aviation: exposure to the burgeoning British and European aircraft industries had revealed that the USA had a lot of catching up to do.

It was the United States Army who encouraged the USA's first steps in flying. Their first sponsorship took place in 1898 when they provided $50,000 to Samuel P. Langley for the development of a man-powered flying machine.

The first step in this process was to successfully fly a quarter-scale model in 1901, followed by a full-size machine named the 'Aerodrome'. The two flight trials of this machine took place off the Potomac River during October and November 1903: they were a failure. This caused a furore in Congress, the press and amongst the public, as the aircraft and its development had been paid for out of public funding. Having been bitten by the failure of the Langley experiment, the US Army was loath to become involved in further aviation programmes, even though the Wright brothers had successfully flown their aircraft at Kill Devil Hills on 17 December 1903. The Wright 'Flyer'

The start of it all: the Wright Flyer on an early flight from Kitty Hawk, North Carolina.
via LOC/Dennis R. Jenkins

introduced the first vestiges of proper flight controls for roll, pitch and yaw, as well as a reasonably reliable engine and fuel supply.

Over the next four years the US Army resisted all attempts to become involved in aviation, and it was only the intervention of President Theodore Roosevelt that swung the services' opinion. The US Army established an Aeronautical Division on 1 August 1907; this, the first Army organization dedicated to supporting heavier-than-air flying, being part of the Office of the Chief Signal Officer of the US Army. Its first commanding officer was Captain Charles de Forrest Chandler, who had a staff of two enlisted men. On 10 February 1908, the Army was encouraged by the President to accept a tender from the Wright brothers for $25,000 to build a single military aircraft that could carry two persons at a maximum speed of 40mph, and the Aeronautical Division accepted the Wright Model A at Fort Myers, near Washington, DC, on 2 August 1909. The Model A remained the Division's only aircraft for the next two years, during which time the first Army Air Base was established at College Park, Maryland. At this base with their single aircraft the first two aviators for the US Army graduated.

The Army gained further funding from Congress in Fiscal Year 1912, allowing the service to purchase further aircraft. This allowed the formation of the 1st Aero Squadron at Texas City, Texas on 5 March 1913; this was the first US Army air combat unit. Commanded by Captain de Forrest Chandler, the squadron was equipped with a mixture of Curtiss JN2 and JN3 machines, better known as 'Jennys'. The day-to-day management of the unit was vested in Lt Thomas D. Milling.

War with Mexico

The creation of the squadron had been precipitated by the possibility of war with Mexico, then under the rule of General Victoriano Huerta. The initial threat of war receded, allowing the 1st Aero Squadron to relocate to North Island, California on 28 November 1913. At its new base the squadron acted as the Army flying training unit, for which purpose it acquired aircraft provided by Burgess, Curtiss, Martin and Wright. It did, however, send a detachment to Fort Crockett, Texas, in April 1914 in response to the Tampico Affair. This incident – which started as a fracas between some US Navy sailors and Mexican soldiers – and its subsequent fallout saw relations between Mexico and the USA strained almost to breaking point, while the Mexican revolution played in the background. Another detachment was sent to Brownsville in March 1915 in response to the civil war that had broken out in Mexico between Pancho Villa and the government of Venustiano Carranza.

On 29 July 1915 the entire complement of the 1st Aero Squadron was packed aboard a train and shipped to Fort Sill, Oklahoma in order to learn artillery spotting. At the completion of this training the 1st Aero Squadron transferred to Fort Sam Houston, near San Antonio, Texas on 15 November 1915.

The 1st Aero Squadron first saw action in

The Curtiss Jenny series of aircraft were the foundation for the flying services of the USA. Here a JN4 awaits its pilot at an unknown training school. via NARA/Dennis R. Jenkins

March 1916 when Mexican forces attacked Columbus, New Mexico, and its resident unit, the 13th Calvary. The US Army sent a force under the command of General Pershing with the air unit in support. Right from the outset there were problems with the Curtiss aircraft: not only were they unable to climb over the mountains, but dust storms grounded the aircraft and the heat delaminated the wooden propellers. Despite this they did provide some useful service, moving despatches and performing reconnaissance and liaison duties. During this period three aircraft crashed and four were grounded to provide spares, leaving two aircraft in service. Further Curtiss machines were supplied to make up the shortfall but, although improved, they too proved to be inadequate.

World War One

The USA declared war on Germany on 16 April 1917. The 1st Aero Squadron was supposed to have shipped out to Europe with the initial deployment of the 1st Army Division, but was delayed and had to make its own way to France. As the air unit was untested and untried over Europe, it was sent to a quiet part of the front. During the winter period of 1917/18 the squadron was based at Avord, flying a mix of Curtiss AR-1s, Spad XIIIs and Salmson 2 observation aircraft; whilst based at Avord, Lt Stephen Thompson

achieved the first aerial victory for the US Army Air Corps. With the end of the war, the squadron returned to the USA in 1919. While units were being despatched overseas the core of the air component was divorced on 20 May 1918 through the Overman Act, the result of which was the creation of the Division of Military Aeronautics and the Bureau of Aircraft Production; the latter was responsible for aircraft procurement, supply and training. Both of the departments would become known as the Air Service. The units despatched to Europe would become known as the American Expeditionary Force of the Air Service, this in turn being sub divided into the 1st, 2nd and 3rd Army components in November 1918.

By 18 July 1914 an enlarged Aviation Section of the Signal Corps had been created, of which the 1st Aero Squadron became part. Starting with a strength of sixty officers and 260 enlisted personnel, the Aviation Section had expanded to include seven squadrons by the time the USA entered the war. The 1st, 3rd, 4th and 5th Squadrons were based in America, the 2nd in the Philippines, and the 6th and 7th in Panama. These seven squadrons expanded to forty-five by the time of the Armistice, while others were either training or under formation. While units were being despatched overseas the core of the air component was divorced on 20 May 1918 through the Overman Act, the result of which was the creation of the Division of Military Aeronautics and

---

Salmson 2

Crew: 2
Length: 8.5m (27ft 10½in)
Wingspan: 11.75m (38ft 6½in)
Height: 2.9m (9ft 6in)
Wing area: 37.27m² (401ft²)
Empty weight: 780kg (1,716lb)
Loaded weight: 1,290kg (2,838lb)
Powerplant: 1 × Salmson 9Za, 172kW (230hp)

Performance
Maximum speed: 188km/h (101kt, 116mph) at sea level
Range: 500km (270nm, 310 miles)
Service ceiling: 6,250m (20,500ft)

Armament
1 × forward synchronized 0.303in Vickers machine gun
2 × rear, ring-mounted 0.303in Lewis Guns

Spad XIII

Crew: 1
Length: 6.25m (20ft 6in)
Wingspan: 8.25m (27ft 1in)
Height: 2.60m (8ft 6.5in)
Wing area: 21.1m² (227ft²)
Empty weight: 566kg (1,245lb)
Loaded weight: 856kg (1,888lb)
Max. take-off weight: 845kg (1,863lb)
Powerplant: 1 × Hispano-Suiza 8Be 8 cylinder vee-type, 220hp (164kW)

Performance
Maximum speed: 218km/h (135mph)
Service ceiling: 6,650 m (21,815ft)
Rate of climb: 2m/s (384ft/min)

Armament
Guns: 2 × 0.303in Vickers machine guns

As the Air Service lacked American-built fighters for combat over the Western Front, its units were equipped with the French-built Spad XIII. via NARA/Dennis R. Jenkins

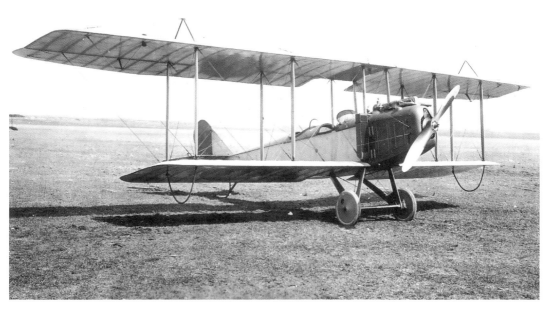

This unmarked Curtiss JN-4 still requires its colour doping before delivery to the US Army. via NARA/Dennis R. Jenkins

The Jenny was extensively used by both the US Army and Navy to train their tyro aviators.
via NARA/Dennis R. Jenkins

the Bureau of Aircraft Production; the latter was responsible for aircraft procurement, supply and training. Both of the departments would become known as the Air Service. The units despatched to Europe would become known as the American Expeditionary Force of the Air Service, this in turn being sub divided into the 1st, 2nd and 3rd Army components in November 1918.

The Air Service returned to Army control under the Army Reorganization Act of 4 June 1920, and the United States Army Air Corps (USAAC) came into existence under the Air Corps Act of 2 July 1926; this state of affairs continued until 1948, when the fully independent United States Air Force (USAF) was created.

After the war the United States armed forces – like those of the other combatant nations –

suffered as successive governments struggled to provide money to implement social programmes and recover from the war effort. With little money available, the Air Service had to fall back on the aircraft already in service, as little funding could be spared to procure new aircraft and equipment.

Curtiss

One of the companies that helped develop the American aircraft industry and, in turn, US Army aviation was the Curtiss Aeroplane and Motor Company. The founder, Glenn H. Curtiss, had been born on 21 May 1878 in Hammondsport, New York. As with many youngsters, Curtiss received a formal education only until his early teen years.

After front-line usage some Curtiss JN-4s were allocated to an infant NACA for test and evaluation purposes as shown here.
via NASA/ Dennis R. Jenkins

Curtiss had a feeling for and fascination with mechanical engineering that gained him employment at Eastman Dry Plate and Film Company, now better known as Kodak. By 1898 Curtiss was involved in the bicycle trade and later he caught the motorcycle bug. His first contribution to this new method of transport was not only a bike, but also the motor needed to power it. Although Curtiss had established himself as a motorcycle manufacturer and, in 1906, a speed record holder, his perspective on transport changed again when he visited the Wright brothers and discussed with them aircraft and aero-engines. In 1907 he was persuaded by Alexander Graham Bell to join Aerial Experimental Association with the intention of building a heavier-than-air machine. This made its first flight on 4 June 1908 and was named the 'June Bug'. While he was congratulated by many for this success, gaining the first American pilot's licence in the process, Curtiss found himself involved in a long-running patent lawsuit with the Wright brothers.

The legal wrangles notwithstanding, Curtiss increased his public profile by flying from Albany along the Hudson River to New York, which won him a prize of $10,000 offered by publisher Joseph Pulitzer. Having arrived over New York, Curtiss then flew over Manhattan and even had the temerity to circle the Statue of Liberty. This success interested the US Navy in aviation and its possible fleet applications. In response, Curtiss set up a small manufacturing facility in San Diego where the first Model 'D' was constructed. On 14 November 1910, Eugene Ely of the US Navy became the first person to take off from a ship, flying a Model D from the cruiser USS *Birmingham*.

Curtiss Model D

Crew: 1
Capacity: 1 passenger
Length: 29ft 3in (8.92m)
Wingspan: 38ft 3in (11.66m)
Height: 7ft 10in (2.39m)
Empty weight: 700lb (318kg)
Loaded weight: 1,300lb (590kg)
Powerplant: 1 × Curtiss E-4 V8 engine, 60hp (45kW)

Performance
Maximum speed: 43kt (50mph, 80km/h)

Curtiss now turned his attention to the US Army, which was in the process of acquiring a Wright biplane. His response was to produce the famous 'Jenny' series of biplanes. The roots of this famous series of aircraft were in Britain, where Curtiss hired the designer/engineer Douglas Thomas from A.V. Roe to design a tractor biplane of the kind that had become the standard in Britain. The first design was the 'J', much of which was completed in Britain, and was followed by the 'N' design. Both models was combined later to create the 'JN', better known as the Jenny. The US Army tested a mix of both types during 1914, the result of which was an order for eight JN-2 aircraft with equal-span wings and a pair of JN-3s with extended upper mainplanes; the JN-2s were later fitted with JN-3 wings.

Having got used to operating the Jenny, the Army began large-scale procurement in 1916 when ninety-four JN-4s were purchased; these were controlled using a control wheel instead of a column. Although the early Jennys suffered from some problems while supporting General Pershing in the Mexican conflict, they were considered good enough to act as trainers for the US Army and were exported to the Royal Flying Corps in Britain. The Curtiss JN series was also one of the first aircraft to be manufactured by subcontractors: the Standard Aircraft Corporation and the Canadian Aeroplane Corporation of Toronto, the latter's output being known as 'Canucks'.

In the closing year of the war Curtiss began building experimental aircraft to trial various improvements. The first of these was the JN-4C, which trialled British 'RAF.6' aerofoils. Also during the war, the patent wrangle between Curtiss and the Wright brothers was concluded as the Wrights pulled out of aircraft manufacture

---

Curtiss JN-4

Crew: 2
Length: 27ft 4in (8.33m)
Wingspan: 43ft 7¾in (13.3m)
Height: 9ft 10½in (3.01m)
Wing area: 352ft² (32.7m²)
Empty weight: 1,390lb (630kg)
Max. take-off weight: 1,920lb (871kg)
Powerplant: 1 × Curtiss OX-5 Inline piston, 90hp (67kW)

Performance
Maximum speed: 65kt (75mph, 121km/h)
Cruise speed: 52kt (60mph, 97km/h)
Service ceiling: 6,500ft (2,000m)

Wright Model A
Crew: 2
Length: 30ft 8in (9.3m)
Wingspan: 36ft 5in (11.1m)
Height: 8ft (2.43m)
Empty weight: 740lb (336kg)
Loaded weight: 1,263lb (573kg)
Powerplant: 1 × Wright Model 4,30hp (22kW)
Performance
Maximum speed: 42mph (67.6km/h)

to concentrate upon engines instead. Eventually, in 1929, the assets of the Wright Aeronautical Corporation was merged with Curtiss to form the Curtiss-Wright Corporation.

Developments by the Wright Brothers

Having successfully made their first flight in December 1903, the Wright brothers formed a slew of companies to promote their aeronautical products: France had an office in 1908, Germany and the USA in 1909, and Britain in 1913. Originally the company was named Wright and Company; in 1916 it was merged with the Glenn L. Martin Company to form the Wright-Martin Aeronautical Corporation,

although Martin resigned in 1917. Other engineers departed at this point to form the Pratt and Whitney Corporation.

Prior to merging with the Martin Corporation the Wright Company had produced a handful of designs, many of which were purchased by the US Army. The first type delivered to the Army was the Model A, which was purchased at a cost of $25,000 including bonus and penalty clauses related to the aircraft's performance. After flight demonstrations at Fort Myers in 1908, the Model A underwent a thorough flight testing before being accepted for service.

Very much a development machine not only for aviation in general, but also for the Wright brothers, the Model A was subject to various trials. One of these included fitting slightly larger pusher propellers that were test-flown by Orville Wright with Lt Thomas Selfridge as the passenger. These slightly bigger propellers caused excessive vibration in a diagonal bracing wire, which fouled one of the propellers. In the resulting crash Selfridge was killed and Wright was injured. The aircraft itself was rebuilt and returned to US Army ownership the following year. Unlike many prototype and development machines the Model

After the Flyer had proven that the aircraft was viable, the company delivered similar machines to the embryo Air Service. This version used a single engine to drive the propellers via chains. via LOC/Dennis R. Jenkins

A survived, and is on display to this day at the Smithsonian Institution.

The Wright Model A was followed by the Models B and C. These were a complete revamp of the original design in which the elevators were relocated to the rear of the aircraft and a wheeled landing gear replaced the original skid assembly. Both models retained the original wing warping with two-lever controls, and the chain-driven propellers behind the wings. Only two Model Bs were constructed; they were used as trainers even though the instructor and pupil had to share some controls. The seven Model Cs had fully duplicated controls, but were otherwise similar to the earlier machine.

Following on from these open-framework aircraft, the Wright Brothers developed the Model F. This aircraft retained the rear-mounted flight surfaces introduced with the B and C, but the open fuselage framework was replaced by an enclosed fuselage. The engine was an Austro-Daimler of 90hp that drove a pair of pusher propellers, while flight control was still by wing warping. An improved version, the HS, featured a 60hp Wright engine with wings of a shorter span. This machine was tested by the US Army at San Diego but was not purchased.

The final aircraft built under the Wright name was the Wright-Martin Model R. In 1916 the Glenn L. Martin company combined with the Simplex Automobile Company and the General Aeronautical Corporation to form the Wright-Martin Company, whose factory was located at Los Angeles. The first two Model Rs were completed under the Curtiss name while the remaining twelve of the Army contract were delivered under the Wright-Martin name.

Burgess

Founded in 1910, the Burgess Company, originally known as Burgess Company and Curtis Inc., after the founders W. Starling Burgess and Greeley S. Curtis, was an offshoot of the W. Starling Burgess Shipyard of Marblehead, Massachusetts. The company became the first licensed aircraft manufacturer in the United States when it began building and selling Wright aircraft under licence in February 1911. The addition of pontoons to the Wright Model F improved sales, but this deviation from the original design infringed

---

Burgess Model D

Crew: 1
Capacity: 1 passenger
Length: 29ft 3in (8.92m)
Wingspan: 38ft 3in (11.66m)
Height: 7ft 10in (2.39m)
Empty weight: 700lb (318kg)
Loaded weight: 1,300lb (590kg)
Powerplant: 1 × Curtiss E-4 V8 engine, 60hp (45kW)

Performance
Maximum speed: 43kt (50mph, 80km/h)

---

the original Wright patent, and the manufacturing agreement between the two companies was terminated in January 1914.

The company now changed its name to the Burgess Company, to avoid confusion with the Curtiss Aeroplane and Engine Company; however, Greeley Curtis continued as chief shareholder and treasurer. While Curtis managed the money, Burgess as the chief designer developed and manufactured aircraft, production operations at the Marblehead plant being managed by Frank Russell. With all its manufacturing and financial elements in place, the Burgess Company was acquired by the Curtiss Aeroplane and Engine Company in February 1914. As a Curtiss subsidiary, it manufactured Curtiss seaplanes for military use. The company remained active until its manufacturing premises were destroyed by fire in November 1918.

During the existence of the Burgess Company it produced the Herring-Burgess Model A; this was a joint effort with Augustus Herring, who was responsible for the controls and powerplant. This was followed by the Burgess Model B, which was purchased by the US Army as the BP trainer in 1916. A series of Wright-licensed machines was then manufactured: these were the Wright Models B and C, which Burgess designated the F and J, respectively. These were followed by the Model D, a license-built Curtiss Model D. The Burgess H followed for the US Army and Navy, and the Navy also purchased the HT-2 Speed Scout. The Burgess I Scout was a single floatplane that drew on the company's Wright experience; it was purchased by the US Army for use in the Philippines and was lost in a crash in 1915.

These small orders were followed by Burgess H trainers, of which six were purchased by the US

One of the first aircraft built by the Curtiss Aircraft Company was the Model E flying boat, which led to an extensive range of similar machines.
via NARA/Dennis R. Jenkins

Army. These were multi-purpose machines that could be converted from landplanes to seaplanes by the simple expedient of removing the wheels and bolting floats on instead. This model still retained the Wright wing-warping method for roll control and featured a tail skid, although this was mainly to protect the rudders. Problems with the engines and the handling of these aircraft – and the similar behaviour of the Wright and Curtiss aircraft – at the Army Aviation Training School at North Island, San Diego, meant that the School gained an undeserved reputation for being dangerous.

In an effort to sort out these problems, four of the Burgess aircraft were handed over to Grover C. Loening in San Diego for rebuilding. The engine and basic fuselage were retained, but the wing warping was replaced by ailerons and handling was improved by replacing the original control by a control column. The twin rudders were replaced by an enlarged single unit mounted onto a single fixed fin. The undercarriage became a cross-axle unit, which was patented by Loening and became a popular choice for many subsequent aircraft. These modifications resulted in a much better-behaved aircraft.

The final aircraft manufactured under the Burgess banner was the unique Burgess-Dunne Tailless aircraft – a radical approach for any period in aviation history. This most different of biplanes was designed in Britain, and a single landplane example was constructed by Burgess for evaluation at San Diego. The Dunne design featured a pusher engine and propeller. Its wings were severely swept: this put the elevators aft of the centre of gravity, which in turn gave the aircraft longitudinal stability.

Loening

Born in Bremen, Germany, on 12 September 1888, Grover Cleveland Loening, son of the American consul to Germany, is very much the unsung hero of the American aircraft industry. After returning to the USA Grover Loening proved to be a more than able scholar, graduating from Colombia University in 1910 with the nation's first degree in aeronautics. After graduation Loening joined the Queen Aeroplane Company in New York where he gained experience in aircraft construction, building Bleriot aircraft for exhibition pilots. Returning to university, Loening published the book *Monoplanes and Biplanes* in 1915 as part of his Masters thesis. His second book, *Military Aeroplanes*, later became a standard work in the US Army, the Royal Flying Corps, the US Navy and many others. After a short period managing the Wright brothers' manufacturing facility at Dayton, Loening moved to the Sturdevant Aeroplane Company where he became vice president and was involved in

---

Loening Model 8

Crew: 2
Length: 21ft 6in (6.6m)
Wingspan: 32ft 9in (9.98m)
Gross weight: 2,068lb (938kg)
Powerplant: 1 × Hispano-Suiza V-8 engine, 300hp (224kW)

Performance
Maximum speed: 145mph (233km/h)

Armament
Twin 0.3in Lewis machine guns

This aircraft was designed and built by the Grover Loening Aircraft Company. The PW2 was a single-seat monoplane that seemed destined for an Army career until the wings came off an early production example, resulting in the cancellation of the contract. via NARA/Dennis R. Jenkins

pioneering the first American aircraft with a steel framework.

Two years later Loening left Sturdevant to form the Loening Aeronautical Engineering Corporation. This company developed and manufactured a small aircraft for the US Navy for shipboard use, followed by the M-8 two-seat pursuit (fighter) aircraft for the Army, which featured rigid wing-strut bracing. At the cessation of hostilities the company produced the five-seater Loening Flying Yacht. Not only was this aircraft successful in setting world records, it also started the push for private ownership and operation by civilian pilots; for this work Loening was awarded the Collier Trophy in 1921. After the Yacht the company marketed the Amphibian. This featured a retractable undercarriage and was used by the US Army, Navy, Marines and Coast Guard, as well as by airlines and private owners throughout the world. Among its many achievements was the famous Pan American goodwill flight of 1926.

After the company merged with the Keystone Corporation in 1928, Loening left to form the Grover Loening Aircraft Company; this company was involved in building various research and development prototypes for both the military and the National Advisory Committee on Aeronautics (NACA), the forerunner of NASA.

In 1937 Loening sold up, the final remnants of his company being subsumed into the Curtiss-Wright empire. In 1937 Loening became a member of NACA and, in 1942, the chief consultant to the War Production Board. Although no longer involved directly with aircraft design and manufacture, he guided various aircraft companies along the path of producing development prototypes in concert with their prospective purchasers.

After the war ended in 1945 Loening remained involved with aviation. When the National Air Museum was founded in 1948, President Truman selected him as the first of two civilian members for its advisory board, an appointment renewed by Presidents Eisenhower, Kennedy and Johnson. He was awarded the Medal for Merit in 1946, Columbia University's Eggleston Medal in 1949, the Wright Memorial Trophy in 1950, the Air Force Medal in 1955, and the Guggenheim Medal in 1960 for a lifetime devoted to the development of aeronautics in America. In 1966 he was awarded the Silver Wings plaque by that organization of aviators. This doyen of aviation pioneers died in Florida on 29 February 1976.

Thomas-Morse

Great Britain provided further impetus to the American aviation industry in the shape of William T. and Oliver W. Thomas, both of whom had been born and raised in Bath. Arriving in the USA, William joined Curtiss and Oliver General electric, both being based in New York. William was very much the aeroplane enthusiast, designing his first aircraft in 1909. The following year he left Curtiss with their blessing to form his own aircraft manufacturing company, the Thomas Bros. Airplane Company. Initially based at Hammondsport, the operation moved to the Hornell/Canisteo area to undertake flight testing of William's first aircraft. The sojourn at Hornell was short as the company moved again later that year to Bath, New York, close to Lake Salubria.

Having finally settled, the company invested in the Kirkham engine, whose first application was in the Thomas Headless Pusher. Test flying was undertaken by a close friend, Walter Johnson, who was also a Curtiss employee and pilot. In 1911 Oliver finally left General Electric to join William on a full-time basis. After a three-year stay at Bath, the Thomas company made their final move to Ithica, also close to New York. By this time the company was engaged in building its T-2 seaplane for the Royal Naval Air Service, a total of twenty-four being delivered; another

Thomas-Morse MB-3
Crew: 1
Length: 20ft 0in (6.10m)
Wingspan: 26ft 0in (7.92m)
Height: 8ft 7in (2.59m)
Wing area: 229ft² (21.28m²)
Empty weight: 1,716lb (778kg)
Loaded weight: 2,539lb (1,151kg)
Powerplant: 1 × Wright H Vee, 300hp (217kW)
Performance
Maximum speed: 141mph (228km/h)
Cruise speed: 125mph (201km/h)
Range: 280 miles (455km)
Service ceiling 19,500ft (5,950m)
Rate of climb: 1,235ft/min (6.3m/s)
Armament
2 × fixed forward-firing 0.30in machine guns or 1 × 0.30in and 1 × 0.50in machine guns or 2 × fixed-forward-firing 0.50in machine guns

fifteen, fitted with floats and designated the SH-4, were delivered to the US Navy between 1915 and 1916. The company also built a single two-seat aircraft, the D-5, for US Army evaluation.

In 1917 the company was in need of a bigger manufacturing facility to keep up with its contracts and the financial capital to fund it. The

The first fighter aircraft delivered to the Air Service was the Thomas-Morse MB-3, which owed much of its design to the Spad XIII. via NARA/Dennis R. Jenkins

answer was to merge with the Morse Chain Company, the new organization becoming the Thomas-Morse Aircraft Corporation; this new company also operated a flying school and an engine development company. In its new guise the company used its own aircraft under contract to train at least 400 pilots for the American and Canadian forces. It was Thomas-Morse that introduced the concept of series production, which not only simplified manufacture and spares support, but also provided consistency in pilot training as the tyro pilot could be sure of the handling of the aircraft he faced. To emphasize this, Thomas-Morse manufactured the S-4 single seat advanced trainer, of which 600 were built while a further quantity with floats was constructed for the US Navy. On the company front, William continued designing aircraft while finding time to undertake some test flying, while Oliver became the chief engineer and the general manager.

At the beginning of 1918 Thomas-Morse was given a contract by the US Army to develop a fighter that would be superior in all respects to the French Spad then in widespread combat use: the military were anxious to fully develop the American aviation industry in their favour. Having worked their way through the MB-1 and MB-2 fighters, the company developed their *piece*

Thomas-Morse O-19

Crew: 2
Length: 28ft 4in (8.64m)
Wingspan: 39ft 9in (12.12m)
Height: 10ft 6in (3.20m)
Wing area: 348ft² (32.33m²)
Empty weight: 2,722lb (1,235kg)
Gross weight: 3,800lb (1,724kg)
Powerplant: 1 × Pratt & Whitney R-1340-7 Wasp radial piston engine, 450hp (336kW)

Performance
Maximum speed: 137mph (220km/h)
Service ceiling: 20,500ft (6,250m)

Armament
2 × 0.3in machine guns (one fixed forward-firing, one movable in rear cockpit)

---

de resistance, the MB-3. Four prototypes were ordered, to be powered by the 300hp Wright 'H'. This was a licence-built version of the French Hispano Suiza engine as Thomas Aircraft had severed their link with Curtiss engines. The resultant aircraft owed much to the Spad XIII, although it did not fly until February 1919, after the war was over. Even with no obvious require-

The Thomas-Morse MB-3A was the primary fighter delivered to the Air Service after 1918, and remained in service during the early post-war years. via NARA/Dennis R. Jenkins

ment in focus, the Army was impressed enough with the MB-3 to order fifty aircraft for squadron use.

The next model, the MB-3A, was in fact manufactured by Boeing under the competitive tendering system then in operation. While it bore a new designation, the MB-3A was changed little from the earlier MB-3, the major alteration being that the engine cooling system was moved from the upper wing to the fuselage sides. Also available with this model was the option to use either two- or four-bladed propellers. The programme seemed to be dogged by mishaps from the beginning. First, the MB-3 pattern aircraft provided by Thomas-Morse flipped over on landing at the military airfield near Seattle, so had to be rebuilt before Boeing could use it. After this inauspicious beginning Boeing decided to fly the first MB-3A from the Army field at Camp Lewis, whence it was moved by road. Having got the new aircraft safely into the air for a successful test flight, the pilot failed to see a small ditch in one part of the airfield, so the MB-3A emulated the pattern aircraft by flipping over on its back. Continuing bad luck saw US Army test pilot Tyndall managing to pull the wings off an MB-3A after a spectacular short take-off, though he managed to parachute to safety at dangerously low altitude.

In response Boeing undertook an extensive test programme that saw structural strengthening applied to the airframe, while the tail surfaces on the final fifty machines were completely redesigned. While the MB-3A was a step in the right direction, it proved to be one of the last all-wood-framed aircraft built for combat use, as the heavy engine had a tendency to shake itself loose from the bulkhead. This failing led to the development of the arc-welded tubular steel fuselage frame for aviation use.

Although Thomas-Morse was one of the biggest aircraft manufacturers in the United States, its days as a separate entity were numbered after the production of the O-19 observation aircraft for the US Army. The O-19 was the result of much development work as the fuselage was of all-metal construction, even though the wings were still fabric-covered. While both the Thomas brothers retained an interest in their company's development, Oliver retired in 1922. William retained his interest until 1929, by which time the O-19 was entering USAAC service. When Thomas-Morse was taken over by Consolidated Aircraft

in 1929 William Thomas retired, the company name finally disappearing in 1934.

Boeing

Possibly the most famous company to start manufacturing aircraft in the World War One period was Boeing. This company was founded in July 1916 by William E. Boeing as the Pacific Aero Products Company. Its first aircraft was a seaplane designed in conjunction with George Conrad Westervelt, a US Navy engineer. Boeing had earned his money working in the timber industry, where he not only learned much about the use of this material, but also gained a strong interest in the nascent aviation industry. Having flown their first – somewhat shaky – aircraft Boeing and Westervelt built a far more robust machine known as the B&W.

The company was renamed the Boeing Aircraft Company in May 1917 and manufactured aircraft such as the MB-3A under contract whilst pursuing its own designs. As the company continued to expand, the Boeing Air Transport airline was created, this along with Pratt & Whitney, Hamilton Standard Propeller Company and Chance Vought becoming United Aircraft and Transport Corporation. While Boeing, like other major manufacturers, struggled to stay in business during the 1930s recession, resorting to manufacturing various wooden products to keep its work force occupied, it eventually became one of the major players in the world market.

Lockheed

The American aerospace giant Lockheed-Martin took its first faltering footsteps in 1912 when Allan and Malcolm Loughead formed the Alco Hydro-Aeroplane Company in San Francisco. The brothers built their first aircraft, the Model G seaplane, during the early months of 1913; it made its maiden flight on 15 June, being the largest flyable seaplane extant in the United States at the time. Although the brothers were unable to find a buyer for their seaplane it did earn them some money by transporting paying passengers.

Alco left San Francisco to set up a new operating base at Santa Rosa, California, and this time

Curtiss HS-2L

Crew: 2 or 3
Length: 39ft 0in (11.90m)
Wingspan: 74ft 1in (22.6m)
Height: 18ft 9in (5.70m)
Wing area: 695ft² (64.6m²)
Empty weight: 4,300lb (1,950kg)
Gross weight: 4,632lb (2,101kg)
Powerplant: 1 × V-12 Liberty engine, 360hp (270kW)

Performance
Maximum speed: 85mph (137km/h)
Range: 517miles (832km)
Rate of climb: 180ft/min (0.9m/s)

Armament
1 × 0.303 Lewis gun in flexible mount
2 × bombs or depth charges carried under wings

the brothers had some financial backing from Burton Rodman and others. The first aircraft built by the company at its new base was the F-1 ten-seat seaplane. The F-1 introduced another major player to the American aviation industry: John K. 'Jack' Northrop was responsible for designing the hull and wings. The F-1 was a twin-engine biplane featuring twin booms and a triple fin and rudders. The aircraft made its maiden flight on 29 March 1918 and its shakedown flights were completed quickly enough for it to undertake a record-breaking flight from Santa Barbara to San Diego on 12 April, during which the aircraft set a flying distance record in 181 minutes. This level of performance impressed the US Navy so much that they purchased the aircraft.

Like others, the Loughead Aircraft Manufacturing Company was severely hit by the post-war recession that saw the cancellation of outstanding contracts. In response the company designed and built the S-1 sport plane, but sales were few. Sub-contracting was the next step, the company building the Curtiss HS-2L flying boats for the US military. Not even this low-level flow of work was enough to keep the company going, and it went into liquidation in 1921. While the brothers searched around to find another way to enter the aircraft industry, Jack Northrop was hired by Douglas Aircraft, later leaving them to return to Lockheed.

The Loughead brothers re-entered the aircraft business in December 1926. By this time the brothers had changed their surname to Lockheed, the new company being known as the Lockheed Aircraft Manufacturing Corporation. Although the company only lasted in this form for three years it did produce the Vega, designed by Jack Northrop, which made its maiden flight on 4 July 1927. It was a high-winged cantilever monoplane with a monocoque fuselage that consisted of two half-shells of plywood that had been steam-formed over a concrete former, after which both parts were bolted together. It could carry four passengers and a single pilot.

After passing through various financial machinations and several owners, the Lockheed Aircraft Corporation rose again in 1932 when Robert Gross purchased the original company's assets. Although neither of the Lockheed brothers was involved with directly managing the new corporation, Allan, having left three years earlier, spent some time as a consultant from 1932. After this rather

The Curtiss H5L was one of the most important flying boats built for the US armed forces during World War One. It was both a viable patrol machine and a capable anti-submarine aircraft. via NARA/Dennis R. Jenkins

The Glenn L. Martin Company was an early aviation pioneer; this is their 1913 pusher aircraft. via NARA/Dennis R. Jenkins

shaky start the Lockheed Martin Corporation has grown to become one of the major players in the international aerospace industry.

Martin

Although it is now part of the Lockheed Martin conglomerate, Glenn L. Martin established his original company in August 1912 at Santa Ana, California. After four years of independent existence the company merged with the Wright Company, although this was apparently not successful as Martin left the Wright-Martin setup to form another company in September 1917, based in Cleveland, Ohio.

From the outset the new Glenn L. Martin Company was a success, its first contract from the US Army arriving in January 1918. This was for the MB-1 twin-engine biplane bomber, although the war had ended before deliveries could begin. The following aircraft, the MB-2, was even more successful: an initial five were ordered as the MB-2, followed by fifteen designated as the NBS-1 (Night Bomber Short Range-1). Unfortunately for Martin the design rights to the MB-2 were retained by the War Department and the company's bid for the following 110 aircraft was too high; therefore, these machines were constructed by Curtiss who built fifty, LWF Engineering (thirty-five) and Aeromarine (twenty-five). This

aircraft was the standard bomber used by the Air Service until 1930.

While the Martin Aircraft Corporation went on to build many aircraft for the US Armed Forces it had one other claim to fame: not only did Glenn L. Martin teach William Boeing how to fly, he sold him his first aircraft as well.

Aeromarine

One of the lesser known manufacturers in the United States was the Aeromarine Company. The Aeromarine Plane and Motor Company existed from 1914 to 1924; its major investor was Inglis Uppercu, who had made his fortune in various fields including the Chrysler Motor Corporation. As an ardent aviation enthusiast, Uppercu was looking for a way to become involved in the American aviation industry. His opportunity came when he was contacted by the Boland brothers, who were the owners of a defunct brickyard. Not only were premises available, but the brothers also had a $2 million contract to manufacture 200 aircraft for the US Navy. The company manufactured entire aircraft including hulls, engines and wings, at their plant in Keypoint, New Jersey. The company later gained another contract with the US Navy to produce seaplanes. Eventually the company formed a subsidiary, Aeromarine Airways, that

The Aeromarine company was founded by Inglis Uppercu in 1914 and remained in operation until 1924. The company's claim to fame was the winning of a contract to transport mail to ships at sea, although most operations ceased in 1924 after restructuring. via NARA/BBA Collection

produced the first aircraft to fly from New York to Havana via Key West and back. During the Great War Aeromarine delivered over 300 aircraft and, at its peak, employed over 1,000 people. They were also assigned the first government contract to deliver mail to seafaring ships.

During the post-war period Aeromarine suffered from the downturn in the aviation industry that afflicted all of America, and their problems were compounded by a disastrous fire that destroyed the factory in 1921. The fire finished Aeromarine in Keyport, although from the ashes rose the Healey-Aeromarine Bus Company based in New York.

Frank Boland acquired the manufacturing right for the Klemm range of aircraft, forming the Aeromarine-Klemm Corporation, but the company went into receivership in 1931. The assets were sold to the Burnelli Aircraft Corporation. While its founder, Vincent Burnelli, did not strike gold in his lifetime, he was responsible for much of the theorizing behind flying-wing aircraft, although it took the arrival of the Northrop B-2 stealth bomber to bring his designs to fruition.

Gallaudet

While not a major player in the technical development of American aviation, Edson Gallaudet was one of the first to establish a dedicated engineering design office and manufacturing facility. In fact, General Dynamics laid claim to Gallaudet's innovations as the basis for their company. Gallaudet had originally received a doctorate in 1886, becoming a physics instructor at Yale the following year. During his tenure at Yale he developed the technique of wing warping and managed to apply it to one full-size design, the DB-1 before his superiors at Yale decided that aeronautics was not covered by the study and teaching of physics. Fortunately for the Wright brothers, Gallaudet had not bothered to patent his wing-warping idea, otherwise their flying machine might have been stillborn. In fact, Gallaudet became involved with the Wright Flyer, helping to design the wings and controls. He died in 1945 after a long career in aviation.

While Edson Gallaudet is unknown to most students of history, his ideas concerning aircraft construction formed the basis for many future designs. This is the DB-1, which was designed for the day bomber role although it did not pass the prototype stage. via NARA/Dennis R. Jenkins

L-W-F

The L-W-F Company was founded by Edward Lowe Jr, Charles Willard and Robert Fowler in December 1915. During their short existence, L-W-F were credited with developing the monocoque fuselage and the art of using laminates to build up fuselage skinning.

Little is known of Edward Lowe, but Charles Willard and Robert Fowler are well recognized as pioneers of early flight. Willard had origi-

nally starred in the world of motor racing after graduating from Harvard. As aviation was slowly growing across America, Willard was taught to fly by Glenn L. Curtiss. Not long after completing his course, he won a spot-landing contest at the Dominguez Air Meet in 1910. Having shown he was a competent pilot, Willard spent a short period of time with the L-W-F Company before joining the Glenn L. Martin Company as the chief engineer in 1917. After a long career in aviation, Charles Willard died in 1977.

The Lowe-Willard and Fowler engineering company was responsible for providing the Army with its earliest bombers. This is the NBS-2. via USAF/ Dennis R. Jenkins

The Martin MB-2 was delivered to the US Army Air Service and remained in use until the mid-1920s.
via NARA/Dennis R. Jenkins

Robert Fowler is best known for his series of record-breaking flights across America in the early days of aviation. When L-W-F ceased operations in 1917, Fowler formed his own company.

While the US aviation industry had got off to a slow start initially, its ability quickly to catch up with its British and European rivals was undoubted. Helping the industry to develop was a disparate band of aviation enthusiasts who were not only capable of putting America on par with its rivals, but also of looking ahead at future developments. Prominent amongst these early pioneers was Glenn L. Curtiss, who laid down many of the foundations that underpin the current aerospace industry, while the torch was carried forward by William Boeing, the company bearing his name still being one of the world's foremost aircraft makers.

The USA had learned that any aircraft entering service required proper testing, and that proper facilities for design and construction had to be available. The primary purchasers – the US Air Service and its numerous offspring, and the US Navy – had learned that they needed to be more aware of buying aircraft for series production and not to rely on their early practice of buying sundry aircraft on an ad hoc basis. All in all, the industry and its customers were well prepared for the decades that followed.

CHAPTER TWO

American Prototyping
The Lean Years

The period between 1919 and 1939 was the lean years, as countries throughout the world converted their economies from a war footing to one more geared to civilian life. Fortunately the government of the USA was well aware that war was possible at any time; in fact, the US War Department was still preparing for a potential war with Great Britain, even though both had only recently been allies! That aside, the federal government was aware of the need to keep the armament industry active, even if only at a low level.

After the war the US Air Service was slowly being equipped with aircraft manufactured in the USA instead of those built in Europe, even though the early designs were based on the European aircraft. It lost its independence to the US Army under the Army Reorganization Act of 4 June 1920. The Air Service also remained a hotchpotch of units as the distinctive fighter and bomber units and commands was yet to emerge.

US Air Service Fighters

The fighters on the strength of the US Air Service included the Thomas-Morse MB-3A built, as related in Chapter One, by Boeing, as until the late 1920s the government owned the copyright to any designs built on their behalf. While the MB-3A was adequate at the time of its introduction, it was obvious that it would soon need replacing: Boeing and Curtiss were therefore approached to design a new fighter. Boeing put forward the XPW-9 while Curtiss offered the XPW-8, which had started life as a private venture but was sufficiently forward-thinking in design for the Army to order a batch of twenty-

---

Boeing PW-9

Crew: 1
Length: 23ft 5in (7.1m)
Wingspan: 32ft 0in (9.7m)
Height: 8ft 2in (2.40m)
Wing area: 260ft² (24.1m²)
Empty weight: 1,936lb (878kg)
Loaded weight: 3,120lb (1,414kg)
Powerplant: 1 × Curtiss D-12 water cooled V-12, 435hp (315kW)

Performance
Maximum speed: 159mph (257km/h, 138kt)
Cruise speed: 142mph (290km/h, 123kt)
Range: 390 miles (628km, 339nm)
Service ceiling 18,925ft (5,768m)
Rate of climb: 1,630ft/min (8.27m/s)

Armament
Guns: 2 × 0.30in machine guns
Bombs: one 244lb bomb

---

five machines. However, it was the Boeing aircraft that became the favourite, the initial order for twenty-five machines being followed by a further forty-six aircraft; in service these were known as the PW-9. Boeing also put forward the P-12 radial-engined biplane fighter and then the P-26 Peashooter, which secured the largest single fighter order ever issued up to that time, totalling 586 of all versions.

The Boeing XP-4

Boeing continued to push forward ideas to what had by now been renamed the US Army Air Corps for fighter aircraft with the XP-4. This was based around the PW-9 that had been ordered in 1924, though the XP-4 was ordered in June 1925 before the PW-9s had even been delivered. The airframe chosen for conversion was the thirtieth PW-9, 25-234, which was taken from the production line and fitted with a Packard 1A-1500 turbocharged engine rated at 500hp; the turbocharger was mounted externally on the starboard side of the fuselage. It was the installation of this engine in the Boeing aircraft to test its performance at high altitude that warranted the designation change. In addition to the new engine, the XP-4 was fitted with a new, more aerodynamic wing profile and an increase in span, which was needed to lift the increased weight of the Packard. Although intended as a test aircraft, the XP-4 was also fitted with an armament that consisted of the original pair of fuselage-mounted machine guns carried by the PW-9, plus a further pair installed in the lower wing, placed so that their line of fire was well clear of the propeller arc. The change in engine required that a new cowling be manufactured, while to absorb the extra power a four-bladed propeller was installed.

The XP-4 was delivered to Wright Field for test flying on 27 July 1927, at the completion of company test flying. Both the Army and Boeing were disappointed by the performance of the Packard engine, as its output was not enough to compensate for the extra 800lb of weight that the engine and the extra modifications had engendered. In comparison with the PW-9 fighter then being delivered to the USAAC, the XP-4 was a very poor performer, so it was decided to ground the aircraft after four hours of test flying. The redundant aircraft was later scrapped, in May 1928.

Boeing XP-7

The next Boeing project also centred around an engine change, and again the aircraft chosen to act as the starting point was the PW-9: the USAAC was very interested to see how much further the PW-9 design could be pushed. The resultant aircraft was the XP-7, which was fitted with the Curtiss Conquerer engine. The XP-7 was ordered on 5 March 1928, and was based on the last PW-9D, 28-041, off the production line. After modifications to the engine bulkhead, the 600hp Curtiss V-1750-1 Conquerer was fitted. As with the earlier Packard experiment, the new Curtiss installation required that a redesigned cowling be manufactured to accommodate the larger radiator, which presented the airflow with a shorter, deeper nose. Further changes saw a modified tail skid and an improved aileron control system,

---

Boeing XP-4

Crew: 1
Length: 23ft 11in (7.29m)
Wingspan: 32ft 1in (9.78m)
Height: 8ft 10in (2.69m)
Wing area: 245ft² (22.8m²)
Empty weight: 2,783lb (1,264kg)
Max. take-off weight: 3,650lb (1,655kg)
Powerplant: 1 × Packard 1A-1500 supercharged liquid-cooled piston engine, 510hp (380kW)

Performance
Maximum speed: 146kt (168mph, 270km/h)
Cruise speed: 104kt (120mph, 193km/h)
Range: 326nm (375 miles, 604km)
Service ceiling: 22,850ft (6,965m)
Rate of climb: 1,400ft/min (7.1m/s)

Armament
Guns: one 0.30in and one 0.50in machine gun firing through propeller disc plus two wing-mounted 0.3in machine guns

---

Boeing XP-7

Crew: 1
Length: 24ft 0in (7.31m)
Wingspan: 32ft 0in (9.75m)
Height: 9ft 0in (2.74m)
Wing area: 252ft² (23.4m²)
Empty weight: 2,358lb (1,070kg)
Gross weight: 3,260lb (1,479kg)
Powerplant: 1 × Curtiss V-1570-1, 600hp (447kW)

Performance
Maximum speed: 167.5mph (270km/h)
Cruise speed: 134mph (216km/h)
Range: 250 miles (402km)
Service ceiling: 22,300ft (6,797m)
Rate of climb: 1,408ft/min (7.2m/s)

Armament
1 × 0.50in machine gun
1 × 0.30in machine gun
125lb (57kg) bombs

and the tailplane being constructed completely of alloy.

Boeing carried out the usual range of manufacturer's flight trials before delivering the XP-7 to the USAAC at Wright Field on 8 September 1928. The Army flight trials proved that the Conqueror engine was suitable for use as a fighter engine, so a tentative specification was drawn up by the Army to purchase four test P-7 airframes. While the initial flight test reports seemed to indicate that a Conquerer-powered PW-9 might be a vast improvement on the original model, close comparison between the PW-9 and the XP-7 during further flights revealed that there was little to choose between them. The four test aircraft were cancelled, while the single XP-7 was converted back to standard PW-9 configuration.

Boeing XP-8

Crew: 1
Length: 23ft 5in (7.14m)
Wingspan: 30ft 1in (9.17m)
Height: 9ft 0in (2.74m)
Wing area: 260ft² (24.15m²)
Empty weight: 2,390lb (1,084kg)
Max. take-off weight: 3,421lb (1,552kg)
Powerplant: 1 × Packard 2A-1530 liquid-cooled piston engine, 600hp (448kW)

Performance
Maximum speed: 153kt (176mph, 283km/h) at 6,000ft (1,830m)
Cruise speed: 129kt (148mph, 238km/h)
Range: 283nm (325 miles, 523km)
Service ceiling: 20,950ft (6,390m)

Armament
1 × 0.30in machine gun
1 × 0.50in machine gun

Boeing XP-8

With the Boeing Model 66, designated the XP-8 by the Army, the company began to move away from rehashes of the PW-9 fighter. The Model 66 was built in response to a US Army request, issued in April 1925, for a new fighter powered by the Packard 2A-1530 inverted liquid-cooled engine, rated at 600hp. This particular aircraft was constructed under a bailment contract, under the terms of which Boeing retained ownership of the airframe while the engine and other equipment was delivered as Government Furnished Items.

While the Model 66 was a new design, it did owe something to the experience gained

The Boeing XP-8, known to the company as the Model 66, was a prototype biplane fighter developed in the 1920s. It was notable for its unusual design, which incorporated the engine coolant radiator in the lower wing. via NARA/Dennis R. Jenkins

during the design and building of the PW-9 and earlier fighters. The Model 66 was a single-bay biplane with staggered wings and alloy N struts. The forward fuselage consisted of a welded steel tubular framework, while the remainder of the fuselage and the rudder were manufactured from duralumin section bolted together; this did introduce the possibility of failure should a bolt fail, and there was the chance of dissimilar metal corrosion. The basic wing structure was wood and the majority of the airframe was fabric-covered. The engine radiator was mounted in the lower fuselage at the point where the lower wing joined the fuselage. The propeller was a twin-blade unit covered by an aerodynamic spinner, while the undercarriage featured oleo pneumatic shock absorbers – a feature that would appear on many subsequent fighters.

The completed Model 66 was delivered unflown to the Army at Wright Field in July 1927, undertaking its maiden flight from there on 14 July. The Model 66 was purchased by the USAAC in January 1928, after which it was serialled 28-359. Flight testing of the XP-8 revealed that the aircraft performed no better than the PW-9, so no production order was forthcoming. While the Army was more than happy with the Boeing airframe, the Packard engine was a different proposition – perhaps this was not surprising given its experimental nature. After the conclusion of its flight trials the XP-8 was grounded, being finally disposed of in June 1929.

Boeing XP-9/XP-15

Following on from the XP-8, Boeing produced the XP-9 in response to a USAAC request for a monoplane fighter issued in 1928. This aircraft was a complete change in design direction for the company, as their previous products had been biplanes. The XP-9, serialled 28-386, made its maiden flight on 18 November 1930 and was delivered to Wright Field soon afterwards. The XP-9 featured a broad-chord wing of 6ft (1.8m) that was carried atop the fuselage. While an innovative feature, the placement of the wing severely obstructed the downward vision of the pilot, so landing was a very hazardous affair.

After the Army pilots had made their initial test flights their reports were quite scathing about the XP-9, highlighting the visibility problem

---

Boeing XP-15

Crew: 1
Length: 21ft 0in (6.40m)
Wingspan: 30ft 6in (9.29m)
Height: 9ft 4.5in (2.84m)
Wing area: 157.3ft² (14.61m²)
Empty weight: 2,052lb (931kg)
Gross weight: 2,746lb (1,246kg)
Powerplant: 1 × Pratt & Whitney SR-1340D, 525hp (392kW)

Performance
Maximum speed: 190.2mph (306km/h)
Cruise speed: 160mph (257km/h)
Range: 420 miles (676km)
Service ceiling: 27,650ft (8,428m)

Armament
2 × 0.30in machine guns

---

and instability around the pitch and yaw axes. In response Boeing fitted the XP-9 with tail surfaces of increased size, the aircraft becoming the XP-15 in the process. However, this modification failed to cure the instability problem, so the aircraft was grounded permanently in August 1931 after fifteen flying hours. While the initial XP-9 was cancelled, there was an intention to purchase five Y1P-9s as part of the P-12D production contract, although these were later cancelled.

All was not lost from the XP-9 fiasco as technical developments introduced with this aircraft were later transferred to other aircraft on the Boeing production line. The semi-monocoque fuselage design of the XP-9 was introduced into the P-12E biplane fighter, also from Boeing, while the undercarriage intended for the P-12C was trialled on the XP-9 before being introduced into the production line.

The XP-15 designation was reused later for another Boeing product, although this one began as a company-funded project. It started as an adaptation of the Model 89 airframe that had been the progenitor of the F4B and P-12 aircraft for the US Navy and USAAC, respectively. This was to have been redesigned as a monoplane, the lower wing being deleted and a support strut fitted to mount the remaining wing, this being moved slightly aft. This reworked aircraft had been known as the Model 97.

The appearance of the XP-9 changed the Boeing approach to the new aircraft. The Model

The Boeing XP-9, or Model 96, was the first monoplane fighter aircraft produced by Boeing. It utilized sophisticated structural refinements, which were carried over to later Boeing designs. via NARA/Dennis R. Jenkins

97 project was abandoned, its replacement being the Model 202. The basis of this aircraft was the XP-9 monocoque fuselage, on top of which was a parasol wing – based on that of the P-12 – attached to the fuselage by numerous struts. The wing itself was constructed of alloy instead of wood and covered with alloy sheeting instead of fabric as previously used. The main wheels were mounted on separate undercarriage legs while the familiar tail skid was replaced by a tail-wheel assembly. The fuselage was similar to that of the XP-9, although the skinning was again alloy instead of fabric. During manufacture the opportunity was taken to build two sets of tail surfaces: one was smooth-skinned with alloy while the other set had corrugated skinning; both sets were externally braced. The engine selected for this new aircraft was the Pratt & Whitney SR-1340D Wasp air-cooled radial, which was rated at 450hp at 8,000ft (2,400m).

As this was a company-funded project, the Model 202 was given the civil registration X-270V. It made its first flight in January 1930. After initial company flying the Model 202 was fitted with the vertical fin that was later fitted to the P-12E fighter, while an engine cowl similar to that carried by the P-12C was fitted. In this new guise the aircraft was despatched to Wright Field. Here the designation 'XP-15' was unofficially

applied when the USAAC accepted the aircraft on a bailment contract on 10 March 1930.

While the XP-15 was a reasonable performer, the deletion of a lower wing meant that the rate of climb, manoeuvrability and the landing speed all suffered in comparison with the P-12s already in service. These parameters would have suffered even more, had the intended machine-gun armament been installed. Although from a technical standpoint the XP-15 was another step forward in fighter evolution, its shortfall in performance meant that no Army contract was forthcoming. After returning to Boeing the aircraft was used for further trials work. This came to an end on 7 February 1931, when it was destroyed in a crash; a propeller blade failed after a high-speed run that had been followed by a zoom climb.

Boeing YP-29

Boeing's final inter-war fighter design was the YP-29; this was an attempt to modernize the P-26 monoplane pursuit aircraft. The YP-29 began as the company-funded Model 264 and differed from the earlier P-26 in having fully cantilevered wings without external bracing, and a fully retractable undercarriage. The undercarriage was similar to that carried by the Boeing Monomail

---

Boeing YP-29

Crew: 1
Length: 22ft 7in (6.8m)
Wingspan: 32ft (9.7m)
Height: 10ft 0in (3.04m)
Loaded weight: 3,857lb (1,749kg)
Powerplant: 1 × Pratt & Whitney R-1340-30 Wasp radial engine, 550hp (420kW)

Performance

Maximum speed: 231mph (200kt, 371km/h) at 6,000ft (1,800m)
Combat radius: 360 miles (310nm, 580km)
Service ceiling: 29,600ft (8,198m)

Armament

2 × 0.30in machine guns
1 × 200lb bomb

---

mailplane, while the tail had been borrowed from the P-26. The chosen powerplant was the Pratt & Whitney R-1340 Wasp air-cooled radial, similar to that carried by the P-26. The armament was also the same as that fitted to the P-26, consisting of single 0.30in and 0.5in machine guns mounted in the fuselage.

The first Model 264 was rolled out in January 1934. There were a few changes from the initial design: it featured an enlarged pilot's windshield, an R-1340-31 Wasp rated at 550hp and a NACA cowling in place of the Thompson cooling ring as fitted to the P-26. The aircraft's first flight was undertaken on 20 January and it flew to Wright Field for Army testing on 25 January; it was test-flown under bailment contract as the XP-940. From the outset the USAAC was impressed by the aircraft, deciding in June 1934 to purchase the XP-940 and two other similar aircraft as the YP-29. The Army only raised one concern, this being that the original cockpit restricted the pilot's vision. Therefore the first machine and then the others were fitted with a standard open cockpit, although the long headrest that faired back to the fin was retained. The modified aircraft was returned to Wright Field as the YP-29A in April 1934, made its first flight on 4 June, and was then purchased outright by the Army and given the serial 34-24. A later engine change to the R-1340-27, rated at 600hp, saw the aircraft redesignated as the P-29A.

The second YP-29 differed from the original machine in that it was completed with a large

and roomy full canopy and an R-1340-35 engine. This machine was delivered to Wright Field in September 1934, serialled 34-23. While the Army was impressed with the new cockpit and the aircraft in general, they were slightly alarmed by the high – for the period – landing speed, which was thought to be too high for general operational use. The cure rested with Boeing, who accepted the aircraft at the factory for the installation of wing flaps. After Boeing and Army test flying that saw the testing of variable-pitch propellers and the installation of a P & W R-1340-39 engine the aircraft was redesignated as the P-29.

The third and final Model 264 was completed as the YP-29B and included features drawn from both predecessors. Serialled 34-25, it had the open cockpit from the YP-29 while the wing flaps from the YP-29A were also installed. The YP-29B was delivered to Wright Field on 11 October 1934 to begin flight testing. Eventually 1 degree of dihedral was applied to the wing, and an oleo tail-wheel installation was fitted. After initial flight trails the YP-29B was sent to Chanute Field for further flight trials, where it was eventually designated the P-29B. After the YP-29 Boeing offered the Army the XP-32, which was a refined YP-29 powered by a Pratt & Whitney R-1535 Twin Wasp Junior, but as no interest was shown it remained a drawing-board concept only.

Martin XP-10

The other main inter-war contender for the few available US Army aircraft contracts was one of the first American aviation pioneers, the Glenn L. Martin Company. Having survived the post-war economic downturn, the company continued to design and manufacture.

One of the first development prototypes that Curtiss produced for the USAAC was the XP-10. This was an experimental biplane ordered by the USAAC on 18 June 1928, and took an innovative approach to speed and manoeuvrability. The Curtiss designers fitted a gull top wing, the roots of which were mounted onto the fuselage, while the lower wing roots were also given an upward cant. The reasoning behind mounting the upper wing in such a manner was to improve pilot visibility. The wings themselves were covered with plywood sheet, while the tubular-steel fuselage

---

Curtiss XP-10

Crew: 1
Length: 24ft 6in (7.47m)
Wingspan: 33ft (10.06m)
Height: 10ft 10in (3.30m)
Wing area: 238ft² (21.1m²)
Empty weight: approx. 2,900lb (1,315kg)
Max. take-off weight: 3,400lb (1,542kg)
Powerplant: 1 × V-1570 Conqueror water-cooled 12-cylinder
vee, 600hp (448kW)

Performance

Maximum speed: 150kt (173mph, 279km/h)
Cruise speed: 113kt (130mph, 209km/h)
Range: 195 miles (170nm, 314km)
Service ceiling: 19,610ft (6,000m)

---

framework was fabric-covered. The XP-10 was powered by the liquid-cooled Curtiss V-1570 Conqueror, rated at 600hp. As this engine used water cooling, its radiator requirements were greater than those of later engines that used ethylene glycol, therefore the radiators were incorporated into the upper wing. The radiator sections themselves were manufactured from corrugated brass, but these were deemed to be vulnerable to enemy fire. The USAAC received the XP-10 at Wright Field in August 1928, although it did not undertake its maiden flight until the following month. Although the XP-10 was a far better performer than the then-current Curtiss fighter, the Hawk, problems with a leaking coolant system and clogging of the radiators saw the engine overheating. As the Army was reluctant to spend further scarce funds on improvements for the XP-10, it was decided to ground the aircraft permanently.

Curtiss XP-14 and XP-17

Curtiss followed up the XP-10 with the XP-14. This was a proposed Curtiss-built version of the Thomas-Morse XP-13 Viper, but extensive development problems with the Chieftain engine that was intended to power both aircraft meant that both were eventually cancelled.

Curtiss was luckier with its next machine, the XP-17. This used the first P-1 fighter of the production line, serialled 25-410, which spent its entire working life as a test bed. The first stage in this

journey was the testing of an Allison air-cooled version of the Liberty engine, although in this condition its designation remained unchanged. When the air-cooled Wright V-1460-3 Tornado engine, rated at 480hp, was installed, the aircraft designation was changed to XP-17. The installation of the Wright engine was undertaken by the USAAC Engineering Division, instead of by the manufacturer as was the norm for machines in the XP designation series. As the aircraft and the engine installation were purely experimental, the cowling was made of sheet metal as there was no need for aerodynamics to be considered. Fortunately the type was not intended for production, as the performance of the engine was disappointing. Once testing had been completed, the XP-17 was grounded and finally scrapped in March 1932.

Curtiss YP-20

The next two Curtiss XP aircraft – the XP-18 and XP-19 – barely made it onto the drawing board, far less off it, as the Wright V-1560 engine intended for them was cancelled, taking the two aircraft projects with it.

With the XP-20, however, Curtiss was far more successful. The YP-20 had originally been ordered as part of the first production contract for the Curtiss P-6 Hawk. The USAAC had decided to order three of the aircraft as the P-11, the intention being to fit them with a Curtiss H-1640

Curtiss YP-20

Crew: 1
Length: 23ft 9in (7.24m)
Wingspan: 31ft 6in (9.6m)
Height: 8ft 10in (2.69m)
Wing area: 252ft² (23.41m²)
Empty weight: 2,447lb (1,110kg)
Max. take-off weight: 3,233lb (1,466kg)
Powerplant: 1 × R-1820 Cyclone air-cooled 9-cylinder radial
engine, 575hp (429kW)

Performance

Maximum speed: 187kt
Range: 248nm (285 miles, 459km)
Service ceiling: 24,700ft (7,529m)

Armament

2 × 0.30in Browning machine guns

Chieftain engine instead of the Conquerer of the P-6. Of the three P-11s ordered, 29-267, -268 and -374, the first two were eventually completed, but the new engine proved to have excessive overheating problems. As a result, 29-374 was fitted with a Wright R-1820-9 Cyclone radial engine rated at 650hp during October 1930 and, to compensate for the greater engine output, the fin and rudder were slightly increased in size. In this new guise the aircraft was designated the YP-20. Other changes to the aircraft included fitting the undercarriage with strut fairings, a Townend ring around the engine and a crank covercase for the engine.

Having completed its initial flight trials, the YP-20 was set against a Curtiss P-6, the Boeing P-12 and the Conqueror-powered XP-22 (see below) during June 1931. During this competition the YP-20 was outclassed by the XP-22, which eventually won a pre-production contract for forty-six machines as the YP-22. At the conclusion of these flight trials the YP-20 was fitted with a V-1570-23 Conqueror engine, a modified forward fuselage and associated radiator and divided undercarriage legs. In its new guise the aircraft was re-designated the XP-6E. Having been thoroughly tested, the XP-6E prototype cleared the type for production, but 29-374 still had further development work ahead. Its next task was to act as the prototype for the Curtiss XP-6F, for which purpose a turbocharger was installed. At the conclusion of this programme the aircraft was withdrawn and scrapped.

Curtiss XP-21

The Curtiss XP-21 began as a P-1A, 26-300, the last of the production run. The original liquid-cooled Curtiss D-12 engine was replaced by a Pratt & Whitney R-1340-1 air-cooled radial. In its new guise the aircraft first flew during April 1928, becoming the prototype for the P-3A fighter. In 1930 the XP-3A, 26-300, and a P-3A, 28-189, were experimentally fitted with Pratt & Whitney R-895 Wasp Junior engines, both being designated XP-21. The first XP-21 made its maiden flight in December 1930. After test-flying both aircraft, the USAAC was not overly convinced that the radial engine was a great improvement over the normal D-12 engine. The P-3A-based XP-21 later had its experimental

engine replaced with a D-12, becoming a standard P-1F. The remaining XP-21, 26-300, was later re-engined with the Wright R-975 Wasp Junior rated at 300hp; in this guise it was designated the XP-21A. This aircraft, too, was scrapped once flight trials of this engine had been completed.

Curtiss XP-22

Only an engine was required to produce the Curtiss XP-22, which was a step in the development of the P-6E pursuit fighter. The third P-6A, 29-262, was chosen to trial the new radiator and oil cooler intended for the V-1570-23 power-plant: this required a new nose section, in which the machine guns were mounted in troughs on the fuselage sides, under the engine cylinder banks, rather than between them as on previous models. The whole was carried on a new undercarriage with individual undercarriage legs. In its new guise the XP-22 first flew in June 1931, taking part in a competition against other fighter hopefuls. The XP-22 produced the highest speed of all four types, so an initial contract for forty-six production machines was issued, the aircraft being designated Y1P-22. Eventually the aircraft was designated the P-6C, although this changed to P-6E before delivery. At the completion of these flight trials the XP-22 was returned to original condition, eventually being redelivered to the USAAC as a stock P-6A.

Curtiss XP-23

The final biplane built by Curtiss was the XP-23, reckoned by many to be one of the most handsome aircraft ever built. The airframe chosen for conversion was the last P-6E of the USAAC, serialled 32-278, which had been held at the Curtiss factory at the request of the Army. The aircraft was completely new as it featured a monocoque aluminium fuselage, new tail surfaces, a new nose assembly, new undercarriage and a Curtiss G1V-1570-C geared powerplant, complete with turbocharger, which drove a three-blade propeller. The revamped fuselage was a more aerodynamic design than on previous aircraft, the only item intruding into the airflow being the cooling radiator that was mounted between the undercarriage legs. The wing design was borrowed from

The Curtiss XP-23, or Model 63, was based on the P-6E with a light alloy monocoque fuselage, modified tail assemblies and powered by a turbocharged G1V-1570-C Conqueror engine and geared propeller. The aircraft was redesignated YP-23 after the turbocharger was removed. via NARA/Dennis R. Jenkins

the P-6E, although the wings were constructed from alloy rather than wood.

The XP-23 was delivered to the USAAC on 16 April 1932. Although it performed as promised, it was obvious that the era of the biplane was coming to an end. This point was driven home when the USAAC purchased the Boeing P-26A monoplane fighter instead of the production version of the XP-23. Although the XP-23 garnered no production orders, the aircraft was used for test flying; for this role its designation was changed to YP-23, as the aircraft had changed from experimental to service test status. After the designation changed, the engine supercharger was removed and the three-blade propeller was replaced by a two-blade unit.

The final trials use of the YP-23 were to determine the increase in aircraft speed when it was flown without the radiator. For this trial the radiator assembly was removed, which required that the cooling water was fed from tanks carried in the airframe, the water being dumped directly overboard rather than being recirculated. At the completion of these flights the aircraft was scrapped.

Curtiss XP-31

The final inter-war prototype produced by Curtiss was the XP-31. This machine owed its roots to the development of the Model 66 Swift; the Swift had been the unsuccessful competitor against the Boeing P-26, the USAAC's interim monoplane fighter ordered in 1932. Although the Swift had not won the fighter competition the Army was impressed enough to ask Curtiss to continue development of the design as a private venture, the USAAC providing the engine and other military equipment under a bailment contract. The internal company designation for this project was the XP-934.

The revamped Swift design was based around the Curtiss A-8 Shrike attack aircraft, the resulting machine being a mix of old and new technologies. The XP-934 was a low-winged monoplane with external bracing struts, while the undercarriage was fixed and came complete with fairings and spats. The cockpit was covered with a sliding canopy to protect the crew. The wings were fitted

Curtiss XP-31

Crew: 1
Length: 26ft 3in (8m)
Wingspan: 36ft (11m)
Height: 7ft 9in (2.4m)
Wing area: 203ft² (18.86m²)
Empty weight: 3,334lb (1,512kg)
Gross weight: 4,143lb (1,879kg)
Powerplant: 1 × Curtiss V-1570 Conqueror water-cooled
12-cylinder vee engine, 600hp (450kW)

Performance
Maximum speed: 208mph (335km/h)
Range: 370 miles (595km)
Service ceiling: 24,400ft (7,440m)

Armament
2 × 0.30 M1919 machine guns – cowl
2 × 0.30 M1919 machine guns – fuselage

with trailing-edge flaps, while the leading edges had slats fitted along the entire leading edge, which would open automatically at 15mph above the aircraft's stalling speed. The armament consisted of four 0.30in machine guns: two carried in troughs in the nose, the others in external blisters on each side of the cockpit. Curtiss had originally planned to fit a 600hp Curtiss Conquerer engine, but the USAAC was convinced that the Conqueror was close to the end of its devel-

opment cycle so they insisted that the 700hp Wright R-1820 Cyclone be used instead.

The XP-934 was rolled out in July 1932, undertaking its flight trials at the Curtiss airfield. The performance of the Wright radial was found to be disappointing, so by the end of August the engine had been changed to the Curtiss Conquerer, the engine that Curtiss had originally wanted to install. While the top speed increased after the engine change, the behaviour of the aircraft overall had suffered as the basic weight had increased. The USAAC purchased the XP-934 in February 1933, the aircraft being designated the XP-31 and gaining the serial 33-178 in the process. After three years of flight trials the XP-31 was redesignated as the ZXP-31, which indicated that the airframe was obsolete. Now unwanted, the aircraft was retired to a USAAC mechanics school for ground training, although it was finally withdrawn from use some six months later.

Thomas-Morse XP-13

The XP-13 – known as the Viper within the company – was the last design put forward to the USAAC by Thomas-Morse before the company completely disappeared. The majority of the aircraft was of alloy construction, although the wing and tail-plane structure was

The Curtiss YA-10, or Model 59B, was a 1930s test and development version of the A-8 Shrike ground-attack aircraft, using various radial engines in place of the inline engine previously used. via NARA/Dennis R. Jenkins

---

Thomas-Morse XP-13

Crew: 1
Length: 23ft 6in (7.16m)
Wingspan: 28ft 0in (8.53m)
Height: 8ft 5in (2.56m)
Wing area: 189ft² (17.6m²)
Empty weight: 2,262lb (1,026kg)
Loaded weight: 3,256lb (1,477kg)
Powerplant: 1 × Curtiss H-1640-1 Chieftain 12-cyliner two-row air-cooled radial engine, 600hp (448kW)

Performance
Maximum speed: 150kt (172mph, 277km/h) (at sea level)
Cruise speed: 113kt (130mph, 209km/h)
Range: 168nm (193 miles, 312km)
Service ceiling: 20,775ft (6,300m)
Rate of climb: 1,700ft/min (8.64m/s)

---

of wood with a fabric covering. The powerplant selected for the Viper was the Curtiss Chieftain, rated at 600hp. Registered as P-559, the Viper was delivered to the US Army for evaluation flying at Wright Field in June 1929; it was quickly purchased by the Army as the XP-13, with the army serial 29-453. While the performance of the aircraft was rated as satisfactory, the Chieftain engine was subject to serious cooling problems. As the chances of sorting out the problems of the engine could not be resolved in a reasonable time, the decision was taken to fit a Pratt & Whitney SR-1340-C engine rated at 535hp instead, this being housed under a NACA cowling. To compensate for the change of engine the aircraft had a modified fin and rudder installed. In its new guise as the XP-13A the aircraft revealed a much improved performance, the pilots praising its smooth handling. While the praise was much appreciated, the USAAC decided against purchasing any production machines as the emerging monoplane fighter was beginning to gain the attention of the Army. The XP-13A was retained for trials purposes, although it was destroyed by fire during its last test flight.

Curtiss had been contracted to build a second Viper as the XP-14, but the problems with the Chieftain engine resulted in its cancellation. As for Thomas-Morse, it was finally absorbed by Consolidated Aircraft of New York, the company name disappearing from the roll of manufacturers soon afterwards.

Consolidated Y1P-35 and Y1A-11

Having absorbed Thomas-Morse, Consolidated Aircraft was the recipient of a contract that had originally been awarded to Lockheed during its short time as part of the Detroit Aircraft Company. When that organization ran into difficulties in 1931 the contract for the YP-24 was awarded to Consolidated, who enlisted the services of the designer Robert Woods to continue leading the design team. A single example of this design was ordered by the USAAC under the designation Y1P-25, the serial 32-321 being applied.

The aircraft that was rolled out by Consolidated was very similar in outline to the proposed Lockheed aircraft, but there were significant differences between the two. While the initial layout of a two-seat, low-wing monoplane with a retractable undercarriage was retained, the wing was changed from being a wooden structure to one that was of all-alloy construction; the tail surfaces of the aircraft underwent a similar alteration, although they were slightly larger that those originally planned. The engine fitted to the Y1P-25 was the same as that proposed for the YP-24 – the Curtiss Conqueror – although the Consolidated aircraft had a turbocharger mounted on the port side of the fuselage. Armament consisted of two fuselage-mounted machine guns and a single flexible machine gun for the gunner/observer in the rear cockpit.

Consolidated Y1P-25 and Y1P-11

Crew: 2
Length: 29ft 10in (9.1m)
Wingspan: 43ft 11in (13.4m)
Height: 8ft 2in (2.5m)
Wing area: 297ft² (27.6m²)
Empty weight: 4,297lb (1,949kg)
Loaded weight: 5,632lb (2,555kg)

Performance
Maximum speed: 274mph (238kt, 441km/h)
Cruise speed: 215mph (187kt, 346km/h)
Range: 510 miles (440nm, 820km)
Service ceiling: 28,000ft (8,500m)
Rate of climb: 1,925ft/min (9.8m/s)

Armament
2 × 0.30in machine guns firing through the propeller
1 × 0.30in machine gun in the rear cockpit

Based on the Consolidated Y1P-25, the Y1A-11 differed from the Y1P-25 in having a Conqueror engine without a supercharger. The Y1A-11 also had two more guns in the nose and underwing racks cleared for a maximum of 400lb (180kg) of bombs. via NARA/Dennis R. Jenkins

A ground-attack version of this aircraft, designated Y1A-11, was also ordered, this being serialled 32-322. The changes between the types was that the supercharger was deleted from the Y1A-11, while two further guns were mounted in the nose and racks were fitted for the carriage of 400lb of bombs.

The Y1P-25 was delivered to the USAAC for flight trials on 9 December 1932 with the Y1A-11 following not long after. Both machines exhibited good flying characteristics, but the Y1P-25 was completely destroyed in a crash on 13 January 1933 and the ground-attack version crashed a week later. While in most cases the loss of both prototypes would result in the cancellation of a programme, the USAAC felt that both versions of the Consolidated aircraft were worthy of further development. As a result a contract was issued for four aircraft serialled 33-204 to -207, these being designated the P-30. The production machines differed from the prototypes in the fitment of a Curtiss V-1570-57 engine driving a two-blade propeller, a modified undercarriage and a revised canopy. The ground-attack version was

also ordered, four A-11s serialled 33-308 to -311 being contracted. The production machine had the same changes applied as the P-30, although the engine lacked a supercharger.

In order to keep this family of aircraft in production Consolidated Aircraft also proposed two other versions powered by Pratt & Whitney engines of different ratings, these being designated the YP-27, YP-28 and XP-33. In the event, none of these designs was proceeded with.

Wedell-Williams XP-34

The final inter-war fighter design submitted to the USAAC was the XP-34. This was the brainchild of the late Harry Williams, owner of Wedell-Williams Air Services Corporation, the design itself being under the control of noted air race pilot Jimmy Wedell. The Army purchased a full set of plans from the widow of Harry Williams in October 1935, the aircraft being known as the Wedell-Williams XP-34. Intensive study of the plans and calculation by Army engineers revealed that, as proposed, the aircraft was under-powered. Although the company proposed substituting a more powerful engine, the USAAC had already decided that there was no real need for the XP-34 and the project was cancelled.

The Wedell-Williams fighter design submitted to the USAAC was based on the company's racing aircraft, one of which is shown here. via NARA/Dennis R. Jenkins

---

Wedell-Williams XP-34

Crew: 1
Length: 23ft 6in (7.2m)
Wingspan: 27ft 8½in (8.45m)
Height: 10ft 9in (3.28m)
Powerplant: 1 × Pratt & Whitney R1535 air-cooled radial, 600hp (450kW)

Performance
Maximum speed: 286mph at 10,000ft (460km/h at 300m)

Huff-Daland XLB-1

It was the bomber force that received the greater attention during this period, as the US Army generals believed that the best use of air power was for attack and that fighter defence was for the bombers.

The first of the Huff-Daland, later Keystone, series of bombers was the Huff-Daland XLB-1, serialled 23-1250. This was a three-place bomber powered by a single Packard engine of 800hp; this was a change from the previous practice of using two lower-powered, wing-mounted engines. The bomb load was carried in the belly while the bomb aimer did his aiming through a window in the aircraft's lower fuselage, instead of the more normal nose position. The prototype was accepted and was followed by a further nine machines designated the LB-9, these being intended for trials and evaluation usage. They were identical to the prototype except for the fitment of a more powerful engine.

Huff-Daland XLB-1

Crew: 4
Length: 46ft 2in (14.07m)
Wingspan: 60ft 6in (18.44m)
Gross weight: 12,415lb (5,631kg)
Powerplant: 1 × Packard 2A-2540 water-cooled vee engine, 800hp (600kW)

Performance
Maximum speed: 120mph (190km/h)
Range: 430 miles (700km)
Service ceiling: 11,150ft (3,400m)

Armament
5 × 0.30in machine guns
2,750lb (1,250kg) of bombs

While the LB-1 managed to pass its evaluation trials, it was decided that the single-engine configuration was not really a viable proposition for such an aircraft. While no further LB-1s were ordered, the original XLB-1 prototype was returned to

Keystone XLB-3A

Crew: 5
Length: 45ft 0in (13.72m)
Wingspan: 67ft 0in (20.42m)
Height: 16ft 10in (5.13m)
Wing area: 105.8ft² (9.83m²)
Empty weight: 6,065lb (2,756kg)
Gross weight: 11,682lb (5,310kg)
Powerplant: 2 × Pratt & Whitney R-1340, 410hp (305kW) each

Performance
Maximum speed: 116mph (186km/h)
Range: 544 miles (870km)
Service ceiling: 11,210ft (3,400m)
Rate of climb: 550ft/min (2.8m/s)

Armament
2 × 0.303in machine guns in nose
2 × 0.303in machine guns in dorsal position
1 × 0.303in machine gun in ventral hatch
2,200lb (1,000kg) of bombs

able, so they were replaced by a pair of air-cooled Pratt & Whitney Wasp R-1340-1 engines; the aircraft was re-designated the XLB-3A in the process. During this period the chief designer was James McDonnell, who later achieved fame as the progenitor of the F-4 Phantom II – a sharp contrast in types and periods!

In 1926 Thomas Huff left the company, leaving Elliot Daland in charge, though soon Hayden, Stone & Co injected a further $1 million capital into the company. It was at this time that its name was changed to Keystone Aircraft, and two years later the company merged with Loening to form Keystone-Loening Aircraft. This independence only lasted for twelve months before the company was absorbed by Curtiss-Wright; within this ever-growing conglomerate Keystone-Loening remained active until 1932, before closing down completely.

While the management and finances were being restructured, the Keystone XLB-3A was undergoing complete flight testing. Although the XLB-3A never entered service, it was used to help develop the following LB-5. The XLB-5 was similar to the earlier aircraft, although the engines were Libertys rated at 420hp. After test-flying, the XLB-5 was cleared for production, an initial order for ten being placed. These were fol-

Huff-Daland for conversion to XLB-3 standard. This saw the single-engine layout replaced by twin-engines mounted between the wings. The engines – air-cooled Liberty engines mounted in the inverted position – were also experimental. The Liberty engine installation proved unsuit-

The Huff-Daland LB-1 was an biplane light bomber operated by the US Army Air Service during the 1920s. It was derived from the XLB-1 prototype purchased by the Army in 1923 and was powered by a single Packard 2A-2540 engine.
via NARA/Dennis R. Jenkins

The Keystone XLB-7 was another variant of the LB-5 design. In this case, the aircraft was the first production aircraft that was used as a test aircraft. The XLB-7 was a LB-6 airframe modified to carry Pratt & Whitney R-1690-3 radial engines; however, in other respects it was identical to the LB-6. via NARA/Dennis R. Jenkins

The Keystone XLB-12 was a modification of the first LB-7 in which Pratt & Whitney R-1860-1 radial engines replaced the LB-7's P & W R-1690-3s. The XLB-12 was an engine test bed used for in-flight evaluation of engine performance. via NARA/ Dennis R. Jenkins

lowed by a further twenty-five aircraft, although these were designated the LB-5A and were fitted with twin fin and rudder assemblies instead of the earlier single fin and rudder; the twin fin and rudder layout remained a distinctive feature of the Keystone bombers until production ceased.

The follow-on bomber first saw the light of day as the XLB-6. This aircraft used the tenth LB-5 airframe, featuring straight-chord wings and Wright R-1750-1 Cyclone engines that were suspended between the wings instead of being mounted on the upper surface of the lower wing. Both the LB-5 and LB-6 were issued to the 2nd Bomb Group, this being the sole US-based bomber unit until 1928.

A follow-on order covered the delivery of eighteen LB-7s, these differing from the LB-6 in that the engine chosen was the Pratt & Whitney R-1690-3 Hornet. A handful of these aircraft were also involved in development work: the LB-10 was an LB-6 powered by R-1750-1s, while another became the LB-11 that was powered by R-1750-3s. The LB-10 saw a return to the single fin and rudder pioneered on the original Huff-Daland aircraft.

In 1930 the USAAC rationalized its aircraft designations, which were becoming far to cumbersome for ordinary usage. Therefore, all of the Keystone aircraft lost their LB- prefix, this being replaced by the more straightforward B- designation. The initial result of this for Keystone was that their next bomber contract covered the LB-10A, LB-13 and LB-14, although the former was delivered as the B-3A complete with single fin and rudder. The LB-13 was delivered in two separate batches: the first group of five aircraft were delivered as Y1B-4s with R-1860-7 engines while the remaining two were delivered as Y1B-6s with the R-1820-1. The final batch of three machines were the LB-14s, which were designated Y1B-5 and should have been completed with R-1750-1 engines, although some doubt exists as to their completion in this configuration. The production of all these aircraft ended in 1932, when Keystone finally disappeared.

Huff-Daland XB-1

While Huff-Daland/Keystone concentrated upon building light bombers they did have one stab at building a heavy bomber, this being designated the XHB-1, later changed to XB-1. The XHB-1, 26-201, had been developed from the earlier LB-1 although it was a bigger and heavier machine in all respects. It carried a crew of four, two in an open cockpit ahead of the wing, one near the tail with twin Lewis guns and the other in a retractable gun platform that could be lowered below the fuselage. Two Browning machine guns were

> ### Huff-Daland XB-1B
>
> Crew: 4
> Length: 61ft 6in (18.7m)
> Wingspan: 85ft 0in (25.9m)
> Height: 19ft 3in (5.9m)
> Wing area: 1,604ft² (149.0m²)
> Empty weight: 9,462lb (4,292kg)
> Loaded weight: 16.500lb (7,480kg)
> Powerplant: 2 × Curtiss V-1570-5 Conqueror liquid-cooled V12 engines, 600hp (450kW) each
>
> **Performance**
> Maximum speed: 100mph (86kt, 160km/h)
> Range: 700 miles (610nm, 1,100km)
> Service ceiling: 15,000ft (4,600m)
>
> **Armament**
> Guns: 6 × 0.30in machine guns
> Bombs: 4,000lb (1,800kg) maximum

mounted in the wings and over 4,000lb (1,800kg) of bombs could be carried. The XHB-1 first flew in October 1926. It was to have been powered by a single 1,200hp engine, but as this engine failed to materialize, a single Packard 2A-2540 engine, rated at 787hp, was substituted; this was the same engine that powered the LB-1. The XHB-1 was known unofficially as the 'Cyclops' by the Huff-Daland company.

The Huff-Daland XHB-1 was an enlarged version of the earlier Huff-Daland LB-1. As this was intended for use in the heavy bomber role, the single-engine layout was rejected by the Air Service on the grounds that it was too vulnerable to attack.
via NARA/Dennis R. Jenkins

ABOVE: The Huff-Daland XB-1 was a development of the earlier XHB-1 although it had two engines and thin fins. The engine nacelles carried defensive gun positions at the rear. via NARA/Dennis R. Jenkins

BELOW: The Curtiss XB-2 was based on the earlier Martin NBS-1 and was built under licence by Curtiss for the Glenn L. Martin Company. There were a few minor differences from the original, such as stronger materials and different engines, but the type was obsolescent before service entry so production was limited. via NARA/Dennis R. Jenkins

However, as early as April 1926, the US Army decided that single-engine bombers were unsatisfactory, concluding that the more conventional twin-engine configuration was safer and had the additional advantage of allowing for a gunner and/or bomb-aiming position to be mounted in the nose. Consequently, the XHB-1 was not ordered into production, and only one example was built.

The XB-1 featured a pair of engines provided by Packard, but these were not powerful enough to fly the aircraft safely. This single machine made its maiden flight in September 1927, although its flight time was short as it was grounded fairly quickly to allow for the fitment of Curtiss Conquerer engines; in this new guise the aircraft was designated the XB-1B. While the XB-1B was a better prospect, the far superior Curtiss XB-2 Condor was chosen to fulfil the heavy bomber role instead.

The Keystone XB-1B was the designation assigned to the Huff-Daland XB-1 after the original Packard 2A-1530 engines had been replaced by Curtiss V-1570-5 Conquerors. Huff-Daland was reorganized and renamed Keystone in 1927.
via NARA/Dennis R. Jenkins

Even with the change of engine, the Keystone XB-1B failed to perform as required, and contract was cancelled.
via NARA/Dennis R. Jenkins

Fokker XO-27

Given the position of the Dutch arm of the Fokker company during the Great War, it was fortunate for the American Fokker Company that it was seen as American enough to garner orders from the US Army. One of these machines was the Fokker XO-27, a twin-engine observation monoplane with seats for three crew. Initially two prototypes were built, the second of which was converted to XB-8 standard in response to an Army requirement. The following six O-7 aircraft were delivered as YO-7 aircraft, while a further six aircraft were ordered as B-8s although they were redesignated Y1O-27 before delivery.

The main innovation introduced by the Fokker machines was the use of a retractable undercarriage; also the fuselage was of tubular steel covered in fabric. Although the Fokker machine was a reasonable performer it was let down by the use of an unsuitable aerofoil, which was known to be incapable of further development. The XB-8 found itself in competition against the Douglas XB-7, which was a far better aircraft in all respects and so won the production contract.

Fokker XO-27/XB-8
Crew: 4
Length: 47ft (14m)
Wingspan: 64ft (20m)
Height: 11ft 6in (3.5m)
Wing area: 619ft² (57.5m²)
Empty weight: 6,861lb (3,112kg)
Loaded weight: 10,545lb (4,783kg)
Powerplant: 2 × Curtiss V-1570-23 Conqueror V-12 engines, 600hp (450kW) each
Performance
Maximum speed: 160mph (140kt, 260km/h)

The Fokker XO-27 was a mixed material aircraft: the wing was built entirely from wood while the fuselage was constructed from steel tubes covered with fabric. The aircraft featured the first retractable undercarriage ever fitted to a large Army Air Corps aircraft. via NARA/Dennis R. Jenkins

The Douglas Y1B-7 was a 1930s bomber aircraft and was the first US monoplane given the 'B' designation for 'Bomber'. At the time the XB-7 was ordered, it was being tested by Douglas Aircraft as an observation aircraft. The Y1B-7 never entered mass production due to its small bomb capacity.
via NARA/Dennis R. Jenkins

The Fokker XB-8 was a bomber built for the United States Army Air Corps in the 1920s, developed from the XO-27 observation aircraft. It was in competition against a design submitted by Douglas, the Y1B-7/XO-36. The XB-7 had a better performance than the XB-8, so no further examples were built. via NARA/Dennis R. Jenkins

Martin XB-10

While various aircraft manufacturers tried to satisfy the need for a reasonably capable bomber, the company that had delivered the Air Services' first aircraft, the MB-1 and MB-2, was also on the lookout for further military contracts. The Glenn L. Martin Company had managed to survive the post-war downturn in the economy, and when the US Army released a request for an all-metal monoplane bomber the company was able to respond quickly. Known as the Model 123, the initial XB-10 prototype had originally been manufactured as a private venture, although it is highly likely that the rumour of the forthcoming requirement had emerged from the War Department.

The resulting prototype was a four-seat machine that still retained open crew positions. While this was a touch retrograde in the light of developments in the civilian airline industry, the aircraft did feature some innovations; these included a deep fuselage that housed the bomb load, and a retractable undercarriage. The engines were a pair of Wright Cyclone SR-1820-Es, which provided more than enough power. The XB-10 made its maiden flight on 16 February 1932 and was delivered for testing at Wright Field on 20 March at the completion of its company flight trials.

Martin XB-10 and variants

Crew: 3
Length: 44ft 9in (13.6m)
Wingspan: 70ft 6in (21.5m)
Height: 15ft 5in (4.7m)
Wing area: 678ft² (63m²)
Empty weight: 9,681lb (4.391kg)
Loaded weight: 14,700lb (6,680kg)
Max. take-off weight: 16,400lb (7,440kg)
Powerplant: 2 × Wright R-1820-33 Cyclone radials, 775hp (578kW) each

Performance
Maximum speed: 213mph (185kt, 343km/h)
Cruise speed: 193mph (167.7kt, 310.6km/h)
Range: 1,240 miles (1,078nm, 1,996km)
Service ceiling: 24,200ft (7,380m)
Rate of climb: 1,380ft/min (7.01m/s)

Armament
Guns: 3 × 0.30in machine guns
Bombs: 2,260lb (1,030kg)

The appearance of the Martin XB-10 started a revolution in bomber design, although in comparison with the aircraft that followed, the Martin machine had a certain quaintness about it. It was the technology that marked it out as a key turning point in aircraft design, as it

The Martin XB-14 was basically a YB-10 airframe modified to carry Pratt & Whitney YR-1830-9 Twin Wasp radial engines. The aircraft was ordered in 1933 in company with the YB-10, YB-10A, YB-12 and B-12A, as part of an order for forty-eight aircraft in total. The only major difference between all these aircraft were the engines installed. via NARA/Dennis R. Jenkins

introduced an all-metal construction that spelled the death-knell for all-wood or composite wood/metal aircraft. Although the initial unit cost per aircraft was higher than those of earlier construction, using all-metal construction resulted in an aircraft that would last longer, was capable of further development and was much less prone to serious damage than aircraft using the older forms of construction.

After completing its evaluation, the prototype XB-10 received modifications that would further improve the type's capabilities: these included closed cockpits, rotating gun turrets and full cowlings. In recognition of Martin's bold design, they were awarded the Collier Trophy, which had been created by Robert J. Collier, the publisher and sports pilot, in 1911. Originally administered by the Aero Club of America, when that organization dissolved in 1922 the administering of the trophy became the responsibility of the National Aeronautic Association, who changed the name to honour Collier's contribution.

The first batch of forty-eight aircraft was ordered on 17 January 1933. The first fourteen machines were designated as YB-10 and delivered to Wright Field in November 1933 for evaluation purposes. As this was still the time of Army ownership of aircraft designs – Martin had to wait until the American orders had been fulfilled before offering the type for export. Some were exported to both Siam (Thailand) and Turkey, both models being upgraded versions of their US Army counterparts.

While the Martin B-10 was quickly superseded by later designs, it still managed to spawn a series of prototypes. The first of these was the YB-12, a re-engined version of the YB-10 that had been fitted with Pratt & Whitney R-1690-11 Hornet engines. As this change in engine resulted in an aircraft that was no faster than the B-10B, only seven were constructed. These were followed by the single XB-14. This utilized the last YB-10 airframe, the original engines being replaced by Pratt & Whitney YR-1830-9 Twin Wasp radial engines. Next came the XA-15 attack version that was to be powered by a pair of P&W R-1820-25 engines, though the Curtiss A-14 Shrike eventually won the competition. The final version of the B-10 was the YO-45, which was a YB-10 converted for the high-speed observation role.

Douglas YB-11

In November 1932 the USAAC ordered the development of an amphibious reconnaissance bomber aircraft that was intended to act as a navigation leader and rescue aircraft for formations of conventional bombers. The resulting aircraft that was ordered under the bomber designation YB-11, was based on the larger Douglas XP3D patrol flying boat for the US Navy. Prior to it being completed, it was redesignated as an observation aircraft YO-44 then later as the YOA-5. The aircraft undertook its maiden flight in January 1935 being delivered to the US Army

The Douglas YB-11 was based on the US Navy XP3D-1 seaplane. The USAAC ordered a smaller version of the aircraft incorporating design changes for amphibious operation. The aircraft was redesignated as an observation plane, YO-44, before construction was completed, although the type never entered service. via NARA/Dennis R. Jenkins

during February. The concept for which it was designed proved unworkable therefore no production order was placed however the YOA-5 did set two world distance records for amphibians before ending as scrap in December 1943. The YB-11 was the only amphibian ever to carry an Army Air Corps bomber designation.

Boeing B-9 and XB-15

The next bomber to make a significant impact on the development of the type was the Boeing XB-15. However, its development began with another aircraft, the Boeing B-9, in 1930. The Boeing design team had begun the development of the Models 214 and 215 in 1930 with the intention of convincing the US Army that it was time to replace their obsolete biplane bombers with more modern designs – the first efforts to replace the biplanes had been made by Fokker with the XO-27 and Douglas with the XO-35, both of which failed to live up to expectations.

Boeing had developed the Model 200 Monomail, an all-metal, low-wing monoplane with a monocoque fuselage, a cantilever wing and a retractable undercarriage. This was later offered to the US Army in 1930 as the basis for a modern bomber. The US Army were impressed enough to order an experimental bomber designated the XB-901. This was very similar to the

Monomail, and powered by a pair of Pratt & Whitney R-1860-13 Hornet engines mounted in nacelles in front of the wing. The prototype undertook its maiden flight on 13 April 1931, piloted by company test pilot Les Tower. After the usual company shakedown flights the XB-901 was delivered to the Army test field at Wright Field for official evaluation that June. The Army

---

Boeing YB-9

Crew: 4
Length: 51ft 6in (15.7m)
Wingspan: 76ft 10in (23.4m)
Height: 12ft 8in (3.86m)
Wing area: 954ft² (88.6m²)
Empty weight: 8,941lb (4,056kg)
Loaded weight: 13,932lb (6,320kg)
Max. take-off weight: 14,320lb (6,500kg)
Powerplant: 2 × Pratt & Whitney R-1860-11 Hornet radial engine, 600hp (450kW) each

Performance
Maximum speed: 188mph (163kt, 302km/h)
Cruise speed: 165mph (143kt, 265km/h)
Range: 540 miles (470nm, 870km)
Service ceiling: 20,750ft (6,325m)

Armament
Guns: 2 × 0.30in machine guns
Bombs: 2,200lb (1,000kg) bombs

The Y1B-9A was an improved version of the earlier YB-9, with a redesigned fin and rudder and more powerful engines. The Y1B-9A carried a crew of four, seated in separate open cockpits along the length of the fuselage. via NARA/Dennis R. Jenkins

test pilots were impressed with the XB-901, their reports convincing the Purchasing Branch to buy the extant aircraft plus a second uncompleted aircraft, which was to be finished with V-1570 engines. This extra machine was followed by a batch of five aircraft ordered in August 1931.

The XB-901 was returned to Boeing for the fitment of supercharged R-1860-11 engines, which increased its top speed to 188mph at 6,000ft (302km/h at 1,800m). In its new guise the aircraft was redesignated the YB-9. The five service test aircraft were designated Y1B-9A, Boeing Model 246, and were delivered during 1922 and 1923. The second prototype was completed with Curtiss Conquerer in-line engines and made its first flight from Seattle on 5 November 1931. In its new guise this Boeing Model 214 was delivered to the US Army as the Y1B-9. After test flying the Y1B-9 was found to have inferior performance compared with the other evaluation machines, so it was re-engined with Hornets. Unfortunately for Boeing its innovative use of materials and technology failed to impress the US Army enough, and so the contracts for the new bomber went to the Martin B-10.

Boeing XB-15

Although Boeing had failed to win any contracts for the Y1B-9 bomber, the company responded quickly to a US Army request for a 'hemisphere defender' long-range bomber that was issued on 14 April 1934. This requirement called for a range of 5,000 miles (3,200km) with a 2,000lb (900kg) bomb load. The Boeing Aircraft Company offered the Army the Model 294. The Army was interested enough in the Boeing proposal to issue a contract on 28 June 1934 that covered the design, wind-tunnel testing and a mock-up, all covered by the designation XBLR-1 (Experimental Bomber Long Range 1). The aircraft passed the design and inspection process successfully and on 29 June 1935 a contract for a single XBLR-1 was issued; the designation was changed to XB-15 in July 1936, when the more

---

Boeing XB-15

Crew: 10
Length: 87ft 7in (26.7m)
Wingspan: 149ft 0in (45.5m)
Height: 18ft 0in (5.5m)
Wing area: 2,780ft² (258m²)
Empty weight: 65,000lb (29,484kg)
Loaded weight: 69,000lb (31,298kg)
Max. take-off weight: 77,000lb (34,927kg)
Powerplant: 4 × 14-cylinder Pratt & Whitney R-1830-11 radial engines, 850hp (640kW) each

Performance
Maximum speed: 200mph (170kt, 320km/h)
Cruise speed: 152mph (132kt, 245km/h)
Combat radius: 3,400 miles (3,000nm, 5,500km)
Service ceiling 18,900ft (5,760m)
Rate of climb: 670ft/min (3.4m/s)

Armament
3 × 0.30in machine guns
3 × 0.50in machine guns
12,000lb (5,400kg) bombs

The Boeing XB-15, or Model 294, was designed in 1934 as a test bed for the USAAC. It was originally designated the XBLR-1. It set a number of load-to-altitude records that included a 31,205lb (14,152kg) flight to 8,200ft (2,500m) on 30 July 1939.
via NARA/Dennis R. Jenkins

long-winded designations were finally dropped from the Army vocabulary.

The aircraft that Boeing produced was a big, four-engined, mid-wing cantilever monoplane of all-metal semi-monocoque construction. Although it was not immediately obvious, the structural design was firmly based around that developed through the Monomail and YB-9 aircraft, the only exception to that rule being that the wing surface area aft of the main spar was covered in fabric instead of metal alloy sheet. It had originally been intended to install four Allison V-1710 liquid-cooled V-12 engines, but before the design was finally confirmed the Allison engine was cancelled and the XB-15's powerplant changed to the Pratt & Whitney R-1830 air-cooled radial. The wings that the engines were mounted on were of sufficient depth to allow the aircraft engineer to enter the space aft of the engines to carry out maintenance in flight, should it be needed – this feature was later covered over to the Boeing Model 314 flying boat.

The ten-man crew was housed in a fuselage that featured heating, pressurization and ventilation as well as crew rest bunks, an in-flight kitchen and a lavatory. The aircraft had a retractable main undercarriage units and tail wheel, the former having two main wheels per leg to reduce the pavement loading factor. The intended defensive armament was the heaviest yet fitted to a combat aircraft consisting of six machine guns. These were located in the nose turret, the forward-facing ventral turret, in the top turret, one in each waist blister and in a rear-facing ventral turret. The basic bomb load was set at 8,000lb (3,600kg), although a maximum overload of 12,000lb (5,400kg) could be carried over a shorter distance.

Even as Boeing was concentrating on getting the XB-15 into the air, its design team was already working on another aircraft, the Model 299, which would eventually emerge as the B-17 Flying Fortress. In fact, the XB-17 took to the air before the XB-15. The soon to be superseded

XB-15, serialled 35-277, made its maiden flight on 15 October 1937 with chief test pilot Eddie Allan at the controls. Although the XB-15 was the biggest and heaviest aircraft to have flown in America up to that date, its very size meant that the Pratt & Whitney engines were never powerful enough to deliver the aircraft's projected performance, the aircraft being limited to a maximum speed of 200mph (320km/h). While the XB-15 performed reasonably enough, in comparison with the B-17 it was found sadly lacking, so only the one example was constructed.

Having completed its company and Wright Field test flying, the XB-15 was handed over to the 2nd Bomb Group in August 1938 for service evaluation and to introduce the concept of the long-range heavy bomber to the USAAC. During this period the XB-15, also known as 'Grandpappy', undertook some long-range flights including visiting many of the capitals in Latin America. As well as long-range flying the aircraft also set some world records for weight carriage. The first took place on 30 June 1939 when the aircraft lifted 31,205lb (14,152kg) to a height of 8,200ft (2,500m) while a later flight saw 4,409lb (2,000kg) carried at a speed of 166mph (267km/h) over a distance of 3,107 miles (5,000km).

Although only one XB-15 was built, it did find some employment as a test bed for both Boeing and the trials teams at Wright Field before the United States became embroiled in World War Two. By 1943 there was little trials work available to the XB-15 so the aircraft was converted into a cargo carrier, for which purpose the bomber equipment was replaced with cargo doors and a cargo hoist. In this new guise the aircraft was redesignated the XC-105 and undertook numerous cargo flights throughout the continental United States. After two years' service the XC-105 found itself standing at Kelly Field just before the war's end, where it was eventually scrapped.

While the XB-15/XC-105 was a one-off, there had been an intention to order two service trials aircraft with the designation Y1B-20. The intended powerplant was the 1,400hp Pratt & Whitney R-2180 radial. Although the XB-15 and the XB-20 never made their mark in the annals of the American bomber, their design and construction did help the Boeing design teams when they were faced with creating the B-29 Superfortress.

Martin XB-16

Boeing at least got their aircraft for the 'hemisphere defender' contract of 1934 into the air; the competition provided by the Glenn L. Martin Company, the Model 145 or XB-16, was not so fortunate. Like the Boeing machine it was intended to carry a 2,000lb bomb load over 5,000 miles, and to be powered by four Allison V-1710s. In 1935 the Martin company decided to revise the XB-16 design, increasing the span from 140ft (42.7m) to 173ft (52.7m) and adding another pair of engines mounted on the trailing edge of wing. To support this increased size and weight, a tricycle landing gear was to be adopted while the original single fin and rudder were replaced by twin fins and rudders. Though this resulted in an impressive-looking machine, the US Army was concerned that the engines then available did not produce enough power to move such an aircraft, so the entire project was cancelled.

Martin XB-16
Crew: 11
Length: 115ft (35.0m)
Wingspan: 173ft (52.7m)
Empty weight: 104,880lb (47,573kg)
Powerplant: 4, later 6 × Allison V-1710, 850hp (640kW) each
Performance
Maximum speed: 190mph (170kt, 310km/h)
Cruise speed: 140mph (120kt, 230km/h)
Range: 3,300 miles (2,900nm, 5,300km)

Douglas XB-19

Another aircraft that entered the Army competition of 1935 was provided by Douglas Aircraft. Initially designated the XBLR-2, this truly was a monstrous machine. The US Army Air Corps had initiated the project on 5 February 1935 as Project 'D', the Boeing XB-15 being known as Project 'A'. While Project 'D' was not intended to end in a production aircraft, the AAF was interested in seeing how far current and imminent technologies could be pushed. Only two companies – Douglas and Sikorsky – responded to this very secret proposal document. The designations for these aircraft were given as the

---

Douglas XB-19

Crew: 16
Length: 132ft 2in (40.2m)
Wingspan: 212ft 0in (64.6m)
Height: 42ft 9in (13.0m)
Wing area: 4,492ft² (417m²)
Empty weight: 140,230lb (63,500kg)
Loaded weight: 158,930lb (72,000kg)
Max. take-off weight: 164,000lb (74,400kg)
Powerplant: 4 × Allison V-3420-11 V24 engines, 2,600hp
(1,940kW) each

Performance

Maximum speed: 265mph (230kt, 426km/h)
Cruise speed: 165mph (143kt, 266km/h)
Range: 4,200 miles (3,600nm, 6,800km)
Service ceiling: 39,000ft (12,000m)
Rate of climb: 650ft/min (3.3m/s)

Armament

5 × 0.50in machine guns
6 × 0.30in machine guns
2 × 37mm cannon
18,700lb (8,480kg) bombs

XBLR-2 for the Douglas machine and XLBR-3 for the Sikorsky. Contracts covering preliminary layouts, detail designs and the testing of critical components were issued to both organizations in October 1935, the AAF stressing that the prototypes had to be ready for delivery by 31 March 1938. Both companies had their mock-ups ready for inspection in March 1936. After detailed inspection of both designs, the Douglas aircraft was cleared for production while the XLBR-3 contract was terminated.

Although Douglas had secured the contract to build the XLBR-2, progress was slow as the economic depression between 1935 and 1937 restricted the monies available for military research and development. The aircraft was a large, four-engined, low-wing monoplane that sat on a tricycle undercarriage – the latter had been trialled on a Douglas OA-4B Dolphin amphibian loaned by the Army for purpose. The intended powerplant was the 2,600hp Allison XV-3420-1 24-cylinder liquid-cooled engine; this had been created by coupling a pair of V-1710 engines to drive a single drive shaft. As this was a very experimental engine and given that Allison was having development trouble with the V-1710, Douglas

Aircraft decided to fit the aircraft with the Wright R-3350 air-cooled radial, rated at 2,000hp.

In 1936 the long-winded XLBR designation was finally dropped by the US Army, and the Douglas aircraft was henceforth known as the XB-19. Funds were made available in late 1937 allowing Douglas to complete the XB-19, although the contract had to be rewritten to allow for the change of powerplant and approval was delayed until March 1938, when the serial 38-471 was allocated. Despite the release of funds, it was fairly obvious that the delivery date could not now be met: by this time Douglas was forced to spend its own funds just to keep the project ticking over. This situation was not to the company's liking as the project was tying up too many design staff who were required for other, more commercial, projects. This was not the only problem: it had become apparent that the XB-19's weight had risen during design, which meant that the available top speed was dropping; also, advances in aircraft design meant that the XB-19 was going to be obsolescent before it had even flown. Therefore, on 8 August 1938 Douglas requested that the Army cancel the XB-19.

The whole project became a bone of contention between Douglas and the Army: while Douglas wanted to cancel the aircraft, the Army Material Division wanted construction to continue. Douglas continued work on the XB-19, albeit slowly, and in 1940 the still-hangared aircraft was removed from the secret list as any design inovations had long lost their significance; none the less, the unveiling of the XB-19's existence to the American press corps led to a flurry of reports proclaiming the Douglas XB-19 as the bomber to attack all enemies of America. After one of the longest development and building periods up to that time, the XB-19 was finally completed in May 1941.

The aircraft that Douglas rolled out to the waiting world had a wingspan that reached 212ft and a maximum gross weight of 162,000lb. It was powered by four 2,000hp Wright R-3350-5 eighteen-cylinder air-cooled radials driving three-blade constant-speed propellers. Normal internal fuel loading was 10,350 US gallons, although there was provision in the bomb bay for overload tanks that could hold another 824 US gallons.

The bomb load could be carried either in the bomb bay or on the ten external racks under the wings. The internal load could consist of eight

The Douglas XB-19 was the largest bomber aircraft built for the USAAC prior to 1946. The aircraft first flew on 27 June 1941 some three years after the construction contract was awarded. In 1943 the original Wright R-3350 engines were replaced by Allison V-3420-11s. After completion of flight testing the XB-19 served in the freight role until it was scrapped in 1949.
via NARA/Dennis R. Jenkins

2,000lb, sixteen 1,100lb or thirty 600lb bombs, while the underwing carriers could tote a further 2,000lb by weight of bombs; thus the maximum bomb load was 37,100lb.

The proposed defensive armament was a 37mm cannon in the nose, single 0.30in machine guns in the nose and the forward dorsal turrets, and 0.50in machine guns in the tail, aft dorsal and ventral turrets, and in the port and starboard waist positions. Further 0.30in machine guns could be mounted on each side of the bomb aimer's position and on each side of the fuselage, just below the tail plane.

The crew for the XB-19 matched the aircraft in size, numbering sixteen in total. There were a pilot, co-pilot, aircraft commander, navigator, flight engineer, radio operator and bomb aimer, while the remainder manned the gun positions. On long-range flights away from base, a support crew of two flight mechanics and six additional flight crew could be carried in a compartment above the bomb bay; this was equipped with eight seats and six bunks. Should their services be needed, the flight mechanics could gain access to the rear of the engines to carry out minor maintenance in flight. As well as good accommodation for the crew and extras, the XB-19 was fitted with a full galley in which it was possible to prepare complete hot meals.

The XB-19 finally made its maiden flight from Clover Field, Santa Monica, on 27 June 1941, three years behind schedule. On this occasion the crew was restricted to seven, the captain being Major Stanley M. Umstead. Once airborne and with initial handling checks completed, the XB-19 was flown to March Field where after landing it was handed over to the US Army for evaluation. Although it was obsolescent, the fuss made by the press was sufficient enough for President Roosevelt to send a congratulatory telegram to Donald Douglas, head of the Douglas Corporation.

The first thirty hours of flight time were spent teaching the Army crew about their new mount as well as carrying out the first set of flight and handling trials. Eventually the Douglas support was reduced and the Army took over full control of the XB-19 in October 1941.

When the Japanese attacked the US Navy fleet at Pearl Harbor on 7 December 1941, the US Army applied olive drab and grey camouflage to the XB-19, while the full armament and ammunition was fitted and gunners allocated to man it; these changes were prominent on the aircraft's last four test flights. While the reality of the situation was that Pearl Harbor was the closest the Japanese forces would ever get to the continental United States apart from a small number of insignificant nuisance raids, the situation was regarded as fluid enough for the XB-19 to be transferred to Wright Field as a protective measure – this location was well outside of the range of Japanese attack aircraft.

The US Army continued their evaluation of the XB-19, during which few modifications were made; the most significant was the replacement of the original brakes by more powerful units. The only other problem encountered was that of engine cooling, which required that the cooling gills be kept open at all times during long flights, reducing the maximum speed to 204mph at 15,700ft, a reduction of 20mph. The Army finally accepted the XB-19 formally and Douglas were accordingly paid $1,400,064 by the government. This represented a considerable loss for the company as it had spent nearly $4 million of its own funding during the design and construction of the XB-19. Given the money already spent by both Douglas and the Army, the investigation and curing of the engine problems was not addressed.

At the completion of the XB-19's flight trials the US Army was a in quandary as to what to do with it. As it was never to enter full-scale production, it was decided to convert it into a cargo transport aircraft in a similar manner to the Boeing XB-15. During the conversion process the opportunity was taken to re-engine the aircraft with 2,600hp Allison V-3420-11 turbocharged 24-cylinder liquid-cooled engines, this being the powerplant that had originally been intended for the aircraft. In its new guise the aircraft was redesignated as the XB-19A. With the change of engine all the problems with engine cooling immediately disappeared, while the maximum speed increased to 275mph. During its time as a transport aircraft the XB-19A was utilized in a similar manner to the Boeing XB-15, carrying cargo and passengers throughout the continental United States.

The aircraft made its final flight on 17 August 1946 when it was delivered to the storage centre at Davis-Monthan Field near Tuscon, Arizona. Originally it was intended that the XB-19A would be preserved, but the majority of the airframe was scrapped by 1949. The nose section was reported to be in a scrapyard in Los Angeles in 1955, but it appears that this, too, was eventually scrapped, and the only surviving item from the wartime behemoth is a main wheel at the Hill AFB Aerospace Museum where it has been on show since 1993.

Douglas XA-2

Although pursuit (fighter) aircraft and bombers featured highly in the USAAC procurement programme, the US Army was well aware that close air support of ground forces was a growing requirement that needed specialist aircraft. The first attempt to provide such a machine began in 1923 when the War Department awarded the Douglas Corporation a contract to manu-

---

Douglas XA-2

Crew: 2
Length: 29ft 7in (9.02m)
Wingspan: 39ft 8in (12.09m)
Height: 11ft (3.4m)
Max. take-off weight: 4,985lb (2,260kg)
Powerplant: 1 × Liberty V-1410 inverted piston engine, 433hp (323kW)

Performance
Maximum speed: 130mph (210km/h)
Cruise speed: 100mph (160km/h)
Range: 400 miles (600km)
Service ceiling: 15,000ft (4,500m)

Armament
6 × forward firing 0.30-cal machine guns
2 × 0.30-cal machine guns
Provision for 100lb (45kg) of bombs mounted on lower wing racks

facture a pair of experimental aircraft designated XO-2 for an observation aircraft. While the XO-2 eventually entered quantity service with the USAAC, the manufacturers thought that there was more life left in the design. The War Department was also aware of this fact as they had awarded Douglas a contract to convert the final O-2, 25-380, as an attack aircraft to be designated the XA-2. This aircraft was to be powered by a Liberty engine; this being air-cooled, there would be no need for a vulnerable radiator. The armament consisted of six forward-firing machine guns of 0.30in calibre, two each in the upper engine cowling, the upper wing and the lower wing. A further pair of machine guns was carried on a flexible mounting in the rear cockpit. The XA-2 was delivered to the USAAC in 1926 and was tested in competition with the Curtiss XA-3, although it lost out in the flight test competition.

General Aviation/Fokker XA-7

The Curtiss A-3 equipped the 3rd Attack Group from 1926, although by 1930 the USAAC was well aware that these aircraft were coming to the end of their service life. At the end of 1929 the Army requested proposals from manufacturers for a replacement type, and one of the first responses was from General Aviation (Fokker)

General Aviation/Fokker XA-7

Crew: 2
Length: 31ft (9.45m)
Wingspan: 46ft 9in (14.25m)
Height: 9ft 5in (2.87m)
Wing area: 333ft² (30.94m²)
Empty weight: 3,866lb (1,754kg)
Max. take-off weight: 5,650lb (2,563kg)
Powerplant: 1 × Curtis Conqueror V-12 liquid cooled, 600hp (448kW)

Performance
Maximum speed: 184mph (296km/h)

Armament
5 × 0.30-cal machine guns and 488lb (221kg) of bombs

---

whose entrant, the XA-7, was ordered by the US Army on 8 January 1930.

This single prototype was a two-seat, low-winged monoplane powered by a Curtiss XV-1570-27 Conqueror engine rated at 600hp. In a slightly backwards step the wing, although cantilever, was thicker than previous aircraft types', while the undercarriage was fixed, covered by large fairings. The cockpits were open while under the fuselage there was a tunnel radiator for engine cooling. Fixed armament consisted of four 0.30in machine guns while the gunner/observer had a single weapon on a flexible mount.

The General Aviation/Fokker XA-7 was a prototype attack aircraft ordered in December 1929, and made its first flight in January 1931. The Curtiss A-8 eventually won the competition so A-7 development was cancelled. The XA-7 was a two-seat, low-wing, all-metal monoplane design featuring a thick cantilever wing, tunnel radiator and two closely spaced open cockpits. via NARA/Dennis R. Jenkins

The Curtiss XA-8 was designed in response to a USAAC requirement for an attack aircraft to replace the Curtiss Falcon, which had been in service since 1927. The Curtiss Model 59 Shrike was designated XA-8 by the Army. The aircraft remained a test-bed aircraft until scrapped in early 1937. via NARA/Dennis R. Jenkins

The Curtiss XA-14 was a 1930s twin-engine attack aircraft tested by the USAAC. Manned by a crew of two, it was as fast as the standard pursuit aircraft in service at the time. No production aircraft were purchased, although thirteen service test aircraft were ordered with a different engine under the designation Y1A-18. via NARA/Dennis R. Jenkins

Curtiss XA-8/Y1A-8A

Crew: 2
Length: 32ft 10in (10m)
Wingspan: 44ft 3in (13.5m)
Loaded weight: 5,710lb (2,590kg)
Powerplant: 1 × Curtiss V-1570-31 Conqueror Vee, 600hp (447kW)

Performance
Maximum speed: 184mph (296km/h)

Armament
4 × 0.30in machine guns in the wheel fairings
1 × 0.30in machine gun in the rear cockpit
4 × 100lb bombs carried under the wings

The XA-7 was rolled out in April 1931, although the undercarriage was modified in June before the aircraft was delivered to Wright Field for testing. Flight testing began in September against the Curtiss XA-8, although the Fokker design was unsuccessful in the event.

Curtiss XA-14

The Curtiss XA-14 was unfortunate in appearing just when the Great Depression was at its peak. Also known as the Model 76, this aircraft was a mid-wing monoplane of all-metal construction, the only fabric-covered areas being the control surfaces and the wing aft of the main spar. Power was provided by a pair of Wright R-1670-5 air-cooled radials driving two-blade propellers. The pilot was seated well forward in the fuselage under a canopy, while the observer was further aft under a separate canopy. The armament consisted of four nose-mounted machine guns and a single weapon on a flexible mount for the observer.

The XA-14 made its maiden flight on 17 July 1935 wearing the registration X15314. After test flying by the USAAC at Wright Field, the XA-14 was returned to Curtiss where new cowlings and propellers were fitted. Post-modification, the aircraft was purchased by the Army in December 1935 and given the serial 36-146. While the XA-14 comfortably outperformed the fighters

of the day, the Army declined to order any production aircraft as each cost $90,000 minus the
engine; however, a service test batch of thirteen
aircraft was ordered as the Y1A-18 in July 1936.
The single XA-14 was originally going to undertake record-attempting flights, but the USAAC
required a test bed for a new 37mm cannon. After
the completion of these trials the XA-14 was
scrapped in August 1938 after 158 flying hours.

**The Curtiss XA-14 was a 1930s twin-engine attack aircraft
tested by the USAAC. Manned by a crew of two, it was as
fast as the standard pursuit aircraft in service at the time. No
production aircraft were purchased although thirteen service
test aircraft were ordered with a different engine under the
Y1A-18 designation.** via NARA/ Dennis R Jenkins

Curtiss XA-14
Crew: 2
Length: 40ft 3in (12.3m)
Wingspan: 59ft 5in (18.11m)
Height: 10ft 9in (3.3m)
Max. take-off weight: 11,750lb (5,330kg)
Powerplant: 2 × Wright R-1670-5 radials, 775hp (578kW) each
Performance
Maximum speed: 220.7kt (254mph, 408.8km/h)
Range: 717nm (825 miles, 1,327.7km)
Service ceiling: 27,100ft (8,260m)
Armament
5 × 0.30in machine guns
650lb (300kg) bombs in internal bay

Northrop Gamma 2C

While Curtiss was trying to sell the Army
expensive ground-attack aircraft, the Northrop
Corporation presented the USAAC with a
slightly cheaper alternative. The aircraft was the
company-financed Gamma 2C, which followed
on from the Gamma 2A and SB research aircraft.
This design retained the wings and trousered
undercarriage units from the earlier machines,
although Northrop designed a new fuselage
that housed a crew of two under a full canopy.
Power was provided by a Wright SR-1820-F2
air-cooled radial rated at 735hp. The fixed armament was four forward-firing machine guns while
the observer had a single weapon that could be
discharged either upward through the canopy or

downwards through a ventral hatch. The bomb
load of 1,100lb was carried on racks between the
undercarriage legs.

The aircraft was purchased by the USAAC
as the YA-13 on 28 June 1934, serial number
34-27. Initial test flying revealed that an engine
of increased power was needed, although its location needed thought, too, as the original engine
obscured the pilot's forward vision. The answer
was to return the YA-13 to Northrop in January
1935 where it was re-engined with a Pratt &
Whitney R-1830-7 Twin Wasp air-cooled radial
that was rated at 950hp yet had a smaller diameter. The change in engine resulted in a change
of designation to XA-16.

In its new guise, the XA-16 first flew in March
1935. Test flying revealed that the aircraft was
now over-powered, so either a lower-powered

The Northrop XA-16 was the final designation of the aircraft that had originated as the Northrop Gamma 2C. Northrop also developed the A-17, the primary single-engine attack aircraft used by the USAAC during the late 1930s. As the A-17 proved successful the XA-16 programme was cancelled. via NARA/Dennis R. Jenkins

---

Northrop YA-13

Crew: 2
Length: 29ft 8in (9.04m)
Wingspan: 48ft 0in (14.63m)
Height: 9ft 2in (2.79m)

Performance
Maximum speed: 184kt (212mph, 341km/h)
Cruise speed: 169.5kt (195mph, 313.8km/h)
Range: 869nm (1,000 miles, 1,609km)
Service ceiling: 22,000ft (67,000m)

Armament
4 × 0.30in machine guns
1 × 0.30in. machine gun
Provision for up to 1,100lb (500kg) of bombs mounted on wing racks

---

engine or tail surfaces of increased area were needed. Fortunately, Northrop had already sold the following Gamma 2F as the A-17, so the XA-16 was cancelled.

Stearman XA-21

Possibly the strangest and bluntest-looking attack aircraft built in the inter-war years was the Stearman XA-21. In 1937 the Army Material Division started researching the possibility of acquiring a twin-engine attack bomber that could outperform the fighters of the day. In March 1938 the USAAC issued Circular Proposal Number 38-385, which laid out the requirements for the new aircraft. All interested parties were invited to construct prototypes at their own expense that would be ready by March 1939 for the Army competition fly-off. The Stearman aircraft – designated the Model X-100 – was a high-wing monoplane powered by a pair of

Pratt & Whitney R-2180 engines. Although the design and construction of the X-100 started under Stearman, the finished article was rolled out under Boeing colours as Stearman had been purchased by the larger company.

The crew for this aircraft consisted of a pilot, bomb aimer and a radio operator/gunner. The first two sat under a single canopy in the smoothly contoured nose while the radio operator/gunner was housed under a separate canopy in the rear of the fuselage, from where he controlled four machine guns. One each was carried in dorsal and ventral turrets while the others sat in flexible mountings on each side of the fuselage. Should he be needed, a fourth crew member could be carried to man the defensive armament. The X-100 featured an electrically driven undercarriage, integral fuel tanks, fully feathering constant-speed

---

Stearman XA-21

Crew: 3
Length: 53ft 1in (16.18m)
Wingspan: 65ft 0in (19.81m)
Height: 14ft 2in (4.32m)
Wing area: 607ft² (56.39m²)
Empty weight: 12,760lb (5,789kg)
Loaded weight: 18,230lb (8,269kg)
Powerplant: 2 × Pratt & Whitney R-2180-7 radial engines, 1,400hp (1,030kW) each

Performance
Maximum speed: 223kt (257mph, 414km/h)
Cruise speed: 174kt (200mph, 322km/h)

Armament
4 × wing-mounted 0.30in machine guns
1 × nose-mounted 0.30in machine gun
4 × aft-firing 0.30in machine guns
2,700lb (1,200kg) of bombs

The Army Air Corps requested design proposals from five aircraft manufacturers for a twin-engine light attack bomber in the late 1930s. Stearman submitted its model X-100; while the USAAC did not order any production aircraft, they did buy the prototype and designate it XA-21. via NARA/Dennis R. Jenkins

propellers and sealed compartments throughout the wings and fuselage, to ensure flotation should the aircraft ditch. In the X-100's initial configuration the pilot was forced to look through the bomb aimer's compartment, but a stepped windscreen was then fitted, slightly disrupting the earlier smooth contour.

The contest that the Army had devised for its new attack aircraft took until 1939 to resolve; the winner was the Douglas DB-7, later redesignated the A-20. Although the X-100 had lost out to the DB-7 it was later purchased by the USAAC, serialled 40-191, the service accepting it in September 1939. After a short period as a trials aircraft the XA-21 was scrapped.

Transport Aircraft

During the inter-war period the USAAC normally purchased its transport aircraft from available commercial stocks, but some designs were purchased for evaluation purposes. The first of these was the Boeing 221A Monomail mail aircraft, which was given the military designation Boeing Y1C-18. As the aircraft would not be available for at least six months Boeing offered the prototype for the intervening period. While the Army was reasonably happy with the Monomail, aircraft from other manufacturers already on order meant that the Monomail prototype was returned to Boeing and the contract for the Y1C-18 was cancelled.

The USAAC also tested a Fokker F.32 civil transport as the YC-20. Although the Fokker had a spacious passenger cabin, its performance and handling was deemed inadequate for military usage so it was returned to the manufacturer.

The final transport aircraft tested by the US Army was the Kreider-Reisner XC-941. This was a single-engine, high-wing monoplane ordered in 1934. While the aircraft, now designated the XC-31 and now produced by Fairchild, was a reasonable performer, the USAAC decided instead to opt for the twin-engine safety factor offered by the forthcoming Douglas transports. However, although the XC-31 never achieved production, the single example was used for transport and cargo carriage throughout the 1930s.

Fokker YC-20

Crew: 2 or 3
Capacity: 32 sitting passengers; 16 sleeping passengers
Length: 73ft 1in (22.2m)
Wingspan: 99ft 1in (30.2m)
Height: 16ft 8in (5.1m)
Powerplant: 4 × Pratt & Whitney Hornet radial, 575hp (429kW) each

---

In 1934 the USAAC evaluated a large single-engine, high-wing monoplane built by Kreider-Reisner as the XC-31. Although it never entered production, the aircraft was used in the staff transport, training, liaison, and light cargo-carrying missions. via NARA/Dennis R. Jenkins

CHAPTER THREE

US Navy Prototypes and Trials Aircraft

The US Navy had provided a complete battle squadron to the Royal Navy's Grand Fleet based in Scapa Flow during World War One. Although there was little for the mighty battleships to do, the American hierarchy had taken note of the number of aircraft carried by the Royal Navy's battleships, battlecruisers and small carrier group. Upon returning to America the US Navy faced numerous problems in introducing carrier aviation into the fleet. There was a major downturn in finances from 1919 as contracts were cancelled and the navy was reduced in size, and looming on the horizon were the ramifications of the Washington Treaty, which limited the size of fleets and the vessels themselves; just over the horizon was the Wall Street Crash and the Great Depression that followed it.

The First US Aircraft Carriers

All of these problems notwithstanding, the Naval Appropriations Act for Fiscal Year 1920 provided funds to purchase the collier *Jupiter* for conversion into a vessel capable of carrying aircraft, these monies being made available in July 1919. Later to become the USS *Langley* (CV-1), this carrier featured a full-length flight deck and, as building continued, other changes were applied including the provision of catapult launchers at both ends of the flight deck. The Langley was formerly commissioned into the US Navy on 20 March 1922 with the executive officer, Commander Kenneth Whiting, assuming command at the vessel's home base of Norfolk, Virginia.

While the *Langley* was working up, various engineering organizations were investigating types of arrestor gear. The specification sent to these parties required that the arresting gear consist of two or more transverse wires stretched across fore-and-aft wires that lead around sheaves placed outboard of hydraulic brakes. The aircraft, after engaging the transverse wire, was to be guided down the deck by the fore-and-aft wires and brought to rest by the action of the transverse wire working with the hydraulic brake. Not only would this be applied to the *Langley* when available, but it was also slated for the vessels to follow.

As the Washington Treaty began to take effect, Congress was faced in 1922 with the decision whether to scrap the two battlecruisers building on their slipways or to finish building them as aircraft carriers. Fortunately, as it turned out, the politicians decided to complete both vessels as aircraft carriers, thus the key ships *Saratoga* and *Lexington* were added to the fleet.

As the building of the next two aircraft carriers continued, the *Langley* undertook its first aircraft launch on 22 October 1922 when a Vought VE-7SF biplane piloted by Lt V.C. Griffin took off from the carrier while it was at anchor in the York River, Virginia. On 26 October a successful aircraft landing was made while the *Langley* was underway by Lt Cdr Godfrey de C. Chevalier piloting an Aeromarine, the vessel cruising off Cape Henry, Virginia. Unfortunately Chevalier was badly injured in an aircraft crash on 12 November, dying from his injuries two days later. *Langley* undertook the first US Navy catapult launch on 18 November 1922 when Cdr Whiting was launched in a PT seaplane.

Langley continued in its trials role for the next two years before officially joining the battle fleet on 17 November 1924; on 1 December the carrier was nominated as flagship for Aircraft

The USS *Langley*, CV-1/AV-3, was the US Navy's first aircraft carrier, being converted in 1920 from the collier USS *Jupiter*, she was also the navy's first electrically propelled ship. Following another conversion to seaplane tender standard, the *Langley* fought in World War Two. The ship was so badly damaged by Japanese bombing attacks on 27 February 1942 that it was sunk by the escort vessels. via US Navy/Dennis R. Jenkins

Squadrons, Battle Fleet. USS *Langley* remained the only active carrier until the USS *Saratoga* (CV-3) commissioned on 16 November 1927 at Camden, New Jersey, the ship's first commanding officer being Captain Harry Yarnell. The *Saratoga* was quickly followed by the *Lexington* (CV-2) on 14 December at Quincy, Massachusetts, Captain Albert Marshell commanding. *Saratoga* achieved a first of its own when Cdr Marc A. Mitscher, the ship's Air Officer, made the first take-off and landing, piloting a Vought UO-1.

Both new carriers took part in fleet exercises between 23 and 27 January 1929, attached to the opposing forces. *Saratoga*, in company with an escorting cruiser, was detached from the main force and sent on a wide southward sweep before turning north to approach within striking distance of the designated target, the Panama Canal. On the morning of the 26th, during the dark hours, the carrier launched its strike group of sixty-nine aircraft, which arrived over the target undetected shortly after dawn, complet-

ing the theoretical destruction of the Miraflores and Pedro Miguel locks without any opposition. This demonstration of naval strike power and the flexibility of the aircraft carrier made a profound impression on naval tacticians.

Although all the operational carriers had arrestor gear fitted, operations aboard the *Saratoga* and *Lexington* revealed that as the aircraft used their own brakes to stop, the arrestor systems were rarely used; thus the Secretary of State for the Navy authorised their removal in April 1929. Aircraft carriers can also provide other services, as *Lexington* proved when it was tied up near Tacoma, Washington, to provide power to the town when the local power station failed. During a thirty-day period electricity from the carrier totalled more than 4.25 million kilowatt-hours.

The US Navy started to look forward to its next aircraft carrier, USS *Ranger* (CV-4), which was laid down 26 September 1931 at the dockyard at Newport News Shipbuilding and Drydock Company, Virginia. The carrier was launched on

25 February 1933 and commissioned on 4 June 1934 at the Norfolk Navy Yard, the commanding officer being Captain Arthur Bristol. Not long after the commissioning of USS *Ranger* the Naval Aircraft Factory was authorized to manufacture and test a flush deck hydraulic catapult, the Type H Mark I. This catapult was designed to launch wheeled aircraft from aircraft carriers and was the initial development of a hydraulic catapult, a type which was to become the primary means of launching aircraft from carriers.

With the fourth carrier in commission and two more on the way (USS *Yorktown* was launched on 4 April 1936 and USS *Enterprise* on 3 October the same year) the decision was taken to retire the *Langley* from front-line naval service. Over a four-month period from April 1937 the vessel was converted into a seaplane tender, being redesignated AV-3 soon afterwards. Six months later, on 30 September, the *Yorktown* was commissioned at Norfolk Naval Operating Base (NOB), Virginia, with Captain Ernest D. McWhorter in command. On 12 May 1938 the *Enterprise* was commissioned at the Newport News Shipbuilding and Drydock Company, Newport News, Virginia, commanded by Captain N. H. White.

Berliner Joyce XF2J-1

Aircraft prototypes for naval use were few as the service spent much of the period between 1919 and 1930 finding the right aircraft types to operate from the new carrier force via a piece-meal process of using small batches from different manufacturers.

One of the first types considered for regular service was the Berliner Joyce XF2J-1; this was the navalized version of the P-16 that had entered service with the USAAC, and the US Navy ordered a single example in 1931 for evaluation. The primary difference between the two versions was that the naval aircraft was fitted with a 625hp Pratt & Whitney R-1510-92 Hornet instead of the inline engine fitted to the Army fighter. The installation of this radial engine required the manufacture of a wider fuselage. This originally had twin open cockpits, although a full canopy was subsequently fitted at the request of the Navy. The aircraft was given the Bureau of Aeronautics serial 8973.

The manufacture of the XF2J-1 took two years

Berliner-Joyce XF2J-1

Crew: 2
Length: 28ft 2in (8.59m)
Wingspan: 34ft 0in (10.36m)
Height: 10ft 2in (3.10m)
Empty weight: 2,734lb (1,240kg)
Max. take-off weight: 3,968lb (1,800kg)
Powerplant: 1 × Pratt & Whitney R-1510-92 Hornet, 625hp

Performance
Maximum speed: 172mph (282km/h)
Range: 650 miles (1046km)

Armament
2 × fixed forward-firing and 1 × flexible-mounted 0.30in machine guns
maximum bombload 224lb (102kg)

---

to complete as Berliner Joyce, like many companies, was experiencing financial difficulties. By the time it was ready the XF2J-1 was up against the Grumman FF-1, a far more capable machine. Although the Grumman aircraft was the outright winner of the competition, the XF2J-1 was put through a full flight test schedule, which revealed that, like the P-16, it suffered from poor visibility during landing, a fatal flaw for a carrier-based aircraft. Another factor that worked against the XF2J-1 was the decision by Wright Engines to cancel the R-1510-92 radial, so the US Navy decided against ordering more aircraft.

The failure of XF2J-1 and the financial problems surrounding the company saw it fade from view. North American Aircraft acquired the assets of Berliner Joyce in 1933; twelve months later Berliner Joyce became a full division of NAA at which time its assets were moved to Inglewood, Berliner Joyce disappearing for ever.

Boeing Carrier-Based Fighters

Boeing entered the carrier aircraft fray with a navalized version of the XP-15 monoplane, this being designated the XF5B-1 by the US Navy and Model 205 by Boeing. As with most such adaptions the naval aircraft was fitted with an arrestor hook and other equipment specific to its role; to cater for the increase in weight a Pratt & Whitney SR-1340C rated at 480hp and fitted with a supercharger was installed. This proto-

Boeing XF7B-1	Boeing XF6B/XBFB-1
Crew: 1 Length: 22ft 7in (6.8m) Wingspan: 32ft (9.7m) Height: 10ft 0in (3.04m) Loaded weight: 3,857lb (1,749kg) Powerplant: 1 × Pratt & Whitney R-1340-30 Wasp radial engine, 550hp (420kW) **Performance** Maximum speed: 231mph (200kt, 371km/h) at 6,000ft (1,800m) Combat radius: 360 miles (310nm, 580km) Ferry range: 635 miles (550nm, 1,020km) Service ceiling: 29,600 (8,200m) **Armament** 2 × 0.30in machine guns 1 × 200lb bomb	Crew: 1 Length: 22ft 1.5in (6.73m) Wingspan: 28ft 6in (8.68m) Height: 10ft 7in (3.22m) Empty weight: 2,823lb (1,281kg) Gross weight: 3,704lb (1,680kg) Powerplant: 1 × Pratt & Whitney R-1535-44, 625hp (466kW) **Performance** Maximum speed: 200mph (322km/h) Cruise speed: 170mph (274km/h) Range: 525 miles (845km) **Armament** 2 × 0.30in machine guns 500lb (227kg) bombs

type was delivered to the US Navy in February 1930 under a bailment contract, wearing the registration X-271V.

Over the following two years the XF5B-1 was put through an intensive trials programme although the US Navy declined to order any production machines as the monoplane was not yet seen as reliable enough for use as a carrier aircraft. Although not slated for production, the XF5B-1 was purchased by the Navy for further trials, being serialled A-8640 in the process. After three years of further test flying the aircraft was grounded to be used as a static test aircraft until it was destroyed.

Boeing followed the XF5B-1 with the XF7B-1,

a sea-going version of the USAAC's P-29 also known as the Boeing Model 273. This aircraft was very similar to its land-based counterpart although the design catered for naval requirements. The XF7B-1, BuNo. 9378, made its maiden flight in September 1933, but its high landing speed militated against its operation from aircraft carriers and so the programme was cancelled.

The final development of the Boeing F4B was the single XF6B that was ordered by the US Navy on 30 June 1931. It differed from the earlier aircraft in being mainly of metal construction, although the wings were fabric-covered. The engine was the Pratt & Whitney R-1535-44 Twin Wasp rated at 625hp. Designated the Model 236

The Boeing XF6B-1/XBFB-1 was the last biplane design for the US Navy from this company. Only the one prototype was constructed, making its first flight in early 1933. The aircraft was badly damaged after ramming into a crash barrier in 1936, which ended the design process. via US Navy/Dennis R. Jenkins

The Boeing P-29 and XF7B-1 were an attempt to produce an improved version of the highly successful P-26. Although improvements were made in performance, the USAAC and US Navy did not order the aircraft as better aircraft were already on the drawing boards of other manufacturers. via US Navy/Dennis R. Jenkins

by Boeing, this was the last aircraft fighter design that the company submitted for consideration by the US Navy. The XF6B made its maiden flight on 1 February 1933. After the required company test flying Boeing modified the engine cowling and fitted a three-blade propeller unit, both changes increasing the aircraft's top speed. Test flying was undertaken at Anacostia and Langley during which period the aircraft was redesignated as the XBFB-1 fighter bomber. The aircraft's flying career ended in 1936 when it rammed into a crash barrier, being written off in the process.

Curtiss XF9C

The final fighter built for the US Navy was destined for an entirely different type of aircraft carrier: the airships USS *Akron* and *Macon*. Contracts for both vessels were issued on 6 October 1928 and both were designed from the outset for the carriage of fighters: the airships were designed to both launch and retrieve their fighters in flight. The aircraft chosen to equip the airships was the Curtiss XF9C Sparrowhawk.

The Curtiss XF9C Sparrowhawk was a lightweight biplane fighter aircraft that was carried by the US Navy airships USS *Akron* and *Macon*. In order to increase their range while flying from the airships, the Sparrowhawks had their landing gear removed and replaced by a fuel tank; the undercarriage was reinstated when they needed to return to land. via US Navy/Dennis R. Jenkins

Curtiss XF9C

Crew: 1
Length: 21.08ft (6.27m)
Wingspan: 25.5ft (7.75m)
Height: 10.92ft (3.34m)
Empty weight: 2,114lb (961kg)
Loaded weight: 2,776lb (1,262kg)
Powerplant: 1 × Wright R-975-22 radial engine, 415hp (310kW)

Performance
Maximum speed: 176mph (153kt, 283km/h)
Range: 297 miles (258nm, 475km)
Service ceiling: 19,200ft (5,853m)
Rate of climb: 1,690ft/min (8.6m/s)

Armament
2 × 0.30in machine guns

The XF9C had its origins as a small, single-seat carrier-borne fighter that was developed in response to a US Navy proposal issued on 10 May 1930, the other contenders being the General Aviation XFA-1 and the Berliner Joyce XFJ-1. The Curtiss XF9C was ordered on 30 June 1930 and made its first flight in March 1931. The aircraft was mainly of metal construction with fabric-covered wings, and the upper wing was mounted onto the upper fuselage to give the pilot excellent upward vision. The powerplant chosen was the Wright R-975C Whirlwind engine rated at 415hp.

A second machine unofficially designated the XF9C-2 was built by Curtiss as a private venture. Changes from the earlier machine included a Wright R-975E-3 rated at 438hp and an upper mainplane raised by 4in, while the main wheels gained a set of spats in order to reduce drag.

Fitted with airship-hooking equipment at the Naval Aircraft Factory, the XF9C-1 was then transferred to Lakehurst for trials. The first airship hook-up was undertaken on 17 October 1931 using the airship USS *Los Angeles*. The success of these trials saw the US Navy order six production machines designated F9C-2 in October 1931. At the same time the service purchased the XF9C-2 prototype making the designation official, the aircraft gaining the serial 9264 in the process; this machine was later brought up to full production standards and redesignated F9C-2.

The first hook-up by a production Sparrowhawk took place on 19 June 1932, the recipient being the USS *Akron*, and the six production machines were accepted in September 1932. While all seven aircraft were assigned to the *Akron* the vessel itself could only carry four machines internally in the

The Curtiss F6C Hawk was a US Navy biplane fighter. A single Hawk was converted to XF6C-6 standard and won the 1930 Curtiss Marine Trophy. After achieving the fastest lap in the 1930 Thompson Trophy race, the XF6C-C crashed when its pilot was overcome by exhaust fumes. via US Navy/Dennis R. Jenkins

The Curtiss F11C Goshawk saw limited service with the US Navy. After flight trials and some modifications the XF11C-2 became the prototype for the F11C-2, of which twenty-eight were ordered as fighter-bombers in October 1932. via US Navy/Dennis R. Jenkins

hangar, with another one carried on the external launch point. The *Akron* was lost over the sea near New Jersey on 4 April 1933, although no aircraft were aboard at the time. The aircraft were transferred from Lakehurst to Moffet Field where they were assigned to the USS *Macon*. By this time the Curtiss XF9C-1 was also at Moffet assigned for training purposes although it ended its days at the Naval Aircraft Factory in January 1935 where it was scrapped.

Aboard USS *Macon* the Sparrowhawks were frequently flown without undercarriages, this

The Curtiss XF13C, or Model 70, was a carrier-based fighter aircraft. The XF13C first flew in 1934 with good results, although no production orders were received. via US Navy/Dennis R. Jenkins

allowing for the carriage of an external fuel tank that increased the available range. The *Macon* was also lost over the sea, off California on 12 February 1935; the airship was carrying four aircraft, which were also lost.

The remaining three aircraft were stripped of their hook-on gear, after which they were redesignated as XF9C-2. Two aircraft were later scrapped while the remaining machine was despatched to the Anacostia Naval Station. By 1939 the aircraft had been gifted to the Smithsonian Institution, fitted with a replacement airship hook from the Naval Aircraft Factory, repainted in an inaccurate colour scheme and placed on display at the Museum of Naval Aviation.

Transport Prototypes

The US Navy also purchased a few transport aircraft for evaluation, mainly from Bellanca.

All were based on the civil CH-400 Skyrocket, this being a high-wing monoplane with a fixed undercarriage and streamlined aerofoil wing struts; the powerplant was a single Pratt & Whitney Wasp. The XRE-1 was purchased for radio trials work, the XRE-2 was used as a light transport while the XRE-3 served as an ambulance aircraft.

Bellanca XRE-1/2/3
Crew: 1
Capacity: 5 passengers
Length: 27ft 9in (8.5m)
Wingspan: 46ft 4in (14.1m)
Powerplant: 1 × Pratt & Whitney Wasp C radial, 420hp (313kW)
Performance
Maximum speed: 155mph (249km/h)
Range: 670 miles (1,080km)

Three examples of the Bellanca CH-400 Skyrocket were purchased by the US Navy under the designation XRE. The aircraft shown was used for radio research at NAS Anacostia. via US Navy/Dennis R. Jenkins

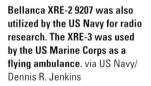

Bellanca XRE-2 9207 was also utilized by the US Navy for radio research. The XRE-3 was used by the US Marine Corps as a flying ambulance. via US Navy/ Dennis R. Jenkins

CHAPTER FOUR

American Fighter Prototypes and Trials Aircraft 1939–45

Although the USA viewed the outbreak of World War Two with serious concern, its isolationist policy – allied to the slow recovery from the Wall Street crash – meant that the government was very reluctant to become involved in events thousands of miles away. There were also concerns about Japanese activity in the Far East: the Japanese invaded Manchuria in 1931, followed by a full-scale invasion of China in 1937. The invasion of China revealed an obvious weakness in the armed forces of the Far Eastern nations: on their own they were incapable of withstanding the might of the Japanese, and the chances of them acting collectively were virtually nil. These failings were quickly revealed when Korea and the various smaller nations in the area such as Cambodia, Laos, Malaya, Siam, Vietnam and other small territories soon fell to invasion.

While America presented an uncaring face to the world it was obvious within the higher circles of the US government that Japan had designs on the whole Pacific region, including those areas already under the control of the USA. In response to this the War Department quietly began the process of developing aircraft capable of withstanding a Japanese attack. At first progress was slow with the Seversky P-35 and the Curtiss P-36 Hawk series of aircraft. Both types were low-wing fighters powered by radial engines that performed in the speed range between 260–300mph (420–500km/h), both types slower than the Japanese Mitsubishi A6M 'Zero' fighter.

Curtiss XP-37

The Curtiss Aircraft Company was one of the first to respond to an Army request to produce a faster fighter. To speed up development, Curtiss was instructed to use a P-36 Hawk airframe to create the prototype. Assigned the company designation Hawk 75-I – the I indicating the fitment of an inline engine – the resulting aircraft was subject to some drastic modifications. The engine chosen to power this conversion was the Allison V-1710-11 liquid-cooled engine rated at 1,150hp with a turbocharger. The contract was signed between the USAAC and Curtiss on 1 April 1937, the former looking forward to flying their first aircraft with a projected top speed of 340mph (550km/h).

To fit the engine and the extra fuel tanks into the aircraft required that the pilot's cockpit be moved further aft behind the wings' trailing edges. While this configuration was adequate for the pylon air racers popular in the USA, such a layout put any combat pilot at a disadvantage. The engine exhaust went through the turbocharger while cooling air for the three radiators was supplied by three scoops around the cowling. The Army followed up its order for the XP-37 with one for thirteen YP-37s as service test vehicles, the intended powerplant being the Allison V-1710-2 with an increased output.

As the XP-37 was required quickly the prototype was converted from the earlier Model 75 prototype, and it was ready for its maiden flight by the end of the month. The first test flights immediately revealed that the XP-37 suffered from engine and supercharger problems, while the pilots complained about the lack of visibility. The XP-37, 37-375, was handed over to the USAAC for intensive testing, but they too were concerned about the engine, supercharger, lack of pilot vision and the fact that the aircraft was not able to reach its intended top speed. Eventually,

Curtiss XP-37

Crew: 1
Length: 31ft (9.45m)
Wingspan: 37ft 4in (11.38m)
Height: 9ft 6in (2.90m)
Empty weight: 5,272lb (2,391kg)
Loaded weight: 6,350lb (2,880kg)
Engine: 1 × Allison V-1710-11 o, 1,000hp

Performance
Maximum speed: 340mph (547km/h)
Cruising speed: 304mph (490km/h)
Range: 485 miles (780km)
Service ceiling: 35,000ft (10,700m)

Armament
1 × 0.30in and 1 × 0.50in machine gun

after 152 hours of flying the XP-37 was grounded in August 1941, ending its days at a mechanics training school.

Hoping for greater things from the YP-37, the USAAC confirmed the contract on 11 December 1937 and assigned the serials 38-472 to 38-484 to the airframes. Besides the modified engine

the fuselage had been lengthened aft of the wing by 25in (635mm). The first YP-37 undertook its first flight in June 1939, the remainder following quickly. The YP-37s suffered from the same engine problems that beset the earlier XP-37 and most were withdrawn from use by early 1942, the highest-time aircraft retiring at 212 hours although one single example, 38-474, was delivered to NACA for flight testing. This example survived until January 1943 when it was scrapped.

Curtiss XP-42

While the Curtiss XP-37 and YP-37 had failed to live up to expectations, the USAAC was convinced that a good fighter could be built with an inline engine. Just to confuse matters the aircraft – designated XP-42 – was the fourth P-36, 38-4. It was powered by a modified Pratt & Whitney R-1830-31 radial powerplant housed under a long streamlined cowling with a streamlined propeller spinner. The cooling air intake was located under the engine while the intake for carburettor air was located above.

The USAAC requested from Curtiss a fighter to match those operating in Europe. The result was the XP-37, which featured two side-mounted radiators behind the engine and a cockpit that was well aft of the wing. The cockpit position limited the forward view and this, combined with poor performance, led to the cancellation of the project. via NARA/Dennis R. Jenkins

Seen here is the Curtiss XP-42 in use with NACA after a protracted development period that saw various cowlings being fitted. After many problems the XP-42 programme was terminated, the production order going instead to the P-40, another Curtiss product. via NASA/Dennis R. Jenkins

Given the company designation Model 75S, this aircraft was delivered in March 1939. Even before the XP-42 had made its first flight there were complaints from the test pilots about visibility problems and engine cooling, which was almost non-existent as the temperature gauge went into the red almost as soon as it was started. During the initial series of test flights there were problems with engine cooling and the propeller shaft was subject to serious vibrations. Over the following months numerous attempts were made to cure these problems, resulting in no fewer than twelve different cowling designs being tested on the XP-42. Also various types of cowl flaps were fitted, and short noses with high and low inlet velocity cowlings were tried with and without cooling fans. The nose was progressively shortened until the aircraft again resembled a standard P-36A.

These problems notwithstanding, the XP-42 was entered into the USAAC fighter competition in 1939. While the XP-42 was faster than the in-service P-36 Hawk it was significantly slower than the Curtiss XP-40, the production versions

of which had entered service with the USAAC and numerous other air forces. No longer needed for trials work, the XP-42 was used as a station hack within the continental USA before being withdrawn and scrapped in January 1947.

Seversky XP-41

Having delivered the P-35 to the USAAC, Seversky Aviation were convinced that the design could be pushed further. To that end the Army requested that the final P-35, 36-430, be put aside and modified to create a fighter with a heavier armament. The Seversky design team concentrated not only on improving the weaponry and the available power, but also on removing some of the less aerodynamic features of the P-35.

The resultant aircraft, designated XP-41, featured a revised wing and a Pratt & Whitney R-1830-19 air-cooled radial engine with a two-stage turbocharger rated for medium-altitude performance of 1,200hp instead of the original

Seversky XP-41

Crew: 1
Length: 27ft 0in (8.2m)
Wingspan: 36ft 0in (11.0m)
Height: 12ft 6in (3.8m)
Wing area: 219.5ft² (20.4m²)
Empty weight: 5,390lb (2,450kg)
Loaded weight: 6,600lb (3,000kg)
Max. take-off weight: 7,200lb (3,273kg)
Powerplant: 1 × Pratt & Whitney R-1830-19 radial engine with a two-speed supercharger, 1,200hp (895kW)

Performance
Maximum speed: 323mph (520km/h)
Cruise speed: 292mph (470km/h)
Range: 730 miles (1,168km)
Service ceiling 31,500ft (9,600m)

Armament
1 × 0.50in machine gun and 1 × 0.30in machine gun

Republic YP-43

While the XP-41 failed to garner any orders, the Republic design team offered the USAAC another aircraft, the high altitude YP-43. A company private venture known as the Model AP-4, it was given the test registration NX2597. The powerplant was the Pratt & Whitney R-1830-19, and chief designer Alexander Kartveli made great efforts to streamline the entire airframe, including the engine.

Part of this process saw a large spinner covering the propeller hub, while engine cooling was to be provided by retractable 'ram' air intakes. Unfortunately the large spinner and intakes meant that the engine would overheat very quickly under all conditions. Even before the YP-43 had flown, experience with the XP-41 had shown that such an arrangement was impractical, so the engine cooling arrangements were redesigned. The AP-4 airframe underwent these modifications as they were discovered, this including the installation of a turbo supercharger. The latter led to the loss of the AP-4 when it exploded during flight, causing a serious fire ending with a crash.

This loss notwithstanding, the USAAC ordered a service test batch of thirteen aircraft on 12 March 1939, these being serialled 39-704 to -716. The aircraft purchased by the USAAC differed from the AP-4 in several respects. The cockpit was lowered as a drag-reducing measure, the rear fuselage upper decking was raised and the transparent area behind the cockpit was greatly reduced. The tail-wheel leg was made longer to compensate for the extended-length fuselage while the turbocharger air intake was moved from the port wing root and mounted under the engine, inside the deep oval-shaped cowling. The two 0.50in machine guns in the engine cowling were supplemented by a pair of wing-mounted 0.30in machine guns. The engine was the Pratt and Whitney R-1830-35 engine rated at 1,200hp at take-off, this reducing to 1,100hp at 20,000ft (6,000m). Other changes were less obvious, these including the box-like centre section of the XP-41 being replaced by the straight-through elliptical wing that would later appear on Republic's P-47 Thunderbolt.

The first YP-43, 39-704, was handed over to the USAAC in September 1940; the last arrived in April 1941, by which time the aircraft had gained the name Lancer. The thirteen aircraft were

850hp R-1830-9 engine. The turbocharger was located in a ventral position just aft of the wing, the air intake being located in the left wing root. Overall length was increased from 25ft 2in (7.67m) to 27ft (8.23m). The aircraft featured a fully retractable undercarriage, the units folding inward into the wings and fuselage. The canopy was lower than that of the standard P-35 and was more aerodynamically streamlined. The XP-41 undertook its maiden flight in March 1939 during which it achieved a maximum speed of 323mph (520km/h) at an altitude of 15,000ft (4,600m).

Not long after this the Seversky CEO, Major Alexander De Seversky, was ousted from the board of the company, the organization becoming the Republic Aircraft Corporation soon afterwards. The XP-41 was entered in a USAAC fighter competition, but the opposition consisted of some strong contenders such as the Lockheed XP-38, Bell XP-39, Curtiss XP-40, XP-42 and the H75R. While the XP-40 was unable to match the altitude performance of the turbocharged aircraft, its lower cost and simpler construction meant that it could reach quantity production a year earlier than the other types. While the XP-41 showed increased performance over that of the standard P-35 the USAAC preferred another Seversky/Republic development, the YP-43, so the XP-41 was not developed any further and was scrapped soon afterwards.

The Republic YP-43 Lancer was a single-engine, all-metal, low-wing monoplane fighter. It was first delivered to the USAAC in 1940 but that service preferred the P-47 Thunderbolt. Eventually the final development of the YP-43 saw active service in the Chinese theatre of operations. via NARA/Dennis R. Jenkins

spread around various airfields where they underwent extensive testing. Unfortunately the YP-43 suffered from poor manoeuvrability and climb rate, and it also lacked such modern innovations as armour protection for the pilot and self-sealing fuel tanks. Such equipment was seen as standard for the fighters operating over Europe, and this failure to impress meant that the USAAC were not in favour of ordering more P-43s beyond the initial service test contract.

While the YP-43 exhibited a lack of performance in the air it also had a tendency to ground loop quite violently, rendering severe damage to the aircraft and sometimes the pilot, a tendency it had inherited from the P-35. The first attempt to cure this hazardous tendency was to fit a stronger tail-wheel lock that, it was thought, would improve directional control on the ground. However, the test aircraft managed an even more violent ground loop on its first test flight, which was strong enough the break the aircraft into sections. The answer to the ground-loop problem was eventually found to be fairly simple: all that

was needed was to increase the length of the tail-wheel leg, which reduced the tendency of the aircraft to end upside-down.

Despite the P-43's problems, because of its lack of advanced fighters the USAAC ordered eighty aircraft based on Republic's advanced AP-4J on 13 September 1939, these being designated P-44. However, combat reports coming out of Europe in the spring of 1940 put paid to the P-44, so Alexander Kartveli recommended that all work on the project be scrapped and that efforts be aimed towards a more refined aircraft: this later emerged as the P-47 Thunderbolt. Some production work was needed by Republic to keep its work force occupied until the P-47 was available so, while the P-43 was not seen as the answer to the USAAC's fighter requirements, a contract was issued for the manufacture of fifty-four P-43As to serve in the advanced fighter training role. A further 125 aircraft were later ordered for the Nationalist Chinese Air Force, whose units were operating alongside their American counterparts in the war against Japan.

Curtiss XP-46

After two unsuccessful and one successful attempts to gain fighter contracts from the USAAC, Curtiss returned to the advanced fighter scene in September 1939. Like other major aircraft manufacturers, Curtiss sent observers to Europe to study the performance of the fighters deployed by the combatants during the Spanish Civil War. The Curtiss representatives returned to America with certain ideas firmly fixed, including the need for a heavy armament of uniform calibre, a speedy and manoeuvrable airframe, and an engine that was capable of operating at full power without overheating at all altitudes. Curtiss distilled all that it had learned into a specification that was presented to the USAAC in September 1939, the Army responding with a contract for two prototypes from Curtiss under CP 39-13 on 29 September. The requested aircraft, designated the XP-46, were serialled 40-3053 and 40-3054.

The XP-46 was slightly smaller than the P-40 and featured a wide-track, inward-retracting undercarriage instead of the aft-retracting units used on the earlier type, while the engine was the newly developed twelve-cylinder, liquid-cooled Allison V-1710-39 (F3R) rated at 1,150hp. As the XP-46 had a high wing loading, automatic leading-edge slots were mounted on the outer

Curtiss XP-46
Crew: 1
Length: 30.17ft (9.20m)
Wingspan: 34.33ft (10.47m)
Height: 13.0ft (3.96m)
Empty weight: 5,625lb (2,551kg)
Loaded weight: 7,322lb (3,321kg)
Max. take-off weight: 7,665lb (3,477kg)
Powerplant: 1 × Allison V-1710-39 V12 engine, 1,150hp (858kW)

Performance
Maximum speed: 355mph (571km/h)
Range: 325 miles (523km)
Service ceiling: 29,500ft (9,000m)

Armament
2 × 0.50in machine guns in forward fuselage
Provision for 8 × 0.30in wing-mounted guns

portions of the wing to give increased aileron control near the onset of the stall. Armament was to be a pair of 0.50in machine guns in the nose below the cylinder banks plus a further eight 0.30in machine guns mounted in the wings; this ensured that the XP-46 was the most heavily armed American fighter at that time. A month after the initial XP-46 order the USAAC altered the requirements and requested the provision of

The XP-46 was developed by Curtiss-Wright in an effort to introduce the best features found in European fighters. It was intended, had it been a successful performer, to succeed the Curtiss P-40 that was already in production. via NARA/Dennis R. Jenkins

self-sealing fuel tanks and armour protection for the pilot. The maximum speed when fully loaded was to be a very ambitious 410mph (660km/h) at 15,000ft (4,600m).

The second prototype, 40-3054, was the first to fly, on 15 February 1941, although this was an aerodynamic test vehicle and so lacked armament and other military equipment. Even in this condition the aircraft, now designated the XP-46A, struggled to reach the required 410mph, this only being possible at 12,000ft (3,700m). The first prototype, retaining the designation XP-46, made its maiden flight on 29 September 1941. It was fully fitted with armament and other military equipment, and in this condition could only achieve 355mph (571km/h) at 12,200ft (3,720m).

Even as the XP-46s were being constructed the USAAC had decided to order further upgraded P-40s using the engine specified for the XP-46. The XP-46 was the last new fighter design from Curtiss, although the company went on to manufacture thousands of their P-40 fighters.

Douglas XP-48

The next aircraft in the fighter series, the Douglas XP-48, never left the drawing board. Known by the company designation of Model 312, the proposal was delivered to the USAAC in 1939. This showed a rather unusual-looking low-wing cantilever monoplane, the wing of which had a high aspect ratio. Power was to be provided by a supercharged Ranger SGV-770 twelve-cylinder liquid-cooled engine developing 525hp and driving a three-blade propeller. A tricycle undercarriage was to be fitted. The wing was so slender that the main undercarriage unit had to be attached to the fuselage the main wheel members retracting rearward into bays in the rear fuselage. The proposed armament was single 0.30in and a 0.50in machine guns, both mounted in the upper fuselage decking and synchronized to fire through the propeller arc.

The USAAC perused the Douglas proposal closely and was interested enough to reserve the pursuit designation of XP-48 for the design. Upon further investigation, the USAAC concluded that the aircraft's performance estimates were grossly over-optimistic, so funding for the design ceased. Douglas also cancelled the Model 312,

---

Douglas XP-48

Crew: 1
Length: 21ft 9in (6.63m)
Wingspan: 32ft 0in (9.75m)
Height: 9ft (2.74m)
Loaded weight: 3,400lb (1,542kg)
Powerplant: 1 × Ranger SGV-770 inverted vee engine, 525hp (392kW)

Armament
1 × 0.30in machine gun
1 × 0.50in machine gun

---

preferring to turn their attentions to progressing their transport aircraft further.

Lockheed XP-49

On 11 March 1939 the Army Materiel Division issued Circular Proposal 39-775 to the major players in the American aircraft industry. This proposal called for a new type of twin-engine, high-performance interceptor fighter, and four contractors submitted proposals. The first, from Lockheed, was a development of the P-38 Lightning, which was given the company designation Model 222. The Model 222 had a similar general arrangement to the P-38, but featured a pressure cabin and was powered by a pair of turbocharged Pratt & Whitney X-1800-SA2-G

Lockheed XP-49

Crew: 1
Length: 40ft 1in (12.2m)
Wingspan: 52ft (15.8m)
Height: 9ft 10in (3.0m)
Wing area: 327.5ft^2 (30m^2)
Empty weight: 15,410lb (6,990kg)
Loaded weight: 18,750lb (8,505kg)
Powerplant: 2 × Continental XI-1430-1 inverted V-12s, 1,600hp (1,193kW) each

Performance
Maximum speed: 406mph (653km/h) at 15,000ft (4,60m)
Range: 679 miles (1,093km)

Armament
2 × 20mm cannons
4 × 0.5 inch machine guns

(Army/Navy designation XH-2600) liquid-cooled engines that were rated between 2,000–2,200hp. Lockheed proposed to replace these engines, should the Model 222 be accepted, with the Wright R-2160 Tornado rated at 2,300hp. Armament was to be a pair of 20mm cannon supplemented by four 0.50in machine guns. Total fuel capacity was increased to 300 US gallons (compared with the 230 US gallons carried by the early production P-38). The Model 222 was rather generously estimated to have a top speed of 473mph (761km/h) at 20,000ft (6,000m) when powered by the XH-2600, this increasing to 500mph (800km/h) at the same altitude when powered by the Wright Tornado.

The USAAC completed its in-depth study of the four proposals in August 1939. The Lockheed proposal, by now re-designated the Model 522, was judged the most promising of the four entries so the USAAC ordered one airframe under the designation XP-49 in October 1939. The competing Grumman entry was the Design 41, a development of the XF5F-1 Skyrocket twin-engine, carrier-based fighter. The Grumman design came in second, but the USAAC considered it sufficiently promising that they ordered one example under the designation XP-50.

A contract for a single XP-49 prototype was officially issued on 8 January 1940. However, Lockheed was heavily preoccupied with manufacturing the P-38 Lightning so work on the XP-49 proceeded slowly during the early months of 1940. Both the USAAC and Lockheed soon came to realize that with either the Pratt & Whitney XH-2600 or the Wright R-2160 engines the XP-49 was seriously overpowered. Therefore in March 1940 it was decided to use the experimental Continental XIV-1430-9/11 liquid-cooled engine, rated at 1,540hp, instead. In order to counteract the problem of torque, the engines were handed to rotate in opposite directions: the port propeller rotated to the left and the starboard propeller to the right. Other changes included the substitution of dummy armour plate of the correct weight instead of the genuine article, this expediting construction of the prototype. A maximum speed of 458mph (737km/h) at 25,000ft (7,600m) was now envisaged.

In late December 1940 detailed design of the XP-49 began under the direction of project engineer M. Carl Haddon. Close to 66 per cent of the XP-49's airframe components were common with the P-38; the primary differences were

the engine installation firewall, a heavier and stronger undercarriage to cope with the increased weight and a pressurized cockpit similar to that of the XP-38A.

The first flight was delayed by problems with the experimental Continental engines, which were still awaiting clearance for flight operations when they were delivered to Lockheed in April 1942. The delays in clearing the engines meant that it was not until 14 November 1942 that the XP-49 took to the air for the first time, flown by test pilot Joe Towle. The XP-49 was grounded only a week later for replacement of the original powerplants by XIV-1430-13/15 engines rated at 1,350hp for take-off, this increasing to 1,600hp at 25,000ft. The original fuel tanks were replaced by self-sealing tanks purloined from a P-38 and a flight engineer's jump seat was added aft of the pilot's seat. Flights were resumed in December, but were constantly delayed due to hydraulic problems. The aircraft was reported as handling fairly well and with good manoeuvrability, but the Continental engines gave the aircraft a rather uninspiring performance as the maximum speed was only 406mph (653km/h) at 15,000ft (4,600m) instead of the promised 458mph at 25,000ft.

On 1 January 1943 the Lockheed XP-49 was damaged during an emergency landing at Muroc Army Air Base following a complete failure of both the hydraulic and the electrical systems. While undergoing repairs it received enlarged vertical tail surfaces and further work was carried out on the hydraulic systems in an attempt to make them more reliable. The XP-49 flew again on 16 February 1943 and was finally delivered to Wright Field on 26 June 1943, nearly twenty-seven months later than originally planned. This extensive delay meant that the Army had lost interest in the XP-49 as its performance was actually inferior to that of the standard P-38J that was already in service. Allied to the disappointing performance was the questionable future of the troublesome Continental engine, which eventually caused the USAAC to abandon any quantity production of the XP-49.

Although the USAAC had decided not to proceed with production of the XP-49, the aircraft continued to be tested at Wright Field. However, continued maintenance difficulties with the Continental engines and problems arising with the fuel system limited the usefulness of the XP-49 and it was flown very rarely. Its final task in its short life was to be dropped from a bridge crane to simulate the possible damage caused by hard landings. The remains of the aircraft were finally scrapped in 1946.

Grumman XP-50

The loser in the Circular Proposal 39-775 was the Grumman XP-50, initially known in the company as Design 41. Design 41 was very similar to the previous Design 34 that had resulted in the F5F-1 Skyrocket, but it was powered by a pair of Wright R-1820 radials fitted with turbochargers. Although Design 41 lost out to the XP-49, the Army saw merit in the design and suggested the company submit a revised design as a backup in case the XP-49 ran into problems. This further proposal, known by the company as Design 45, incorporated a tricycle undercarriage, the nose leg being housed in the longer nose. Provision was to be made for self-sealing fuel tanks and armour protection for the pilot. The contract for the manufacture of a single prototype was issued on 25 November 1939, the Army giving the aircraft the designation XP-50. The XP-50 was to be powered by two Wright R-1820-67/69 radials rated at 1,200hp and fitted with turbochargers. Intended armament was to be two 20mm cannon and two 0.50in machine guns, all mounted in the nose.

The single XP-50, serialled 40-3057, undertook its maiden flight on 18 February 1941 with Grumman test pilot Robert L. Hall at the

Grumman XP-50
Crew: 1
Length: 31ft 11in (9.73m)
Wingspan: 42ft (12.80m)
Height: 12ft (3.66m)
Wing area: 304ft^2 (28.24m^2)
Empty weight: 8,310lb (3,770kg)
Loaded weight: 10,560lb (4,790kg)
Max. take-off weight: 13,060lb (5,925kg)
Powerplant: 2 × Wright R-1820-67/69 9-cylinder air-cooled radial engines, 1,200hp (895kW) each
Performance
Maximum speed: 424mph (680km/h) at 25,000ft (7,620m)
Range: 1,250 miles (2,010km)
Service ceiling: 40,000ft (12,190m)
Armament
2 × 20mm cannons
2 × 0.5 inch machine guns
2 × 100lb bombs

controls. Early flight trials were encouraging, the XP-50 handling much better than the earlier XF5F-1. The installation of supercharged engines in the XP-50 gave it an improved performance at medium and high altitudes. Unfortunately, on 14 May 1941 the XP-50 experienced an in-flight turbocharger explosion while on a flight over Long Island Sound, the pilot Robert Hall being forced to parachute to safety. The loss of the aircraft brought the XP-50 development programme to a close.

The Grumman XP-50 was a development of the shipboard F5F-1 Skyrocket that was entered into a USAAC contest for a twin-engine heavy interceptor. The Army Air Corps initially placed an order for a prototype on 25 November 1939, but the XP-50 lost out to the Lockheed P-38. via NARA/ Dennis R. Jenkins

Bell XP-52/XP-59

While Bell Aircraft are better known for their P-39 and P-63 fighters and their later domination of the helicopter field, they made an earlier entry into fighter design; this was in response to the USAAC requirement issued to the aircraft industry in the form of a Request for Data R-40C. At least fifty companies responded including Bell, whose Model 16 had been developed some months earlier. Bell had, by this time, become well known for submitting unconventional designs, the Model 16 being no exception.

This unusual machine seated the pilot in the nose of the round, barrel-shaped fuselage; a Continental XIV-1430-5 liquid-cooled engine rated at 1,250hp was mounted aft of the pilot driving a pair of contra-rotating co-axial pusher propellers. The wing was mounted in the mid-fuselage position and swept back at an angle of approximately 20 degrees. Twin booms were mounted about one third span along each wing and a horizontal tail plane at the rear connected the two booms together. The XP-52 was to be carried on a tricycle landing gear, the nose wheel retracting into the fuselage while the main wheels retracted into the booms. Yet another unusual feature of the XP-52 was the presence of an air inlet for the engine radiators mounted in the extreme nose, a feature that was later carried over to jet-powered fighters. Two 20mm cannon were to be mounted in the lower fuselage while two blocks each of three 0.50in machine guns were to be mounted in the front of each of the twin booms.

At the end of 1940 the USAAC purchasing commission chose six of the submissions for further development, one of which was the Model 16. A single prototype was ordered under the USAAC designation XP-52, although this order was cancelled in November 1941 before any metal was cut. It was replaced by an order for another Bell design that was based on the XP-52 but fitted with a more powerful Pratt & Whitney R-2800-52 air-cooled radial engine. The resulting design was given the designation XP-59 by the USAAC, but this was quickly cancelled as fighters from other manufacturers were seen as better prospects for production and development. The XP-59 designation was used again later for another Bell aircraft of much greater significance: the Airacomet, the USA's first jet fighter.

Vultee XP-54

Another twin-boom fighter that featured in the lexicon of the USAAC was the Vultee XP-54. Vultee was one of the respondees to Circular Proposal R-40C on 27 November 1939. The Vultee Aircraft Corporation had only made one previous venture into the field of fighter design, this being the Model 48 Vanguard that had been unsuccessful in attracting any Army production contracts. However, Richard Palmer and the design team at Vultee came up with a proposal that was judged the best of all the entrants. An initial USAAC contract covering engineering data and wind-tunnel models was issued on 22 June 1940. This was followed by a contract for one prototype that was confirmed on 8 January 1941, the aircraft being designated XP-54 with the serial 41-1210. A further XP-54, 42-108994, was ordered on 17 March 1942; for a short period this machine was painted with the serial 41-1211 on the fins, this being swiftly changed when it was discovered that it had already been allocated to a BT-13A Valiant.

The XP-54, designated the Model 84 by Vultee, was a twin-boom machine with a low-mounted inverted gull wing powered by a pusher engine. This was the Pratt & Whitney X-1800-A4G that gave a power output of 1,850hp and drove contra-rotating pusher propellers. The Model 84 was actually a development of an earlier Vultee proposal known as Model 78, which was of similar configuration but powered by a unsupercharged Allison V-1710 liquid-cooled engine. The single-seat cockpit was placed in the centre section of the bullet-shaped fuselage. Magnesium alloy construction was used throughout the fuselage. A tricycle landing gear was fitted with the nose wheel retracting into the fuselage and the main wheels into the booms. The centre wing section was designed around the newly developed NACA 'ducted wing', in which air was taken in through narrow slots in the wing leading edge and directed over the oil and coolant radiators and then to the intercoolers, and eventually fed into the engine via ducts in the wing trailing edge. The landing flaps were so designed that their secondary function was to regulate the airflow through the coolers; this innovation made it possible to house the coolant radiators and the associated intercooler entirely within the wings.

The XP-54 was designed as a fast interceptor powered by the Pratt & Whitney X-1800 engine. When this engine was cancelled the aircraft was redesigned for the Lycoming XH-2470. The first of two XP-54s built made its initial flight in January 1943, flying eighty-six times before it was grounded by engine problems. The second aircraft flew only once. via NARA/Dennis R. Jenkins

The original mission envisaged for the XP-54 was that of low- and medium-altitude interception and combat, to which end six 0.50in machine guns were to be mounted in the nose. On 7 September 1940 the USAAC informed Vultee that they were interested in changing the mission of the XP-54 to high-altitude bomber interception. This required the development of a pressurized cockpit and the installation of turbo-

charging equipment. Armament was changed to a pair of 37mm T-12/T-13 cannon with sixty rounds per gun and twin 0.50in M2 machine guns with 500 rounds per gun, all mounted in the nose. The Army also required the fitting of heavy armour protection for the engine and pilot. These changes increased the estimated gross weight of the aircraft to 18,000lb (8,000kg).

The need for a pressurized cockpit combined with the height of the aircraft from the ground meant that cockpit entry and exit were a problem. In order to solve this Vultee developed a unique solution that used the pilot's seat as an elevator. In order to enter the aircraft the seat was electrically lowered from the bottom of the fuselage by a switch mounted on the outside of the aircraft. The pilot would then sit on the seat and move another switch, and the seat would electrically raise itself up into the aircraft until it reached the flight position, where locks would engage to hold it into the aircraft. Exit was the reverse of entry. Flight-control cables were routed around the opening in the floor while an inverted U-shaped column was used to support the control wheel. This ventral access was also helpful as it was possible to design a fixed cockpit canopy that ensured a good, pressure-tight seal. In an emergency with sufficient altitude available the elevator seat assembly could be catapulted downward and clear of the propeller: thus the XP-54 was the

Vultee XP-54

Crew: 1
Length: 54ft 9in (16.69m)
Wingspan: 53ft 10in (16.41m)
Height: 14ft 6in (4.42m)
Wing area: 456ft² (42.4m²)
Empty weight: 15,262lb (6,923kg)
Loaded weight: 18,233lb (8,270kg)
Max. take-off weight: 19,337lb (8,771kg)
Powerplant: 1 × Lycoming XH-2470-1 liquid-cooled piston engine, 2,300shp (1,715kW)

Performance
Maximum speed: 381mph at 28,500ft (613km/h at 8,700m)
Range: 500 miles (805km)
Service ceiling: 37,000ft (11,300m)

Armament
2 × 37mm cannon
2 × 0.50in machine guns

first American fighter to be fitted with a simple ejector seat.

The nacelle-shaped fuselage incorporated another unusual feature. Due to the different muzzle velocities of the cannon and machine guns, the entire nose section was moveable so that the direction of fire of the machine guns could be elevated by up to 3 degrees or depressed by as much as 6 degrees without changing the flight attitude. The cannon were fixed and were not movable. The movement of the nose section and the integrated machine guns was controlled by a specially developed compensating gunsight.

In October 1940 Pratt & Whitney decided to discontinue all work on the X-1800 engine, so Vultee decided to substitute the liquid-cooled Lycoming XH-2470 rated at 2,200hp in its place. The Lycoming engine was still under development for the US Navy at the time as one of their prime powerplants; it was to be fitted with a turbocharger, which was a primary requirement in view of the XP-54's assigned high-altitude role.

With all of these changes being undertaken it was no surprise that the delivery date slipped quickly from the promised date of July 1942. The first XP-54, 41-1210, did not fly until 15 January 1943 when test pilot Frank Davis took it for an inaugural 31-minute test flight from Muroc Dry Lake (later to become Edwards AFB). This flight went reasonably well although the Curtiss propeller malfunctioned, and was later replaced by a Hamilton Standard unit. By 11 March ten test flights had been undertaken, but it was clear that performance was far below that projected. In addition, the engine began to show metal traces in the oil during routine inspections, which indicated the possible break-up of a bearing, so the aircraft was returned to Downey for an engine change. A further eighty-six test flights were carried out at Ontario AFB, California, after which the XP-54 was flown to Wright Field on 28 October for USAAC service testing. However, once again the Lycoming engine developed serious problems – this time the entire engine had to be returned to the manufacturer for repairs. After a pre-repair survey the costs turned out to be prohibitive, so the engine was scrapped.

By late 1943 the ongoing troubles with the Lycoming H-2470 engine saw the US Navy deciding to abandon the entire programme; the XP-54 was therefore left without its preferred powerplant. A proposal to fit the Wright R-2160

Tornado radial engine driving a set of contra-rotating propellers to the XP-54 airframe was briefly considered, the resulting machine had been designated P-68. However, the Tornado engine also failed to achieve production, the result being the abandonment of the P-68 project. Although it appeared possible to install the Allison W-3420 in the XP-54 without major structural changes, the delay and expense involved in making such an alteration resulted in the decision being made not to try to introduce the XP-54 into quantity production. There was even a proposal to install a jet engine in the XP-54 airframe, but this proposal was also rejected, on grounds of cost.

The second XP-54, 42-108994, was delayed by the need to change from the originally planned twin Wright turbochargers to a single experimental General Electric XCM unit. The installation of this unit plus the associated ground testing meant that the first flight was seriously delayed. The second XP-54 finally took to the air on 24 May 1944, undertaking a twenty-minute flight from Downey to Norton AFB, California. The engine and turbocharger combination was found to be unsatisfactory and they were returned to the manufacturer for further investigation. Although a replacement unit was fitted to the second XP-54, it was never flown again. The nose section was sent to Elgin AFB for armament tests while the remainder of the airframe was scrapped. After grounding, the first XP-54 was static-tested to destruction at Wright Field.

The XP-54 fighter was the last project that the Vultee corporation carried out for the USAAF under its own name, as in June 1943 Vultee Aircraft Inc. was merged with Consolidated to form the Consolidated Vultee Aircraft Corporation. Although the name of the new conglomerate was contracted to Convair internally, this name was not officially registered until 1954 when Convair became a division of General Dynamics.

Curtiss-Wright XP-55

When USAAC issued its Circular R-40C the Curtiss-Wright entry, designated CW-24 by the company, was one of the most unconventional of the four finalists. It was to be one of the last projects supervised by designer Donovan Berlin before he left Curtiss to take up a similar position with Fisher Aviation to work on the P-75 fighter. The CW-24 was a pusher aircraft with canard elevators; the low-mounted, swept-back wings had both ailerons and flaps on the trailing edges, while the fins and rudders were mounted near the wingtips both above and below the wing. The aircraft was carried on a tricycle undercarriage, this being the first time that this type of undercarriage was employed on a Curtiss fighter. Curtiss proposed to use the new and untried Pratt & Whitney X-1800-A3G liquid-cooled engine.

On 22 June 1940 the Curtiss-Wright company received a USAAC contract for preliminary engineering data, a powered wind-tunnel model and an engineering mock-up. The designation P-55 was reserved by the USAAC for the aircraft. At the completion of the wind-tunnel test the USAAC was not satisfied with the results delivered and was on the verge of cancelling the contract, so Curtiss-Wright took it upon itself to build a full-scale flying model. This new version was designated CW-24B by Curtiss and powered by the 275hp Menasco C68-5 engine. The aircraft consisted of a welded steel-tube fuselage with a fabric covering and a wooden wing, while the undercarriage was fixed.

Once fully assembled and flight tested the CW-24B was moved to the Army flight test centre at Muroc Dry Lake in California. It made its maiden flight on 2 December 1941. Although the maximum speed was only 180mph (290km/h) due to the low engine power, the CW-24B proved the basic feasibility of the concept. However, these early flights also indicated that there was a certain amount of directional instability, the cure for which was to increase the area of the auxiliary wingtip fins and move them 4ft (1.2m) farther outboard on the wings. The wingtips were extended and further improvements were obtained by adding vertical fins to both the top and bottom of the engine cowling. The CW-24B made 169 flights from Muroc between December 1941 and May 1942, at the conclusion of which it was given the serial 42-39347 and transferred to Langley Field, Virginia, for further testing by NACA.

While the CW-24B was being flight tested, work on the CW-24 continued. On 10 July 1942 a USAAF contract was issued for three prototypes under the designation XP-55, the assigned serial numbers being 42-78845 to -78847. The stability problem having been sorted out with the

---

Curtiss-Wright XP-55 Ascender

Crew: 1
Length: 29ft 7in (9.0m)
Wingspan: 40ft 7in (12.4m)
Height: 10ft 0in (3.0m)
Wing area: 235ft² (21.83m²)
Empty weight: 6,354lb (2,882kg)
Loaded weight: 7,710lb (3,497kg)
Max. take-off weight: 7,930lb (3,600kg)
Powerplant: 1 × Allison V-1710-95 liquid-cooled V12 engine, 1,275hp (951kW)

Performance
Maximum speed: 390mph (628km/h) at 19,300ft (5,900m)
Service ceiling: 34,600ft (10,500m)

Armament
4 × 0.50in machine guns in the nose

CW-24B, another problem arose with the X-1800 engine, which was experiencing developmental delays that were eventually serious enough to cause outright cancellation. Curtiss chose as a replacement the Allison V-1710 liquid-cooled inline engine, as it was both reliable and available. The proposed armament was two 20mm cannon plus a pair of 0.50in machine guns. During the mock-up phase it was decided to change the powerplant to the Allison V-1710-95 engine rated at 1,275hp while the 20mm cannon were replaced by 0.50in machine guns.

The first XP-55, serialled 42-78845, was rolled out on 13 July 1943 and the maiden flight was made on 19 July from the USAAC's Scott Field, close to the Curtiss-Wright St Louis plant, the pilot being the Curtiss test pilot J. Harvey Gray. Initial flight testing revealed that the take-off run was longer than forecast, this being cured by increasing the size of the nose-mounted elevators while the aileron 'up' trim was interconnected with the flaps so that it operated when the flaps were lowered.

On 15 November test pilot Harvey Gray was putting the first XP-55 through a series of stall and recovery tests when the aircraft suddenly flipped over on its back and fell into an uncontrolled inverted dive. Recovery action proved impossible and the plane fell out of control for 16,000ft (4,900m) before the pilot was able to parachute to safety, the aircraft being destroyed in the ensuing crash. At the time of the crash

The Curtiss-Wright XP-55 Ascender resulted from proposal R-40C issued by the USAAC on 27 November 1939. An unusual design, it featured a canard configuration, a rear-mounted engine, swept wings and twin fins. This was also the first Curtiss fighter aircraft to use tricycle landing gear. via NARA/Dennis R. Jenkins

the second XP-55, serialled 42-78846, was near to completion so its configuration could not be modified to incorporate any changes resulting from an analysis of the crash of the first XP-55.

The second XP-55 was therefore similar to the first one except for the larger nose elevators, a modified elevator tab system and a change from balance tabs to spring tabs on the ailerons. It flew for the first time on 9 January 1944 but all flight tests were restricted so that the stall zone part of the flight envelope was carefully avoided until the third XP-55 had been satisfactorily flight tested.

This aircraft, 42-78847, flew for the first time on 25 April 1944 and was fitted with the designed complement of four machine guns. It incorporated some of the modifications that resulted from the loss of the first XP-55. It was found that stall characteristics could be greatly improved by adding extensions to increase the wingtip area and by increasing the range of nose elevator travel. However, the first flight revealed that the increased elevator limits resulted in the pilot being able to hold such a high elevator angle of attack during take-off that the elevator could actually stall. After further modifications stall tests were performed satisfactorily, although the complete lack of any warning prior to the stall

and the excessive loss of altitude needed to return to level flight after the stall were undesirable characteristics: the answer was an artificial stall-warning device.

After modification between 16 September and 2 October 1944 42078847, in company with the second XP-55, by now modified to the same standard, underwent official USAAF trials. The trials indicated that the XP-55 had satisfactory handling characteristics during level and climbing flight, but at low speeds and during landings there was a tendency on the part of the pilot to over-control on the elevators because of a lack of any useful feel feedback from the controls. Stall warning was still inadequate and stall recovery still involved an excessive loss of altitude, while engine cooling was also a problem. The performance of the XP-55 overall was not very impressive and was lower than that of the more conventional fighters already in service. In addition, by 1944 jet-powered fighter aircraft were clearly the future. As a consequence, no production was authorized and further development was abandoned. A Curtiss engineer had called the aircraft the 'Ascender', and the name stuck and was later given official confirmation. The third prototype completed the testing programme, but was later destroyed in a crash during an airshow at Wright Field, Ohio, on 27 May 1945, the pilot being killed. The surviving XP-55, 42-78846, was later flown to Warner Robins Field in Georgia in May 1945. It was then transferred to Freeman Field to await transfer to the National Air Museum at the Smithsonian Institution in Washington. For a long period its fuselage was on display at the Paul Garber facility in Suitland, Maryland. In December 2001 the aircraft was sent to the Kalamazoo Aviation History Museum for restoration. By 2007 the work was complete, and the plane is now on display at the Main Campus building of the Kalamazoo Airzoo.

Northrop XP-56

The Northrop Company was another respondent to the Circular Proposal R-40C issued by the USAAC. Designated N2B by the company, this was the last design delivered to USAAC under this proposal. Constructed entirely of magnesium alloy, the N2B was very unusual: a swept-wing tailless 'flying wing' aircraft, all of whose flight control surfaces were carried on the wings' trailing edges. The Northrop proposal for the aircraft's powerplant was the new and untried Pratt & Whitney X-1800-A3G liquid-cooled engine; this was to be mounted behind the cockpit, its power being absorbed by a contra-rotating pusher propeller assembly. On 22 June 1940 Northrop received a contract for preliminary engineering data and a powered wind-tunnel model. The designation P-56 was reserved for the project by the USAAC, and on 26 September 1940 an order was placed for a single prototype designated XP-56 with the serial number 41-786.

Northrop encountered a problem shortly after development of the XP-56 began as Pratt & Whitney decided to abandon development of its X-1800 liquid-cooled engine. This left the XP-56 – and the competing XP-54 and XP-55 – without an engine. The Northrop design team were forced to select the less suitable Pratt & Whitney R-2800 air-cooled radial engine, rated at 2,000hp. Changing to this engine required that the fuselage be widened to accommodate it, and the aircraft increased in weight. The resulting aircraft had a fuselage that was stubby and rounded with an unpressurized cockpit situated well forward. Aft, the airframe had a short dorsal fin and a very large ventral fin that was very close to the ground when the aircraft stood on its landing gear. The cantilever mid-mounted wing had elevons on the trailing edge that functioned both as ailerons and elevators, while the wing flaps were mounted on the trailing edges of the drooped wingtips. Air

The Northrop XP-56 Black Bullet was another design that resulted from the R-40C proposal. This all-magnesium aircraft was first flown on 30 September 1943, later being destroyed during a taxi test. The second prototype was first flown in March 1944 and featured an enlarged vertical stabilizer plus an improved wingtip design incorporating a yaw control system.
via NARA/Dennis R. Jenkins

ducts with inset guide vanes for engine cooling were located on the wing leading edge. The main wheels retracted into the wing and the nose wheel into the fuselage. The proposed armament was two 20mm cannon and four 0.50in machine guns, all mounted in the nose.

The USAAC followed up the initial contract on 13 February 1942 with a further one that covered the construction of the second XP-56 prototype; the serial number for this machine was 42-38353. By this time the nickname 'Black Bullet' has been given to the aircraft, although there is no record of this being made official.

The first XP-56, 41-786, was rolled out in April 1943 and moved by road soon afterwards to Muroc Dry Lake for flight testing. During initial ground-handling trials the pilots reported that the aircraft tended to yaw sharply and dangerously while taxiing at high speeds. It was thought that this problem was caused by faulty wheel brakes so the trials were halted until the aircraft was fitted with modified brake units. This in turn delayed the maiden flight until 30 September 1943, when test pilot John Myers lifted the XP-56 into the air for the first time. An altitude of 5 feet was maintained and the XP-56 appeared to fly normally in ground effect, but during subsequent test flights at higher altitudes the results were not so encouraging. The aircraft had a persistent tendency to be nose-heavy, while lateral control was

difficult to maintain throughout the flight envelope. Before any of these aerodynamic problems could be addressed the port main wheel deflated during a high-speed taxi run, causing the aircraft to somersault onto its back; it was totally wrecked in the process.

To correct the flight deficiencies encountered with the first prototype the second XP-56, 42-38353, underwent major airframe changes. The first involved moving the centre of gravity further forward while there was a major increase in the size of the upper vertical surface. A new type of rudder control was fitted in which air bellows at the wingtips operated a set of split flaps for directional control; control of the bellows was achieved by valves that drew air to or from the bellows by means of wingtip venturi.

On 23 March 1944 test pilot Harry Crosby took the second XP-56 on its maiden flight, during which he found it impossible to lift the nose wheel off the ground at speeds below 160mph (160km/h), and the test flight lasted only a few minutes. The second flight was more positive and it was found that the nose-heaviness went away after the landing gear was retracted. However, the aircraft was found to be severely underpowered for its weight: the relatively low speeds that could be attained were far less than the projected maximum speed of 465mph (750km/h) at 25,000ft (7,600m). To investigate this deficiency it was decided in May 1944 that NACA would use their wind tunnel at Moffett Field, California to look into the causes of the low performance of the XP-56. However, higher priority given to other projects led to postponement of the XP-56 wind-tunnel tests until late October 1944.

Although the wind-tunnel testing was delayed, further flight test trials were undertaken with the XP-56. During the tenth test flight the pilot reported extreme tail-heaviness on the ground, low engine power and excessive fuel consumption. After extensive investigation it was concluded that the XP-56 was basically not of an airworthy standard and that it was just too dangerous to continue flight tests with the aircraft. In the light of this report and with jet-powered aircraft already under development, the whole project was then abandoned. While the XP-56 project was deemed a failure it was not a total loss for Northrop, since the company had learned a lot about flying-wing designs and the data gained

---

Northrop XP-56 Black Bullet

Crew: 1
Length: 27ft 6in (8.38m)
Wingspan: 42ft 6in (12.96m)
Height: 11ft 0in (3.35m)
Wing area: 306ft² (28.44m²)
Empty weight: 8,700lb (3,955kg)
Loaded weight: 11,350lb (5,159kg)
Max. take-off weight: 12,145lb (5,520kg)
Powerplant: 1 × Pratt & Whitney R-2800-29 radial, 2,000hp (1,492kW)

Performance
Maximum speed: 465mph at 25,000ft (749km/h)
Range: 660 miles (1,063km)
Service ceiling: 33,000ft (10,000m)
Rate of climb: 3,125ft/min (953 m/min) at 15,000ft (4,600m)

Armament
2 × 20mm cannons
4 × 0.50in machine guns

during the XP-56 project were put to good use in later Northrop designs such as the XB-35 and YB-49 bombers.

Tucker XP-57

While four of the major aircraft manufacturers were building unconventional aircraft for the USAAC there were other, smaller companies that were bold enough to present their own proposals to the service. One of these was the Tucker Aviation Company of Detroit, Michigan, which delivered a proposal to the USAAC in May 1940 for the construction of a lightweight fighter. Preliminary drawings revealed a small, single-seat aircraft built around the small 720hp Miller L-510 eight-cylinder inline engine. The engine was mounted in a mid-fuselage position aft of the pilot and drove a two-blade propeller by means of an extended propellor shaft. The all-wood wing was mounted low on the fuselage while a retractable tricycle undercarriage was fitted. Loaded weight was estimated to be 3,400lb (1,540kg). The proposed armament was to have consisted of three 0.50in machine guns or a single 0.50in and two 20mm cannon, all mounted in the nose. The Tucker Aviation Company had some very optimistic estimates for the performance of their proposed fighter: it was claimed that the aircraft could attain a speed of 308mph (496km/h) with a range of up to 960 miles (1,540km).

The USAAC were intrigued enough by the Tucker proposal that they decided to order a single prototype under the designation XP-57. However, by February 1941 and prior to the creation of any construction drawings the Tucker company had run into severe financial difficul-

---

Tucker XP-57

Crew: 1
Loaded weight: 3,400lb (1,542kg)
Powerplant: 1 × Miller L-510, 720hp (537kW)

Performance (projected)
Maximum speed: 308mph (495km/h)
Range: 600 miles (960km)

Armament
3 × 0.50in machine guns or 1 × 0.50in machine gun and 2 × 20mm cannon

---

ties so the XP-57 project was placed in abeyance. Since the fighter development trend was toward fighters of increasing weight and complexity the XP-57 contract was allowed to lapse and no prototype was completed.

Lockheed XP-58

The next experimental offering came from Lockheed, who were busily involved in developing and gearing up for production of the P-38 Lightning. This aircraft was also wanted by the French and British air forces, but in early 1940 the US Army reserved for itself the right to refuse permission for its aircraft suppliers to export vital aircraft to overseas customers, as it was felt that foreign orders might result in delays in delivering aircraft to its own units. Therefore, when Britain and France wanted to purchase the Lightning from Lockheed the Army was unwilling to give its approval as it had already ordered the type. After much governmental pressure the USAAC did grant export authorization of a Lightning version minus the turbochargers to Britain and France, with the caveat that Lockheed agree to develop and produce at no cost to the US government a prototype of an advanced version of the Lightning. The formal agreement was signed on 12 April 1940.

The advanced Lightning was given the company designation of L-121 while James Gerschler was named as project engineer. The L-121 was to be powered by a pair of turbocharged Continental IV-1430 liquid-cooled engines and was offered in two distinct versions, single- and two-seater. The single-seat version would retain the standard P-38 armament of one 20mm cannon and four 0.50in machine guns carried in the nose, while the two-seat version had additional armament consisting of a single 0.50in machine gun mounted in a remotely controlled barbette situated at the end of each tail boom. Gross weight was estimated at 16,500lb (7,500kg) while the aircraft was expected to attain 450mph (720km/h) at 25,000ft (7,600m).

During a planning and development meeting at Wright Field in May 1940 it was decided to drop the single-seat version; only the two-seat version was now to be built, this being assigned the designation XP-58. In July 1940 it was concluded that the XP-58 was underpowered with

Lockheed XP-58 Chain Lightning

Crew: 2
Length: 49ft 4in (15.0m)
Wingspan: 70ft (21.3m)
Height: 16ft (4.9m)
Wing area: 600ft² (56m²)
Empty weight: 21,624lb (9,808kg)
Max. take-off weight: 39,192lb (17,777kg)
Powerplant: 2 × Allison V-3420 24-cylinder liquid-cooled
engines, 3,000hp (2,200kW) each

Performance
Maximum speed: 436mph (702km/h) at 25,000ft (7,600m)
Service ceiling: 38,400ft (11,700m)
Rate of climb: 2,660ft/min (810m/min)

Armament
4 × 37mm cannon in an articulated nose; 4 × 0.50in machine
guns in two remotely controlled flexible turrets aft.
1 × 75mm cannon and 2 × 0.50in machine guns in the nose,
4 × 0.50in machine guns in two remotely controlled flexible
turrets in the rear

the Continental engines so it was decided to substitute a pair of Pratt & Whitney XH-2600-9/11 liquid-cooled engines rated at 1,800hp. The re-engined XP-58 was given the company designation of Model 20-14 and a revised specification was issued by Lockheed in September 1940. A second 20mm cannon was later added to the forward-firing armament. The tail-boom guns, although innovative, were thought to be impractical so they were replaced by a single remotely controlled dorsal turret containing a pair of 0.50in machine guns. The serial number 41-2670 was assigned to the prototype. Estimated gross weight had increased to 24,000lb (11,000kg) while estimated top speed had dropped to 402mph (647km/h). Range on internal fuel was projected to be 1,600 miles (2,800km).

Barely a month had passed after these revised specifications had been issued when Neil Harrison, the Lockheed project engineer, was informed that Pratt & Whitney was suspending development of the XH-2600 engine. The design team looked at the XH-2470, the Continental XH-2860 and the Pratt & Whitney R-2800 as possible alternatives for the XP-58 powerplants; they preferred the Pratt & Whitney R-2800 radial engine, estimating that with these powerplants the XP-58 had a a loaded weight of 26,000lb (12,000kg) and a maximum speed of 418mph (673km/h)

at 25,000ft (7,600m). However, the USAAC considered that this performance was inadequate and suggested that Lockheed look at the experimental Wright XR-2160 Tornado engine that offered an output of 2,350hp. This engine had an extremely small frontal area although the engine itself was highly complex, and its development had been dogged by problems from the outset. Even so, in March 1941 the USAAC confirmed that it was going to go with this powerplant for the XP-58.

Two months later, just as Lockheed was starting to sketch out the XP-58, the USAAC issued a change order for the installation of cabin pressurization for the pilot and the aft-facing gunner, and for the addition of a remotely controlled ventral turret to supplement the dorsal turret. These changes caused the estimated gross weight to rise to 34,242lb (15,529kg) while estimated range had been reduced to 1,300 miles (2,100km). In contrast, the top speed of the Tornado-powered XP-58 was estimated to be 450mph (720km/h).

In its revised form the XP-58 was scheduled for delivery to the USAAC in August 1942 and in order to meet this deadline the project team peaked at 187 by October 1941. This underwent a radical change after the events at Pearl Harbor on 7 December with the XP-58, amongst other projects, being assigned a lower priority. As a result, most of the engineering staff were moved to other projects. By early 1942 the entire XP-58 design and development staff numbered just twelve. Although the aircraft was operating under a reduced priority, in March 1942 Lockheed suggested that a second XP-58 prototype be ordered using Government funds. Since the Tornado engines were already experiencing serious developmental delays and were not expected to be ready until early 1943, Lockheed felt that there was sufficient time to redesign the second XP-58 machine in order to provide it with enough fuel capacity to increase the range to 3,000 miles (4,800km). The USAAC agreed to this request and placed an order in May 1942.

Even as this order was being confirmed the USAAC began to go through a yet another in-depth review about the correct mission for the XP-58. Originally, the USAAC suggested that the nose-mounted armament be replaced by a 75mm cannon with a twenty-round automatic feeder, this being supplemented by a pair

The XP-58 Chain Lightning was initially designed as a long-range bomber escort, although it was later redesigned as a low-altitude ground-attack aircraft before reverting to a bomber escort/attack aircraft. Engine and supercharger problems caused the project to be cancelled after one aircraft was built. via NARA/ Dennis R. Jenkins

of 0.50in machine guns. This was an unusual choice of armament for an escort fighter so the USAAF began to think seriously of the XP-58 as a ground-attack aircraft. This, however, led to the consideration of several different configurations, including a two-seat attack aircraft with six 20mm cannon or a three-seat bomber with a bombardier in the nose, an enlarged central nacelle containing an internal bomb bay and the capability to carry a 75mm nose cannon. In both the attack and bomber versions, the dorsal and ventral turrets was deleted while unsupercharged engines were to be installed. However, the Douglas A-26 Invader were already in production and it more than adequately filled all USAAF attack bomber requirements; in addition, the experimental Beech XA-38 Grizzly, then under development, showed considerable promise as a low-altitude tank buster and ground-attack aircraft. Therefore, the USAAF decided that neither XP-58 option was needed.

The XP-58 project then returned to its original role as a high-altitude fighter aircraft, although this time it was to be bomber destroyer rather than an escort fighter. The turbochargers and the dorsal and ventral turrets were reinstated. The first prototype had four 37mm cannon in the nose while the second had a 75mm cannon and two 0.50in machine guns. Gross weight had now risen to 38,275lb (17,358kg) while top speed had dropped to 414mph (666km/h) at 25,000ft (7,600m) and range was only 1,150 miles (1,850km).

By late 1942 the bomber threat from Germany and Japan had largely evaporated in the European and in the Pacific theatres: the P-58 was therefore being designed for a role it was never to perform. All this chaos meant that in early 1943 the XP-58 programme was in utter chaos due to the constantly changing Army requirements, so Lockheed recommended in January 1943 that only one prototype be built and that it have interchangeable noses that would permit the fitting of either type of forward-firing armament. Making things even worse was the fault-ridden Tornado engine, which was finally cancelled in February 1943; the XP-58 was without engines once again. Lockheed and the USAAF both agreed to substitute to a pair of turbocharged Allison V-3420-11/13 liquid-cooled engines rated at 2,600hp for take-off and 3,000hp at 28,000ft (8,500m).

With these engines installed the XP-58, serialled 41-2670, was finally rolled out in June 1944, over four years after its design had been initiated. Its company designation was now Model 20-86. The XP-58 rolled out of the factory in an incomplete state as no cabin pressurization equipment was provided, no forward-firing armament was installed, and dummy dorsal and ventral turrets were fitted in place of the proper assemblies. The aircraft made its initial flight from the Lockheed Air Terminal at Burbank on 6 June 1944 piloted by test pilot Joe Towle. At the conclusion of its first flight it was ferried to Muroc AB. A total of twenty-five flights was made at Muroc prior to the delivery of the XP-58 to Wright Field, Ohio, on 22 October 1944 for further testing. Throughout, these flights were marred by turbocharger problems. Once at Wright Field the XP-58 quickly became a white elephant, especially as the USAAF had no further need for bomber destroyers. Maintenance of the prototype proved to be so difficult that it was very rarely flown. By early 1945 it was transferred for use as an instructional airframe, although it was scrapped soon afterwards.

Bell XP-59A

Following on from the piston-powered XP-58 came the first American jet combat aircraft, the Bell XP-59A. Having already produced unusual aircraft in the XP-52 and its follow-on the XP-59, Bell was one of the companies asked to investigate the development of another kind of fighter aircraft – one powered by the newly emerging jet engine. The development of this engine had caught the Americans unawares. Work on jet-powered aircraft was well underway in Britain, and similar projects were being investigated in both Germany and Italy. America was far behind the other major aircraft-manufacturing nations in using this revolutionary new form of aircraft propulsion. General 'Hap' Arnold, C-in-C USAAF, had been so impressed by the possibilities offered by this new technology that he requested that American engineers be given the blueprints of the new jet engine so that manufacture could take

Bell XP-59
Crew: 1
Length: 38ft 2in (11.63m)
Wingspan: 45ft 6in (13.87m)
Height: 12ft 4in (3.76m)
Wing area: 386ft² (35.9m²)
Empty weight: 7,940lb (3,600kg)
Max. take-off weight: 12,700lb (5,760kg)
Powerplant: 2 × General Electric I-A turbojets, 2,000lb (7,3kN) each

Performance
Maximum speed: 413mph (664km/h)
Range: 240 miles (386km)
Service ceiling: 46,200ft (14,080m)
Rate of climb: 3,200ft/min (16.26m/s)

Armament
1 × 37mm cannon
3 × 0.50in machine guns

place under licence in the USA. Since the USA had been generous with Lend Lease aid to Britain, the British government felt compelled to oblige.

With access to the engine technology secured, a meeting was held at Wright Field on 4 September 1941, General Arnold asking the executives of the General Electric Corporation if they would act as the primary American contractor for licence

Designed and built during the closing months of the War, the Bell P-59A was the first USAAF jet fighter aircraft. The service was not impressed by its performance and cancelled the contract when fewer than half of the aircraft ordered had been produced. via NARA/Dennis R. Jenkins

production of the British jet engine. General Electric had been selected for this role as the company had extensive experience with turbines for industrial and aviation applications. Fifteen jet engines were ordered initially with all aspects of production, assembly and testing being carried out under the utmost secrecy. The following day, Bell Aircraft was approached with the request to build a fighter aircraft powered by the new engines. The choice of Bell as prime contractor for the manufacture of the first American jet fighter was due to its lack of primary war work and its available capacity to manufacture a new aircraft; strict secrecy being a concern, Bell's proximity to the General Electric plant also helped.

Bell Aircraft were happy to accept the contract for three aircraft, the deadline for the first prototype being eight months after signing the contract on 30 September 1941. The assigned serial numbers of the three prototypes were 42-108784 to -108786. As strict secrecy was paramount, the previous Bell XP-59 project was offered up as a cover and the new jet fighter was designated the 'XP-59A'. The premise behind such a move was to persuade Axis intelligence that the XP-59A project was no more than a modification of the totally unrelated XP-59 piston-engined pusher fighter. Even while the jet fighter contract was being signed Bell engineers were already developing the XP-59 pusher, but work on this project was quietly abandoned in the following months as work on the jet fighter got under way and the original XP-59 project was officially cancelled on 1 December 1941.

The General Electric jet engine was given the cover designation I-A and was portrayed as a new turbocharger. With the XP-59A project operating under the highest priority, work proceeded rapidly. As the General Electric jet engines were being designed and built in parallel with the XP-59A, the Bell designers had little knowledge about the possible performance of the engines, so they adopted a conservative design approach.

Two months after the initial order had been confirmed the Bell design team submitted a design that showed a fairly conventional aircraft with a cantilever, laminar-flow, mid-mounted wing and a fully retractable tricycle undercarriage. The aircraft was fitted with a pair of 1,400lb (5.12kN) static thrust General Electric I-A jet engines, one carried on each side of the fuselage under the wing roots. The aircraft had a high-set tail plane well clear of the exhausts and jet efflux. It featured a pressurized cockpit – not a normal option for the time – while access to the cockpit was through a side-hinged canopy. The fuselage itself was built in two sections, the forward section comprising armament bay and cockpit while the rear section was of stressed-skin, semi-monocoque construction. All control surfaces were fabric-covered and manually operated, the ailerons being of the pressure-balance type with pressure seals while the fabric-covered flaps were mounted inboard of the ailerons on the wings' trailing edges.

While the XP-59A was primarily intended as an engine test bed, the USAAF also viewed it as a potential combat aircraft, so it was to carry a nose-mounted armament of two 37mm cannon, each with forty-four rounds. The USAAF approved the initial design and subsequent construction of the three prototypes on 9 January 1942.

Even though the first XP-59A prototype had not flown, the USAAF ordered thirteen service test YP-59As in March 1942; serial numbers assigned were 42-108771 to 108783. These were powered by an improved version of the General Electric engine designated the I-16 (later changed to J31) rated at 1,650lb st (6.04kN). The YP-59As had aft-sliding cockpit canopies in place of the hinged originals of the prototypes.

The first XP-59A prototype was ready for flight by late summer of 1942 and was moved by rail to Muroc Dry Lake, California, on 12 September. After arrival in California and re-assembly and testing, as a deception security measure it was fitted with a dummy propeller attached to its nose just in case curious observers might see it and start asking why this aircraft had no propeller. On 1 October 1942 the Bell test pilot Robert Stanley was undergoing some high-speed taxiing trials with the XP-59A when the aircraft accidentally became airborne for a short time. It made its first official flight the following day, this time with a USAAF pilot at the controls, only thirteen months after the contract had first been awarded. The second XP-59A flew on 15 February 1943 and the third late in April.

However, this revolutionary system of aircraft propulsion created serious problems right from the outset. The jet engines were heavier than forecast in relation to the amount of power they could develop, in addition to which the exhaust was so hot that the turbine blades frequently overheated and detached with catastrophic results.

The maximum achievable speed was 404mph (650km/h) at 25,000ft (7,600m), this being below expectations, while the engine installation was found to generate a significant amount of aerodynamic interference that created severe directional snaking, resulting in an unstable gun platform. However, work on the P-59 continued unabated and modifications were eventually found for its list of faults.

The first YP-59A arrived at Muroc in June 1943 where the USAAF gave the aircraft the name Airacomet, the aircraft undertaking its maiden flight in August 1943. The YP-59A had more powerful 1,650lb st (6.04kN) General Electric I-16/J31 turbojets installed. Even with the slightly increased power, the YP-59A showed little improvement in performance over the XP-59A with a maximum speed of only 409mph (658km/h) at 35,000ft (11,000m). The final four YP-59As had a heavier armament consisting of three 0.50in machine guns and a single 37mm cannon that was standardized for the production P-59A.

The third YP-59A, 42-22611, was taken by ship to Britain in exchange for the first production Gloster Meteor I. After arrival in England it was reassembled by Gloster Aircraft at Moreton Valance where it was flown for the first time by a Bell test pilot on 28 September 1943. The aircraft was assigned the RAF serial number RJ362/G and finished in standard RAF day fighter camouflage. After initial test flying the YP-59A was transferred to the Royal Aircraft Establishment at Farnborough, arriving on 5 November 1943. The aircraft was immediately placed on the top secret Jet Flight list in company with the Gloster E.28/39, de Havilland Vampire and Gloster Meteor.

At Farnborough the Airacomet flew very little due to unserviceability and a lack of spares. The RAF test pilots found the aircraft to be seriously underpowered and with an unacceptably long take-off run: in common with other early jet-powered fighters, the Airacomet suffered from very poor engine acceleration.

Having expressed an interest in the type, the US Navy received the eighth and ninth YP-59As, 42-108778 and -108779, in December 1943 for trial work. During these trials the Airacomet was found to be totally unsuited for carrier operations due to the poor view from its cockpit and the slow acceleration of its engines. In addition,

the Airacomet suffered from a lack of adequate drag during landing approaches, so that there was a lot of 'float' prior to touchdown when the power was cut. The lack of drag was due to the absence of dive brakes, these having been deliberately omitted because of the aircraft's anticipated mediocre performance.

Just prior to the first flight of the XP-59A the USAAF had placed an order for 100 P-59A Airacomets, but as the performance of the YP-59A service test aircraft had been less than expected and it was considered unlikely that any great improvement would be forthcoming, in late 1943 the Airacomet was no longer considered by the USAAF as being an operational combat type. Therefore the Airacomet was relegated to the operational training role, the P-59A order being halved on 30 October 1943. The last YP-59A was delivered by the end of June 1944.

Curtiss XP-53 and XP-60

The Curtiss XP-60 saw a return to piston-engined aircraft, although in this case it was the company trying to develop its successful P-40 further. The original step had been to develop the XP-46, which failed to impress the USAAC therefore no orders were placed. Never ones to shirk a challenge, the Curtiss Aircraft Company returned to the US Army with another pair of designs. The first of these was the Model 88, an improved XP-46 that was powered by the in-development Continental XIV-1430-3 liquid-cooled engine rated at 1,600hp. The Model 88 borrowed the fuselage and tail assembly of the P-40D and combined them with a NACA laminar-flow wing. Armament was to have consisted of eight wing-mounted 0.50in machine guns. The main-wheel retraction sequence was that used by the original P-40: the main wheels rotated 90 degrees before retracting rearwards into the wheel bays.

Impressed by Curtiss' efforts, the USAAC ordered two examples of the Model 88 on 1 October 1940 with the designation XP-53, assigned the serials 41-140 and -19508. This all changed at a conference held six weeks later where the USAAC informed Curtiss of its need for a fighter that combined laminar-flow wing technology with the Rolls-Royce Merlin engine. Curtiss suggested that the second XP-53 airframe, 41-19508, be converted to accept the Merlin engine while it was undergoing construction. This airframe was redesignated Model 90 by the company and the USAAC assigned the designation XP-60 to the new aircraft. It was intended that the XP-60 be fitted with the Packard-built Merlin V-1650-1 engine rated at 1,300hp as this was also used in the XP-40F then under development by Curtiss.

Even as the XP-53 and XP-60 were being built the USAAC cancelled the XP-53 contract due to excessive delays in the Continental XIV-1430 engine. The XP-53 never flew, as with many of the aircraft that were due to use the XIV-1430. As the XP-53 airframe was similar to the XP-60 it was decided in November 1941 to use it as a static test airframe in support of the P-60 project while its bulletproof windshield, self-sealing fuel tanks and armament were removed and fitted to the XP-60. While under construction it was decided to replace the rearward-retracting P-40-style landing gear with a new inward-retracting undercarriage, similar to that which had been fitted to the abortive XP-46.

Initially the XP-60 was fitted with a British-built Rolls-Royce Merlin 28 engine, the aircraft flying for the first time on 18 September 1941 – just eleven days before the first flight of the XP-46. The aircraft's performance was disap-pointing: the top speed was 387mph (623km/h) at 22,000ft (6,700m) and it took 7.3 minutes to reach an altitude of 15,000ft (4,500m), while the service ceiling was limited to 29,000ft (8,800m). One of the reasons given for the disappointing performance was the poor finish to the wing surface, which was not finished to the standard required for a laminar-flow wing. It was also found that the Merlin engine was not delivering the guaranteed output. During the flight test period the XP-60 suffered damage as the result of under-carriage failures. Also as a result of the test flights it was found necessary to enlarge the vertical fin and rudder and implement some other minor modifications. These alterations resulted in the company designation changing to Model 90A.

The XP-60 was modified in August 1942 when a Packard Merlin V-1650-3 of 1,350hp with a two-stage supercharger was installed, this being complemented by a four-blade propeller. In this guise the aircraft was redesignated XP-60D by the USAAC and Model 90B by Curtiss; by the time that the changes were made the intervening B and C designations had been given to other improved versions of the XP-60. 41-19508 was destroyed in a crash on 6 May 1943.

In late 1941 the Packard Merlin engine was in such great demand for other aircraft that there

The Curtiss XP-53/XP-60 was a single-engine, low-wing monoplane fighter aircraft developed as a successor to P-40. It underwent a lengthy development process, but did not reach production. via NARA/Dennis R. Jenkins

was a shortage of engines; this led to a delay in the XP-60 development programme. Therefore consideration was given to alternative powerplants, the liquid-cooled Allison V-1710 engine being the frontrunner as it was reliable and available. Although engine availability was a problem, a contract for 1,950 P-60s was confirmed on 21 October 1941, with the turbocharged Allison V-1710-75 engine rated at 1,425hp specified as the powerplant.

Concerns were raised in November 1941 that the P-60A would be underpowered with the Allison engine, meaning that either a more powerful engine was needed or that another fighter should be built instead of the P-60. After the attack on Pearl Harbor government officials raised doubts about interrupting the P-40 and its introduction to service. In December 1941 all work on the P-60 project was halted, this being followed in January 1942 by the cancellation of the production order for the 1,950 P-60s, which were replaced by more P-40Ks and -Ls, plus some Curtiss-built P-47G Thunderbolts.

While the main P-60 project had been cancelled, the USAAC requested that three experimental P-60s should be constructed: XP-60A, XP-60B and XP-60C. The XP-60A, serial number 42-79423, was to be powered by the Allison V-1701-75 engine with a General Electric B-14 turbocharger while the XP-60B, serial number 42-79425, had the same engine with the Wright SU-504-2 turbocharger. The XP-60C, serial number 42-79424, was to use the experimental Chrysler XIV-2220 engine.

The XP-60A was given the company designation of Model 95A. The nose and fuselage contours of the XP-60A had to be revised to accommodate the Allison engine, while the armament was reduced to six 0.50in guns in the wings, these being borrowed from the XP-60. The XP-60A undertook its initial ground taxi tests in late October 1942. However, during one of these runs a minor fire occurred in the engine due to the lack of cooling air in the shrouds surrounding the exhaust manifold. To ensure that this did not occur again the turbocharger and long exhaust manifold were removed and replaced by short exhausts. The XP-60A undertook its maiden flight on 11 November 1942. During the flight-test regime the aircraft's maximum speed at lower altitudes plus the initial climb rate were lower than expected; it was decided to cease flying the

Curtiss YP-60	
Crew: 1	
Length: 33.92ft (10.34m)	
Wingspan: 41.33ft (12.60m)	
Height: 12.33ft (3.76m)	
Wing area: 275ft^2 (25.6m^2)	
Empty weight: 8,698lb (3,945kg)	
Loaded weight: 10,785lb (4,892kg)	
Powerplant: 1 × Pratt & Whitney R-2800-53 radial engine, 2,000hp (1,492kW)	

XP-60A, so it was dismantled and some of its components were used in the later XP-60C and XP-60E.

The poor performance figures from the XP-60A flight trials resulted in official interest in the P-60 fighter waning therefore the entire project was in danger of being cancelled. However, Curtiss made a proposal to the USAAC that the XP-60C prototype then under construction be fitted with the Pratt & Whitney R-2800 radial air-cooled engine driving a pair of three-blade contra-rotating propellers. The substantial improvement in performance that this modification generated aroused sufficient interest that in November 1942 the USAAC issued a contract for the production of 500 R-2800-powered P-60A-1-CU fighters. The first twenty-six aircraft on this production contract, serialled 43-32762 to -32787, were to be delivered as service test aircraft with the designation YP-60A.

The XP-60C, designated Model 95C by Curtiss and serialled 42-79424, was originally intended to have had an airframe similar to that of the earlier XP-60A and XP-60B, but fitted with the new and experimental 2,300hp Chrysler XIV-2220 engine. However, this engine was experiencing development problems, therefore it was decided in September 1942 to install a Pratt & Whitney R-2800-53 engine driving a pair of three-blade contra-rotating propellers. Armament was further reduced to four 0.50in machine guns. First flight of the XP-60C occurred on 27 January 1943 during which the pilot reported high elevator and rudder forces although the overall flight characteristics were generally satisfactory.

The single XP-60B, known by Curtiss as the Model 95B and serialled 42-79425, was similar in outline to the XP-60A but fitted with a Wright instead of a General Electric supercharger for the V-1710-75 engine. This machine was never completed in this configuration as on 2 December 1942 the Army requested that the Pratt & Whitney R-2800-10 radial engine be installed in place of the original V-1710; in this configuration the aircraft was redesignated XP-60E. As the XP-60E featured a lighter propeller assembly it was found necessary to move the R-2800 engine bulkhead forward by 10in (25cm). The initial flight of the XP-60E was delayed until 26 May 1943 as the engine failed during the initial ground-running tests and had to be changed.

During April 1943 the USAAF decided to undertake a series of comparative trials at Patterson Field with currently available fighter types in an attempt to reduce the number of types under test and development, so that resources could be concentrated on those more likely to succeed. Curtiss-Wright was notified by the Army that the XP-60E was required for these tests within a matter of days. As it had not yet undertaken its maiden flight it was decided to substitute the XP-60C in its place, although it needed reassembling before delivery to Patterson Field. The flight trials with the XP-60C revealed that it was impossible to obtain the engine's full rated power. To add to the problems the experimental wing finish peeled off from the leading edge of the wing, destroying the smooth laminar flow and resulting in a further loss of speed. These defects meant that the XP-60C made a very poor impression on the USAAF as its performance was inferior to that of the Republic P-47D and the North American P-51B. The result was that the P-60 series of aircraft was eliminated from any further manufacture, and in June 1943 the Army contract for the P-60A-1-CU was reduced from 500 to just two aircraft.

After the XP-60C returned to Curtiss-Wright a short period of flight testing was undertaken, but a forced landing caused enough damage to terminate all testing work with this aircraft. Although there was no further need for the P-60, as the P-47 and P-51 would satisfy all the Army fighter requirements, the USAAF agreed to test the delayed XP-60E that had missed the trials at Patterson Field. In January 1944 the XP-60E, or Curtiss Model 95D, was flown to Elgin Field for official service testing. The installed engine was a Pratt & Whitney R2800-10 radial rated at 2,000hp. The USAAF test pilots found that the XP-60E did not compare very favourably in level-flight performance with the current in-service

fighters, although it could match them in the climb. The aircraft was sensitive to slight changes in flight condition around all axes and required constant trimming during flight. Stability in level flight was also found to be poor, while the climb speed was difficult to maintain.

In May 1944 Curtiss-Wright finally recognized that the P-60 would never enter production, and requested that the Army cancel the project. However, the USAAF insisted that the company complete one of the two YP-60A aircraft that were still under construction. These aircraft were later redesignated YP-60E, reflecting the number of design modifications that had been incorporated. The second YP-60A, 43-32763, was used as a YP-60E test bed. It undertook its maiden flight on 15 July 1944 powered by a Pratt & Whitney R-2800-18 radial engine that drove a single four-blade propeller unit. It differed from previous P-60s in that a bubble canopy was fitted over the cockpit, which resulted in a revised fuselage and vertical tail shapes, so that it strongly resembled a P-47D Thunderbolt. Only two test flights of the YP-60E were undertaken by Curtiss-Wright before the aircraft was transferred to Wright Field. By this time, the Army had absolutely no need for the P-60 series, so no further trials were undertaken and the YP-60E was disposed of as surplus after the war. It was later purchased by James DeSanto and was entered in the 1947 National Air Races with Race Numger 80 and civil registration NX21979, although it was destroyed in a crash during a qualifying flight.

Curtiss XP-62

During January 1941 the Army issued a requirement for a heavily armed, high-performance fighter aircraft to be based around the Wright R-3350-17 Duplex Cyclone air-cooled radial engine rated at 2,300hp. This was the heaviest engine yet mounted in a fighter and was the same engine intended for the Boeing B-29 Superfortress bomber. The armament was to be eight 20mm cannon or twelve 0.50in machine guns. The Curtiss proposal was submitted to the Army on 29 April 1941; the design was a cantilever low-wing monoplane with a retractable main landing gear and tail wheel. The Wright engine was intended to drive a pair of contra-rotating three-blade propellers. As the aircraft was intended for high-altitude operation, the engine required a turbocharger and the aircraft was to be equipped with a pressurized cockpit for pilot comfort. On 27 June 1941, the USAAC ordered two prototypes, one being designated the XP-62 and the other the XP-62A. The XP-62 prototype was scheduled for delivery within fifteen months while the XP-62A was to be delivered three months later.

During August 1941 some changes in specifications were submitted for approval by Curtiss. The principal request was that the maximum speed be reduced to 448mph (721km/h), this being due to an increase of 1,537lb (697kg) in loaded weight. The mock-up inspection took place during December, after which some ninety changes were recommended. The status of the XP-62 project was placed under review in January 1942 and it was recommended that a weight reduction programme be undertaken to reduce the projected weight from 15,568lb (7,060kg) to 14,000lb (6,350kg). This was achieved by lightening the aircraft's structure, removing four of the eight cannon and deleting the propeller anti-icing equipment. At the conclusion of the weight-reduction programme Curtiss delivered a proposal in January 1942 for 100 production P-62 fighters, the first of which was intended for delivery in May 1943. The contract for 100 P-62s was approved on 25 May 1942 although the contract was terminated by the USAAF in July 1942 as it was feared that production of the new P-62 had adversely affected deliveries of desperately needed Curtiss-built P-47G Thunderbolts.

Even though the production P-62 was cancelled, development work on the XP-62 continued. The pressure cabin initially caused problems, and delays in its delivery caused the first flight to the XP-62 to be delayed. As the delay was unacceptable it was decided that the maiden flight of the XP-62 should be undertaken without the pressurization system installed. The first flight of the XP-62, serialled 41-35873, took place on 21 July 1943 and was reported as successful. As the P-62 family aircraft had been cancelled the section of the contract covering the XP-62A was cancelled during September 1943. A limited amount of flight testing had been conducted on the XP-62 by February 1944 when it was decided to install the pressure cabin for general development work. However, at this time the XP-62 project had a very low engineering priority so work proceeded very slowly. Such was the lowly

---

Curtiss XP-62

Crew: 1
Length: 39.5ft (12.04m)
Wingspan: 53.67ft (16.36m)
Height: 16.25ft (4.95m)
Wing area: 420ft² (39.0m²)
Empty weight: 11,773lb (5,340kg)
Loaded weight: 14,660lb (6,650kg)
Max. take-off weight: 16,651lb (7,553kg)
Powerplant: 1 × Wright R-3350-17 radial engine, 2,300hp (1,716kW)

Performance
Maximum speed: 448mph (389kt, 721km/h)
Range: 1,500 miles (1,300nm, 2,400km)
Service ceiling: 35,700ft (10,900m)

Armament
4 × 20mm cannon

---

status of the XP-62 that in August 1944 the aircraft was finally scrapped without undertaking any further flight testing.

Grumman XP-65

The Grumman XP-65 was intended to be the USAAF equivalent of the US Navy's Grumman F7F Tigercat twin-engine carrier fighter. Grumman had succeeded in interesting the Army in Design 46, a large twin-engine fighter powered by a pair of supercharged Wright R-2600 radials. Initial design work had begun in October 1939 with the Army and the Navy both deciding to push for the development of twin-engine fighters from Grumman. In order to speed up development they were basically the same aircraft, but the Army version had turbocharged engines while the Navy version was to have supercharged engines. It was intended that both versions would be armed with four 0.50in machine guns, in addition to which the USAAF version had had an additional pair of 37mm cannon and the USN version a quartet of 20mm cannon. The Army ordered two prototypes of the fighter under the designation XP-65 on 16 June 1941 while the Navy ordered two prototypes under the designation XF7F-1 some two weeks after. Eventually, both services concluded that a single design did not cover both sets of individual requirements, so in January 1942 the USAAF decided to withdraw from the programme in order to allow Grumman to develop their design to meet naval requirements.

McDonnell XP-67

Possibly one of the most elegant fighters *never* to enter production was the McDonnell XP-67 Bat. In June 1940 the company submitted an unsolicited proposal to the USAAC for an unconventional fighter powered by either an Allison V-3420-B2 or a Pratt & Whitney H-3130 engine equipped with a two-stage supercharger. The engine was to be located in the fuselage behind the pilot. The engine would drive a pair of pusher propellers situated to the rear of the wings via a complicated system of extension shafts and gear drives. Although the USAAC rejected the proposal because of the excessive weight and complexity, it was sufficiently interested that it bought the engineering information from McDonnell during June 1940 and suggested that the company continue trying.

The next company proposal delivered to the USAAC followed later that month. This time the proposal covered a twin-engine, two-seat heavy fighter powered by a pair of Continental I-1430

McDonnell XP-67 Bat
Crew: 1
Length: 44ft 9in (13.64m)
Wingspan: 55ft (16.76m)
Height: 15ft 9in (4.80m)
Empty weight: 17,745lb (8,050kg)
Loaded weight: 22,114lb (10,030kg)
Max. take-off weight: 25,400lb (11,520kg)
Powerplant: 2 × Continental XI-1430-17/19 12-cylinder inverted vee liquid-cooled engine, 1,350hp (1,000kW) each
Performance
Maximum speed: 405mph (650km/h) at 25,000ft (7,600m)
Range: 2,385 miles (3,840km)
Service ceiling: 37,400ft (11,400m)
Rate of climb: 2,600ft/min (13m/s)
Armament
6 × 37mm M-4 cannon

liquid-cooled engines. Initially the USAAC expressed a lack of enthusiasm, but after further discussions with McDonnell some revisions were made and on 5 May 1941 a formal proposal was submitted to the Army for serious consideration. The project was given the designation of Model S-23-A and changed to a single-seat, long-range fighter with a pressurized cabin. The proposed

The XP-67 was submitted under the 1939 Army Air Corps Proposal R-40C and McDonnell was awarded a contract for two aircraft in May 1941. The first aircraft was ready in December 1943, although it was destroyed in a fire in September 1944. This crash resulted in the project being terminated. via NARA/Dennis R. Jenkins

armament comprised of six 0.50in machine guns and four 20mm cannon. The McDonnell design team attempted to maintain true aerofoil sections throughout the entire airframe: the centre fuselage and the rear portions of the engine nacelles were merged smoothly together, which gave the aircraft a unique bat-like planform. The nose leg of the tricycle undercarriage retracted into the fuselage and the main wheels retracted into the engine nacelles.

Having seen the new design the Army expressed interest and on 2 August 1941 the USAAF issued the authority for the purchase of two prototypes. The contract was formally approved on 29 October 1941, the new aircraft being designated XP-67, while the serial numbers of the two prototypes were 42-11677 and -11678. During the detailed design stage of the XP-67 the armament was changed to six 37mm cannon with forty-five rounds per gun in the inboard wing sections. The two Continental XI-1430-1 engines were fitted with General Electric D-1 turbochargers and drove four-blade propellers. In order to gain the most from the engines' output the engine exhaust was used to augment the thrust. The increased armament and other changes caused the estimated gross weight to rise to 20,000lb (18,000kg).

In order to get the XP-67 flying reasonably quickly the armament, cabin pressurization equipment and oxygen system were not initially installed. The initial flight tests of the XP-67 were delayed by fires in both engines that occurred during a high-speed taxi run undertaken at Lambert Field in St Louis on 8 December 1943. After repairs, the XP-67 was moved by road to Scott Field, Illinois. The first flight of the XP-67 took place there on 6 January 1944 with test pilot E.E. Elliott at the controls, but it had to be abruptly terminated after six minutes due to engine problems. The XP-67 was grounded while modifications were made to the engine compartments. A stainless steel fireproof bulkhead was installed to seal off the turbocharger compartment from the rest of the engine, modifications were made to the cooling air system and the aft ends of the engine cowlings were shortened. With these modifications, two test flights were completed successfully; however, on the fourth flight, undertaken on 1 February 1944, the engines oversped and caused the shaft bearings to burn out, this requiring another emergency landing.

As the mishap had damaged the Continental engines beyond economical repair, the XP-67 was returned to McDonnell in St Louis for modifications while awaiting the delivery of replacement engines. Further wind-tunnel testing had suggested that the tail plane should be raised 1ft (30cm) in order to improve longitudinal stability, this being carried out while the aircraft was awaiting replacement engines. Test flying resumed on 23 March 1944 and five more successful flights were made during the month of May by USAAF test pilots. During this time further problems were encountered with the engine running rough, while the aileron balance was out of adjustment. The main undercarriage door closure sequence was also reported as defective. All was not in the negative as the USAAF test pilots reported that the cockpit layout was adequate and that ground handling was satisfactory. Handling in the air was reported as being satisfactory and the roll rate was deemed to be good at high speed. The fighter was stable longitudinally, but was neutrally stable laterally and tended to Dutch roll. While initial reports described the aircraft as adequate, the performance of the XP-67 fell far short of that promised. In particular, the take-off run was too long, the initial climb rate was poor and acceleration was slow. The aircraft was obviously under-powered by its troublesome Continental engines, which consistently failed to develop their design rating of 1,350hp: in practice they struggled to reach 1,060hp even under ideal conditions.

Test flying continued during the summer of 1944; the aircraft gained a dorsal fin and an additional 2 degrees of dihedral were added to the tail plane to improve lateral stability. In this new guise the XP-67 was due to begin official performance tests in September, but before they could begin a fire broke out in the right engine nacelle while E.E. Elliott was taking off for a test flight. Elliott landed the aircraft safely, but a crosswind blew the flames over the fuselage and caused major damage to the structure. This first XP-67 was deemed to have been damaged beyond economical repair – the accident allied to the seemingly endless problems caused by the temperamental Continental engines resulted in the USAAF recommending that work on the XP-67 project be stopped. In September both McDonnell and the USAAF agreed that the project should be terminated and the contract was formally cancelled six weeks later. The second prototype, 42-11678, was cancelled before it was completed. This prototype was to have been powered by I-1430 liquid-cooled engines with war emergency power ratings increased to 2,100hp. Contra-rotating propeller units were to be fitted in place of the handed propellers of the first prototype.

Republic XP-69

In 1940 the Republic Aircraft Corporation initiated development of a new escort fighter based around the proposed Wright R-2160 Tornado rated at 2,350hp, this being an experimental 42-cylinder, six-row liquid-cooled radial engine driving contra-rotating propellers. Designated Model AP-18 by the company, the aircraft was seen as a potential replacement for the

P-47 Thunderbolt when that aircraft became obsolescent.

In the XP-69 the Tornado engine was to be located immediately aft of the pilot, driving the propellers via an extension shaft through to the nose. The air intake and the cooling system were located under the fuselage. The pressurized cockpit featured a large bubble canopy to ensure good all-round vision for the pilot. The wing was designed to make use of laminar flow while the proposed armament was two 37mm cannon and four 0.50in machine guns, all being mounted in the wings so that they fired outside the radius of the propeller assembly. In July 1941 the USAAF ordered two prototypes, and the XP-69 mock-up was undergoing inspection by June 1942. However, delays in the delivery of the Wright Tornado engine caused the XP-69 project to be cancelled in May 1943 as the

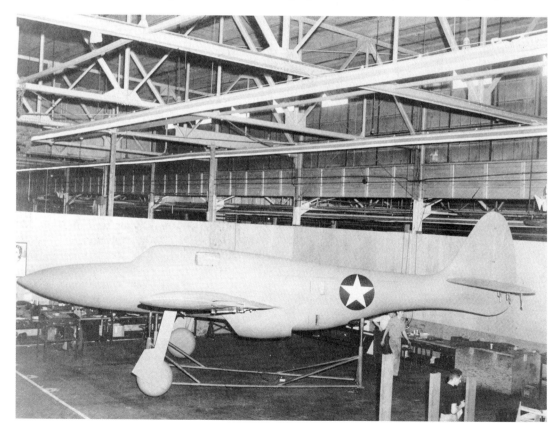

The Republic XP-69 was designed as a large fighter and was powered by a Wright R-2160 engine mounted behind the cockpit. When the engine ran into development problems, the USAAF cancelled the contract in favour of the Republic XP-72.
via NARA/Dennis R. Jenkins

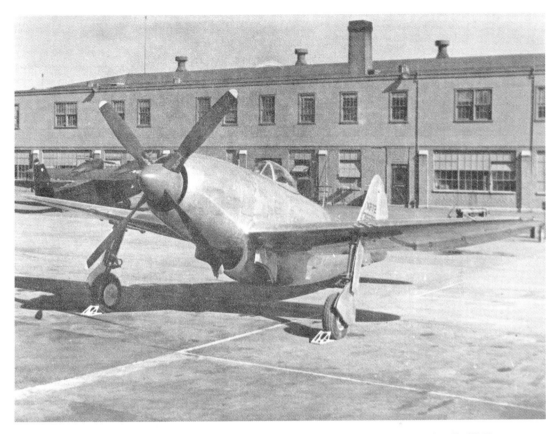

The XP-72 was a modification of the P-47 redesigned for the Pratt & Whitney Wasp Major radial engine. The XP-72 was capable of accelerating to 490mph at 25,000ft and was to be used to intercept German V-1 flying bombs. These aircraft were to be armed with four 37mm cannon instead of machine guns, but the USAAF cancelled the contract because of the need for long-range escort fighters in Europe. via NARA/Dennis R. Jenkins

USAAF favoured the Republic XP-72 project, which showed greater promise.

Republic XP-72

Whereas the XP-69 was a completely new design, the following XP-72 was a development of the earlier P-47 Thunderbolt. The XP-72 was the first fighter to be designed around the huge Pratt & Whitney R-4360 Wasp Major – the most powerful piston engine manufactured during World War Two. In the XP-72 the engine was close-cowled and used fan cooling. It was intended that the Wasp Major would drive a pair of three-blade Aeroproducts contra-rotating propellers.

The wings and tail assembly of the P-47D were retained, but the fuselage was to be enlarged and strengthened. The turbocharger was located aft of the cockpit in a similar manner to that of the P-47, although the turbocharger intake was moved to a new location just below the cockpit rather than in the extreme nose; the lower fuselage was modified to allow for the larger air intake for the turbocharger. The XP-72 was to have been fitted with a bubble canopy for improved all-round vision, this being similar to that used by the late-production blocks of the P-47D. Compressibility recovery flaps were fitted to assist in diving manoeuvres. The proposed armament was to consist of six wing-mounted 0.50in machine guns while underwing mountings and shackles were to be provided for two 1,000lb bombs.

Republic XP-72

Crew: 1
Length: 36ft 7in (11.15m)
Wingspan: 40ft 11in (12.47m)
Height: 16ft (4.88m)
Empty weight: 11,476lb (5,216kg)
Loaded weight: 14,433lb (6,560kg)
Max. take-off weight: 17,490lb (7,950kg)
Powerplant: 1 × Pratt & Whitney R-4360-13 radial engine,
3,000hp at sea level (dash 13 engine) (2,574kW)

Performance
Maximum speed: 480mph (789km/h at sea level)
Range: 1,200 miles (1,932km)
Service ceiling: 42,000ft (12,800m)
Rate of climb: 5,280ft/min (26.8m/s)

Armament
6 × 0.50in machine guns
2 × 1,000lb bombs

As the XP-72 showed great promise the USAAF decided to cancel the more radical and complicated XP-69 project. Two XP-72 prototypes were then ordered on 18 June 1943, being allocated the serials 43-36598 and -36599. The first XP-72 undertook its maiden flight on 2 February 1944. Although the engine was a Wasp Major as planned, the Aeroproducts propeller had been delayed, so the first XP-72 was fitted with a single four-bladed propeller as a temporary measure. Even with the stand-in propellor the performance of the aircraft was rated as excellent, a maximum speed of 490mph (788km/h) being reached in flight tests. The second XP-72 flew for the first time on 26 June 1944, fitted with the Aeroproducts propellers.

Unfortunately the second XP-72 was written off in a take-off crash early in its test-flight programme. Although this held back the flight-test programme, the USAAF was impressed enough with the results already achieved by the XP-72 that it ordered 100 P-72 production aircraft. It was intended that these P-72s would have the R-4360-19 engine and would be provided with a choice of four 37mm cannon or six 0.50in machine guns. It was anticipated that speeds in excess of 500mph (800km/h) could be attained by these machines.

While the XP-72 was seen as promising, the changing face of the war created a greater need for long-range escort fighters than for pure high-speed fighters, and so the USAAF lost interest in the XP-72 project and cancelled the order for the 100 production P-72s. As the jet-powered fighter was beginning to reach fighter units and promised even more spectacular performance than the piston-powered machines in service, the odds were stacked against the XP-72. The surviving XP-72, 43-36598, was scrapped at Wright Field not long after V-J Day.

Curtiss XP-71

The Curtiss-Wright Corporation offered the XP-71 as a private proposal to the Army in 1941. In contrast to their earlier offerings this was a large escort fighter, a high-wing monoplane carried on a tricycle landing gear. It was powered by a pair of turbocharged Pratt & Whitney R-4360-13 Wasp Major air-cooled radials rated at 3,450hp each. The engines were situated in underwing nacelles and each drove a pair of contra-rotating pusher propellers. The pressurized cockpit was to have had two crew members seated in tandem and the proposed armament consisted of two 37mm cannon and one 75mm cannon, these being mounted in the nose. The USAAF ordered a pair of XP-71s but the Army had doubts that such a large and heavy warplane would ever be a viable prospect, so the project never departed the drawing board: it was officially cancelled on 26 August 1943.

Curtiss XP-71

Crew: 2
Length: 61.83ft (18.85m)
Wingspan: 82.25ft (25.07m)
Height: 19.0ft (5.79m)
Empty weight: 31,060lb (14,090kg)
Max. take-off weight: 46,950lb (21,295kg)
Powerplant: 2 × Pratt & Whitney R-4360-13 'Wasp Major'
radial engines, 3,450hp (2,574kW) each

Performance
Maximum speed: 428mph (371kt, 690km/h) at 25,000ft (7,620m)
Range: 3,000 miles (2,600nm, 4,800km)
Service ceiling: 40,000ft (12,200m)

Armament
1 × 75mm cannon
2 × 37mm cannon

General Motors XP-75

In February 1942 the USAAF issued a Request For Proposals to the aircraft companies for a fighter interceptor with an exceptional performance. Maximum speed was to be 440mph (710km/h) at 2,000ft (600m) with an operational ceiling of 38,000ft (12,000m) and the range was to be at least 2,500 miles (4,000km). A special requirement was later added that the initial climb rate was to be no less than 5,600ft/min (28.5m/s).

In April 1942 Donovan Berlin, responsible for the design of the P-36 and the P-40, left the Curtiss-Wright Aircraft Company to take over the directorship of the Aircraft Development Division of the Fisher Body Division of the General Motors Corporation. As one of his first tasks he undertook the design in response to the USAAF request. In September 1942 the Fisher division submitted their proposal to the USAAF. It used the Allison V-3420 liquid-cooled engine, the most powerful powerplant then available. This engine was basically a pair of coupled V-1710 engines mounted in a W-type configuration. Significant savings in cost and time were to be gained by employing major assemblies from aircraft already in production in the construction of the new interceptor.

Fisher XP-75

Crew: 1
Length: 40ft 5in (12.32m)
Wingspan: 49ft 4in (15.04m)
Height: 15ft 6in (4.72m)
Wing area: 347ft² (32.24m²)
Empty weight: 11,495lb (5,214kg)
Loaded weight: 13,807lb (6,263kg)
Max. take-off weight: 18,210lb (8,260kg)
Powerplant: 1 × Allison V-3420-23 liquid-cooled 24-cylinder double-Vee, 2,885hp (2,150kW)

Performance
Maximum speed: 433mph (697km/h) at 20,000ft (6,100m)
Range: 2,050 miles (3,300km)
Service ceiling: 36,400ft (11,100m)
Rate of climb: 4,200ft/min (21.3m/s)

Armament
6 × 0.50in wing-mounted machine guns
4 × 0.50in fuselage-mounted machine guns
2 × 500lb bombs

On 10 October 1942 a contract was issued that covered the construction of two prototypes, designated XP-75; the serials 43-46950 and -46951 were assigned to these prototypes. The Allison engine was located aft of the cockpit, driving a set of contra-rotating propellers via an extension shaft and a reduction gearbox. The engine was cooled by means of a large duct in the ventral fuselage. It was originally planned that the outer wing panels of the P-51 Mustang would be used in an inverted gull configuration, along with the tail assembly of the Douglas A-24 and the undercarriage of the Vought F4U Corsair. However, this was changed at an early stage in the design process when it was decided to drop the gull-wing configuration and instead use a straight-wing design utilizing the outer wing panels from a Curtiss P-40. In mid-1943 the USAAF had an urgent need for long-range escort fighters, these being deemed more important that straightforward fast-climbing interceptors.

On 6 July 1943 the Army ordered six more prototypes that were modified to fulfil the long-range escort role, these being designated the XP-75A with the serial numbers 44-32161 to -32166. They were powered by an Allison V-3420-23 engine and armed with six 0.50in machine guns in the wings plus four 0.50in guns in the nose. The first XP-75 undertook its maiden flight on 17 November 1943 and the following six XP-75A had joined the test programme by early 1944. Some problems were encountered with instability as calculation errors had been made in the initial estimate of the centre of gravity. The coupled Allison engine also give concern as it consistently failed to develop its full intended power. The engine cooling was found to be inadequate, while the aileron forces were excessively high and the aircraft's spinning characteristics were poor. The P-75A production machine featured a modified tail assembly while a clear bubble canopy replaced the original framed and braced canopy of the earlier versions. This version utilized the V-3420-23 engine as installed in the XP-75A.

In parallel with the test aircraft contract the USAAF ordered 2,500 production P-75As, although the Army stipulated that if the production aircraft did not meet the required specifications the order could be cancelled. Proposed maximum speed was to be 434mph (698km/h) at 20,000ft (6,000m) whilst the aircraft had to achieve 389mph (626km/h) at sea level. The first P-75A flew on 15 September 1944, by which time the majority of faults had been eliminated from the design. At this late stage in the war the Republic P-47D Thunderbolt and the North American P-51D Mustang were more than adequately fulfilling the long-range escort role, so the USAAF decided that there was no longer any need for a new escort fighter. Consequently it was decided to terminate the P-75 development programme and the production contract, this being cancelled on 27 October 1944 after just six examples – 44-44549 to -44553 – had been constructed.

When the contract was cancelled the first two P-75As had been delivered to Elgin Field, Florida for tactical and flight trials, the third aircraft was in the process of being fitted with an experimental intercooler while the fourth and fifth machines were almost complete. Even though the USAAF no longer had any requirement for the P-75, it was decided to go ahead and finish these machines and use them for development work. The sixth machine was completed minus its engine and held back for spare parts to keep the remainder flying. As the five production aircraft were to be used for test and trials they never completed official performance trials, but enough flying was undertaken to reveal the fact that the maximum speed was at least 30mph (50km/h) below that stated by the manufacturer. The final production P-75A, 44-44553, is now on display at the USAF Museum in Dayton, Ohio.

Bell XP-76

The P-76 project began life as the XP-39E, the purpose of which was to improve the high-altitude performance of the Airacobra. The proposed powerplant was the experimental Continental I-1430-1 supercharged liquid-cooled engine. The company internal designation for this project was the Model 23 and the first two machines were ordered on 10 April 1941 with a third being added on 17 October 1941. The contract used three production P-39Ds – 41-19501, 41-19502 and 42-7164 – that were taken off the line to be modified to XP-39E standard. As the Continental engine was not available when the XP-39E airframes were completed, the Allison V-1710-47 engine rated at 1,325hp was installed in its place. The carburettor air intake was relocated and the

---

Bell XP-76

Crew: 1
Length: 31ft 11in (9.7m)
Wingspan: 35ft 10in (10.9m)
Wing area: 236ft² (21.9m²)
Empty weight: 6,936lb (3,150kg)
Max. take-off weight: 8,918lb (4,050kg)
Powerplant: 1 × Continental I-1430-1, 2,100hp (1,600kW)

Performance
Maximum speed: 386mph (335kt, 620km/h)
Rate of climb: 2,150ft/min (11m/s)

Armament
Guns:
1 × 37mm cannon
2 × 0.50in machine guns
4 × 0.30in machine guns
Bombs: 500lb externally

---

wing-root radiator intakes were enlarged. The XP-39E also featured laminar-flow wings with square-cut tips.

Each of the XP-39Es was used to test a different configuration for the vertical tail surfaces: the first had rounded and tapered surfaces, the second had surfaces that were square in outline and the third had a configuration similar to that of the P-51. Armament was the same as that of the P-39D, but the XP-39E was considered by the Army as being sufficiently different from the normal P-39 that it was redesignated the XP-76 in February 1942.

The USAAF was confident enough in the new design that it ordered 4,000 production P-76s from Bell, all of which were to be manufactured at the new Bell plant in Atlanta, Georgia. Three months later the Army expressed doubts about this contract even though the XP-76 had been faster in trials than the P-39D. In other respects the new design was found to be inferior to the basic Airacobra and so the order for the P-76 was cancelled on 20 May 1942, the Atlanta plant being used for the licensed manufacture of the B-29 Superfortress.

Bell XP-77

Although Bell Aircraft were normally involved in the design of fighters for the Army, they did

The Bell XP-77, Tri-4, was a lightweight fighter and was constructed mainly of wood, being designed to be highly manoeuvrable. The completion of the first aircraft took nearly two years by which time the aircraft was no longer needed, so the contract was cancelled. via NARA/Dennis R. Jenkins

undertake a diversion into the field of lightweight fighters built of non-strategic materials. On 30 October 1941 the USAAF requested that the Bell Chief Designer, Robert Woods, investigate such a machine. Six month later Woods submitted a design for a low-wing monoplane with a tricycle undercarriage and a laminar-flow wing equipped with manually operated flaps. The structure was of wood covered by an alloy laminate skin. The company designation for this project was Tri-4 and the intended engine was the twelve-cylinder Ranger XV-770-9 air-cooled, supercharged engine rated at 500hp. The estimated top speed was 410mph (660km/h) at 27,000ft (8,000m) while the armament was to have been a pair of 0.50in machine guns mounted in the fuselage and a single 20mm cannon that fired through the propeller hub.

The Army issued a contract for twenty-five Tri-4s on 16 May 1942; it was requested that provision be made to carry either a 300lb bomb or a 325lb depth charge, although the carriage of either required that the 20mm cannon be removed. Delays in the delivery of the XV-770-9 engine saw the contract reduced to six aircraft on 20 August 1942, by which time the designation

XP-77 had been assigned. In a formal contract issued on 10 October 1942 the Army ordered six prototypes of the XP-77, the serials being 43-34915 to -34920. Two further airframes were ordered for static tests.

The programme was given the company designation of Model 32. The mock-up was inspected during September 1942, after which fifty-four changes were requested by the USAAF. It was also decided to install the unsupercharged XV-770-6 engine as a temporary measure for initial flight test trials until the supercharged XV-770-9 became available. It soon became obvious to the Bell design team that the XP-77 as planned was overweight, which, if left uncorrected, would result in an aircraft that offered no appreciable advantage in performance over aircraft already in production. Therefore the Bell team undertook a weight reduction programme to cut the weight of the aircraft down by 3,000lb (1,400kg). This work caused costs to rise and the date of delivery of the first prototypes to be delayed, as a result of which the XP-77 order was cut to only two machines on 3 August 1943. The USAAF did agree that the engine should be the V-770-7, this being the Army designation for the Navy V-770-6.

Bell XP-77

Crew: 1
Length: 22ft 10in (6.96m)
Wingspan: 27ft 6in (8.38m)
Height: 8ft 2in (2.49m)
Empty weight: 2,855lb (1,295kg)
Max. take-off weight: 4,028lb (1,827kg)
Powerplant: 1 × Ranger V-770-7 inverted V12 engine, 520hp (388kW)

Performance
Maximum speed: 330mph (290kt, 530km/h)
Range: 550 miles (480nm, 890km)
Service ceiling: 30,100ft (9,180m)

Armament
Guns:
1 × 20mm cannon, firing through the spinner
2 × 0.50in machine guns
Bombs:
1 × 300lb bomb or
1 × 325lb depth charge

As Bell Aircraft was already heavily committed to P-39, P-63 and P-59 production, the company began to request more and more delays in the XP-77 programme. Also causing problems were delays in the delivery of the wooden wings from the Vidal Research Corporation, who were acting as a subcontractor, and there were problems with undercarriage retraction. The two XP-77s were finally delivered in the spring of 1944, their serial numbers being 43-34915 and -34916. The low-mounted cantilever wing had a single spar structure covered by a stressed skin, and the wing and the fuselage were largely constructed of resin-bonded laminated wood. The tricycle landing gear was electrically operated with the nose wheel retracting aft into the fuselage while the main undercarriage units retracted inwards into wheel wells located in the wings. The flaps retained manual control.

The first XP-77 made its maiden flight on 1 April 1944 piloted by test pilot Jack Woolams. Test flights revealed that the performance was disappointing as the top speed was only 330mph (550km/h) at 4,000ft (1,200m). The take-off run was found to be excessively long while the test pilots complained that there were unfavourable vibrations at certain engine speeds due to the lack of engine support vibration damping mounts. The second XP-77 was despatched to Elgin Field

for fuel consumption and operational suitability trials but on 2 October 1944 the aircraft crashed after getting into an inverted spin, the pilot parachuting to safety.

Flight trials continued with the first XP-77 but the USAAF was still disappointed by the aircraft's poor performance; in fact the performance of the XP-77 was actually inferior to that of aircraft already in service. In addition, any chance of an aluminium shortage had passed and so the ultra-light fighter project was officially abandoned on 2 December 1944. Post-cancellation, the remaining XP-77 was despatched to Wright Field for trials, later returning to Elgin before finally returning to Wright Field. It was later shown at various post-war airshows, sometimes wearing spurious markings.

Northrop XP-79

The Northrop XP-79 began in 1942 as a high-speed flying-wing fighter aircraft powered by a rocket engine, and close-to-supersonic speeds were envisaged. The Northrop fighter project was powered by a 2,000lb (7.32kN)-thrust Aerojet rocket engine while take-off was assisted by a pair of 1,000lb (3.66kN)-thrust rocket boosters that was jettisoned after take-off. Northrop proposed that this aircraft be flown by a pilot lying in a prone position in the cockpit, the hope being that this would reduce strain on the pilot during violent manoeuvres and present the smallest possible target area to enemy gunners. During January 1943 the USAAF issued a contract for three prototypes under the designation XP-79. The availability of jet engines led to a decision in March to use two Westinghouse 19-B turbojets in the third prototype instead, this being redesignated the XP-79B.

As the layout of the fighter was radical, it was felt that glider prototypes should be built to verify the validity of the concept. One of these was designated the MX-324, and was fitted with a fixed tricycle landing gear. The MX-324 was towed into the air by a P-38 on 5 July 1944 and became the first American-built, rocket-powered aircraft to fly.

Delays in the development of the Aerojet rocket engine resulted in the Army cancelling the two XP-79s, leaving only the XP-79B. which was given the serial number 43-52437. The XP-79B

Northrop XP-79

Crew: 1
Length: 14ft 0in (4.27m)
Wingspan: 28ft 0in (8.54m)
Height: 7ft 0in (2.13m)
Empty weight: 5,840lb (2,650kg)
Loaded weight: 8,669lb (3,932kg)
Powerplant: 2 × Westinghouse 19-B turbojet, 1,150lbft (4.2kN) each

Performance
Maximum speed: 547mph (880km/h)
Range: 993 miles (1,598km)
Service ceiling: 40,000ft (12,200m)
Rate of climb: 4,000ft/min (20.3m/s)

Armament
4 × 0.50in machine guns (never fitted)

was finally ready for flight testing in mid-1945. The pilot lay prone in an unpressurized cockpit situated between the two turbojets. The flying wing was of semi-monocoque construction and was built mainly from magnesium to save weight.

Instead of conventional ailerons, the wing had air intakes at the tips for lateral control – in a similar manner to the XP-56 – while the aircraft was equipped with a pair of fins. The retractable landing gear consisted of four units mounted two at the front and two at the back.

The XP-79B was to have used a rather unusual technique for destroying enemy aircraft: the leading edge was reinforced so that it could slice off the wings or tails of enemy aircraft by ramming, although the XP-79B was also equipped with a conventional armament of four 0.50in machine guns in the wing.

The XP-79B was transferred to Muroc Dry Lake in June 1945 but flight testing was delayed by problems with bursting tyres during ground taxi trials. On 12 September 1945 test pilot Harry Crosby finally lifted the XP-79B up into the air for the first time. After just under fifteen minutes, however, the aircraft went into a spin from which it was impossible to recover. The pilot attempted to parachute to safety but his parachute failed to deploy correctly and he was killed, while the XP-79B crashed in the desert and was destroyed in the resulting fire.

The Northrop XP-79 Flying Ram was a design as a 'flying wing' fighter aircraft in which the pilot lay in a prone position, this allowing him to withstand greater 'g' forces. The airframe was a welded magnesium monocoque structure instead of the usual riveted aluminium. via NARA/Dennis R. Jenkins

Convair XP-81

In March 1943 the Consolidated Aircraft Corporation merged with Vultee Aircraft Inc. to form the Consolidated Vultee Aircraft. One of the first designs from the new corporation was the XP-81 mixed-powerplant fighter. The main drawback that faced the early jet fighters was their high fuel consumption, which limited the available range compared with existing piston-engine fighters. In 1943 the USAAF was investigating a way of combining the improved performance offered by jet propulsion with the long range that was being demanded by the Pacific campaign. The result was a requirement for a long-range escort fighter to be powered by the combination of a turboprop and a jet engine. It was intended that the turboprop engine would be used for cruising flight while the turbojet engine was used for take-off and high-speed flight. The specification called for a 1,250-mile (2,000km) range with a maximum speed of 500mph (800km/h).

As this was a bold venture both Convair and the USAAF collaborated and came up with an all-metal, cantilever low-winged monoplane that was powered by an experimental General Electric

TG-100 – later re-designated XT31 – turboprop mounted in the nose with a ventral exhaust and an Allison J33-GE-5 turbojet in the rear fuselage that was fed by a pair of dorsal intakes. A retractable tricycle undercarriage was fitted instead of the then-usual tail-wheel arrangement, as it allowed both the jet engine and turboprop to be presented to the airflow at the optimum angle. The pressurized cockpit was housed underneath the bubble canopy.

Convair began detailed design work on the Model 102 on 5 January 1944 with two prototypes being ordered from Convair on 11 February 1944. The designation XP-81 was assigned, while the serials were 44-91000 and -91001. The contract was subsequently updated to include thirteen service-test YP-81s, although these machines were to be powered by the lighter and more powerful TG-110 turboprop with the wing moving aft by 10in (25cm) to compensate, while an armament of six 0.50in machine guns or six 20mm cannon could have been fitted.

The TG-100 turboprop engine ran into an extensive series of teething troubles and was not available when the first XP-81, 44-91000, was ready for its first flight. A Packard Merlin V-1560-7 engine from a P-51D Mustang was

The Convair twin-engine XP-81 was powered by a conventional turbojet engine plus a turboprop engine. At first, turboprops offered greater fuel economy than turbojets, but this marginal advantage was lost due to improvements in turbojet design. via NARA/Dennis R. Jenkins

---

Consolidated-Vultee XP-81

Crew: 1
Length: 44ft 10in (13.67m)
Wingspan: 50ft 6in (15.39m)
Height: 14ft 0in (4.27m)
Empty weight: 12,755lb (5,786kg)
Loaded weight: 19,500lb (8,850kg)
Max. take-off weight: 24,650lb (11,180kg)
Powerplant:
1 × General Electric J33-GE-5 turbojet, 3,750lbf (16.7kN)
1 × General Electric XT31-GE-1 turboprop, 2,300hp (1,715kW)

Performance
Maximum speed: 507mph (440kt, 811km/h)
Range: 2,500 miles (2,200nm, 4,000km)
Service ceiling 35,500ft (10,800m)
Rate of climb: 5,300ft/min (27m/s)

Armament (projected)
Guns: 6 × 20mm cannon
Bombs: 2,000lb

---

installed in its place while a P-38J-type radiator intake was mounted below the propeller spinner. The Merlin-powered XP-81 was moved by road to Muroc Dry Lake where it undertook its maiden flight on 11 February 1945. The handling overall proved to be exceptionally good although the directional stability was marginal, therefore a 15in (38cm) fin extension and a short ventral fin were later added. The second XP-81 was fitted with a rounded fin extension and a long ventral fin at the factory, prior to delivery.

While Convair was making great strides in developing their composite aircraft, the war against Japan had progressed to such a point where the capture of such islands as Guam and Saipan removed the need for long-range, high-speed fighters. In the face of these conquests the thirteen pre-production YP-81s were cancelled shortly before VJ Day, but work continued on the two prototypes.

The first XP-81 was flown back to Vultee Field to be fitted with the TG-100, though the work was not completed until after Japan had surrendered. The first flight with the TG-100 took place on 21 December 1945. The TG-100 was supposed to deliver 2,300hp (1,750kW), although in reality it only delivered 1,400hp (1,044kW). The performance of the turboprop-powered XP-81 was no better than that of the Merlin-powered version and excess propeller vibration and oil leaks were

persistent problems. The XP-81 programme was officially terminated on 9 May 1947 with both prototypes being re-designated ZXF-81 in 1948; the designation change indicated that the aircraft had been transferred to test-bed status. In 1949 both were stripped of useful parts and placed on the bombing range at Edwards AFB. The remains of both machines were stored for a long time at the Flight Test Museum at Edwards before being moved to the USAF Museum.

Bell XP-83

Bell Aircraft had been working on a jet-powered interceptor design since March 1943, with the company designation of Model 40. In April, in response to a USAAF requirement, the Model 40 was reworked as a long-range fighter. It retained the basic overall configuration of the earlier P-59A Airacomet with twin General Electric I-40 (J33) turbojets installed underneath the wing roots, close to the fuselage. This arrangement had the advantage in that no appreciable asymmetric forces were exerted if one engine failed. In addition, no fuselage space was occupied by the engines, which left the internal fuselage capacity free for fuel tanks and armament.

The rather large and bulky fuselage was of all-metal semi-monocóque construction, while a fully retractable tricycle undercarriage was fitted. Internal fuel capacity was 1,150 US gallons while a pair of 250 US gallon drop-tanks could be fitted. The ailerons were hydraulically boosted, while the flaps were electrically driven. A pressurized, air-conditioned cabin was provided for the pilot, covered by a small, low canopy with a sharply sloping windscreen. The proposed armament was to be six 0.50in machine guns with 300 rounds per gun, all guns being mounted in the nose.

A USAAF contract for two XP-83 prototypes was awarded on 21 July 1944, this being followed by a confirmatory Letter of Contract in March; the serials assigned were 44-84990 and -84991. Seven months after the awarding of the contract the first prototype, 44-84990, undertook its maiden flight on 25 February 1945 with chief Bell test pilot Jack Woolams at the controls. The aircraft proved to be underpowered and somewhat unstable around all axes. The close proximity of the turbojets to the fuselage had the detrimental side effect of allowing the hot

The Bell XP-83 was a prototype jet escort fighter designed by Bell near the end of the war. Based on the earlier YP-59, it first flew in 1945. The XP-83 suffered the usual limitations of the time, including a lack of power. via NARA/Dennis R. Jenkins

jet exhaust gases to buckle the tail plane's skin during ground power runs unless the fire services were standing by to spray cooling water on the rear fuselage.

The second prototype, 44-84991, first flew on 19 October 1945. This aircraft had a slightly different bubble canopy and a longer nose that could easily accommodate a heavier armament of six 0.60in T17E3 machine guns. This aircraft was used for gunnery trials at Wright Field, Ohio. The tail plane overheating problem was later cured by modifying the jet pipes so that they angled slightly outwards. Wind-tunnel tests had showed that an 18in (45cm) extension of the fin would cure the stability problems, though it is unlikely that this modification was ever carried out. As the performance of the XP-83 was disappointing it was decided that no production aircraft would be ordered. Other than its range, the XP-83 offered no significant gains over the Lockheed P-80 Shooting Star, which was already in production and had already been deployed to Italy, so further work on the XP-83 project was abandoned.

Bell XP-83

Crew: 1
Length: 44ft 10in (13.67m)
Wingspan: 53ft 0in (16.15m)
Height: 15ft 3in (4.65m)
Empty weight: 14,105lb (6,400kg)
Loaded weight: 24,090lb (10,930kg)
Max. take-off weight: 27,500lb (12,500kg)
Powerplant: 2 × General Electric J33-GE-5 turbojets, 4,000lbf (18kN) each

Performance
Maximum speed: 522mph (453kt, 840km/h) at 15,660ft (4,775m)
Range: 1,730 miles (1,500nm, 2,785km)
Service ceiling: 45,000ft (14,000m)
Rate of climb: 5,650ft/min (28.7m/s)

Armament
Guns:
6 × 0.50in machine guns or
6 × 0.60in machine guns or
4 × 20mm cannons or
1 × 37mm cannon in the nose

America Embraces the Attack Aircraft

Although the United States armed forces had investigated the use of attack aircraft for ground attack in support of ground forces, they had never invested time and money in developing a dedicated aircraft for the purpose in the inter-war period.

The Brewster XA-32 was designed as an attack aircraft. It was a mid-wing design with an internal bomb bay and powered by a R-2800 engine, although it could take the intended R-4360 powerplant. After a disappointing series of flight test results the XA-32 contract was cancelled. via NARA/Dennis R. Jenkins

With no further development authorized, the two prototypes were used for as test beds for other development work. The first XP-83 was to trial ram-jet engine tests, during which a pair of experimental ram-jets were fitted under the wings. It was intended that the aircraft would be able to fly on ram-jet power once sufficient forward airspeed was obtained. To monitor the trials a hatch was cut in the under-fuselage to provide entry into an engineer station that was provided in the fuselage behind the pilot. However, on 14 September 1946, right at the start of the test programme, one of the ram-jets caught fire during an initial test flight, forcing pilot Chalmers Goodlin and engineer Charles Fay to parachute to safety. The XP-83 was destroyed in the ensuing crash. The second XP-83 remained extant until 1947 after which it was scrapped.

Hughes XF-11

The Hughes XF-11 would have been no more than a footnote in history had it not made a starring appearance in the film *The Aviator* about Howard Hughes. The XF-11 was designed to meet an USAAF requirement for a long-range reconnaissance aircraft. It as a twin-engined, twin-boomed monoplane carried on a tricycle undercarriage, with a pressurised nacelle for the crew. The Pratt & Whitney R-4360-31 28 cylinder radial engines drove four-blade contra-rotating propellers.

The USAAF ordered 100 aircraft, but like many such contracts the entire production run was cancelled at war's end. Two already-completed prototypes, however, were cleared to fly. The first, 44-70155, undertook its maiden flight

The Hughes XF-11 was a prototype military reconnaissance aircraft designed by Hughes Aircraft for the USAAF. The first prototype was lost in a crash while the second was eventually scrapped. via NARA/ Dennis R Jenkins

on 7 July 1946 with Hughes at the controls. This sortie ended in disaster when the rear section of the right-hand propeller unit failed due to an oil leak that in turn caused the aircraft to yaw violently to the right. Hughes made strenuous effort to save the aircraft, even attempting to crash-land it, but the aircraft was destroyed and Hughes badly injured.

Having recovered from his injuries Hughes took the maiden flight of the second prototype on 5 April 1947; this machine, 44-70156, was not fitted with contra-rotating propellers. After landing he reported that the aircraft handled well although it lacked stability and the ailerons were found to be ineffective at low altitudes. Even so the USAAF decided to pit the XF-11 against the Republic XF-12. During these trials it was found that the Hughes machine was harder to fly, maintain and manufacture. The order was for XF-11s was cancelled, to be replaced by conversions of the Boeing Superfortress and a handful of Northrop F-15 Reporters, though the latter in fact spent their time engaged in trials duties.

Republic XF-12

Developed in parallel with the Hughes XF-11, the Republic XF-12 was the epitome of 'big is beautiful': it looked more like a bomber than a reconnaissance fighter. The specification for this machine and the Hughes aircraft had been issued by the USAAF Air Technical Service Command in late 1943. The proposal required an aircraft that had a top speed of 400mph (640km/h), an operating ceiling of 40,000ft (12,000m) and a range of 4,000nm (7,400km) for high-speed flights over the Japanese main Islands and other key installations.

The massive XF-12 undertook its maiden flight on 4 February 1946 without incident. After this flight the aircraft underwent extensive trials during which it operated comfortably at 45,000ft (14,000m) at a speed in the region of 470mph (760km/h) with a range of 4,500 miles (7,200km). To attain this level of performance the aircraft featured some interesting technical advances to reduce drag: the high-aspect wing was slightly tapered with squared-off tips; and the engine were fitted with a sliding cowl that moved

The XF-12 Rainbow was designed by Republic to meet the same requirement as the Hughes XF-11. The aircraft was designed with maximum aerodynamic efficiency in mind. While it was highly innovative, the Rainbow was in competition against the emerging jet engine and did not enter production. via NARA/ Dennis R Jenkins

back and forth instead of the normal cowling flaps. Further cooling was supplied by a two-stage impeller fan mounted behind the propeller hubs. The air drawn through the sliding cowls and the impellors also provided cooling for the oil coolers and the engine inter-coolers.

Like the Hughes XF-11, the Republic XF-12's contracts were cancelled at war's end although two prototypes were completed. As the XF-12 showed great promise it was decided to modify both machines as reconnaissance trials machines. Improved engines allowed for short burst of extra power to and from a target, and improved navigation and radar equipment was also fitted. In this form the XF-12s became potent reconnaissance platforms as they could operate in all weathers and conditions over long ranges and at high speed.

The XF-12s were fitted out with a complete range of photographic equipment. The three equipment bays aft of the wing were fitted with the latest cameras, which were based around the Fairchild K-17 unit. Versions of this unit included a vertical, split vertical and a tri-metrogon unit. all having heated lenses to combat the cold at altitude. A large hold under the fuselage held eighteen high-intensity flash bombs. The camera and flash bay had electrically driven doors that moved at speed, not only to reduce drag but also to keep exposure of the equipment to a minimum. The XF-12 was equipped with an onboard darkroom so that the films could be processed in flight.

The second prototype, 44-91003, crashed into the Gulf of Mexico soon after take-off from Elgin AFB in October 1948 after the No.2 engine exploded; fortunately the entire crew escaped. The first prototype, 44-91002, had been damaged previously in an accident during 1947, but it had been repaired and was able to complete the development programme. The aircraft was then withdrawn from use in June 1952 for use as a target at the Aberdeen Proving Ground.

Beechcraft XA-38

The contract for the Model 28 Destroyer – as it was initially known by the company – was awarded to Beechcraft by the USAAF in December 1942. The intention was to create an aircraft that would replace the Douglas A-20 Havoc, and the Model 28 was designed from the outset as a ground-attack machine capable of destroying tanks, troops and their equipment. The new machine was constructed around a T15E1 75mm cannon with twenty rounds of ammunition, which was supplemented by six Browning 0.50in machine guns, two of which were fixed facing forward in the nose and two each housed in the dorsal and ventral turrets. The aircraft carried a crew of two, a pilot and an observer/gunner who would control the turrets via remote-control sighting.

Beechcraft XA-38

Crew: 2
Length: 51ft 9in (15.8m)
Wingspan: 67ft 4in (20.5m)
Height: 13ft 6in (4.1m)
Empty weight: 22,480lb (10,197kg)
Max. take-off weight: 32,000lb (14,515kg)

Performance
Maximum speed: 376mph (605km/h)
Service ceiling: 27,800ft (8,500m)

Armament
1 × 75mm cannon
6 × 0.50in machine guns
2,000lb (907kg) of external stores

Although a fully loaded XA-38 Grizzly weighed 31,250lb (14,170kg) it was a speedy beast and could easily outpace the fastest fighters available in mid-1944. This performance was provided by a pair of Wright Cyclone R-3350 engines allied with careful attention to the external skinning, which was flush-riveted throughout. The fuselage was constructed in four sections to ease manufacture and repair; it consisted of bulkhead formers and longitudinal beams and stringers, and extra strengthening was applied to the access cut-outs. To reach the cockpit the crew had to mount the wing and board through a hinged canopy section; once there, the nose had a steep forward curve, which gave the pilot good forward and downwards visibility. The extreme nose section, which housed the cannon, could be opened for re-arming and maintenance; this section could also be removed altogether and replaced by other nose sections containing alternative armament configurations or reconnaissance systems.

As the XA-38 was similar in size to a medium bomber its wings were of a commensurate size. The airfoil profile was NACA 2300, although the wing tapered gradually from root to tip. The wings themselves were of conventional all-metal construction with the main spar located at the 25 per cent chord point and the rear spar at the 75 per cent chord point. To enable repair and

The Beechcraft XA-38 Grizzly was a ground-attack aircraft fitted with a forward-firing 75mm cannon to attack armoured targets. The prototype first flew on 7 May 1944 but it used the same engine as the B-29 Superfortress, which had priority. It was then cancelled after two prototypes had been completed. via NARA/Dennis R. Jenkins

maintenance the wingtips were removable, while the wing outer sections could be removed completely. The aircraft had slotted flaps under the inner wing sections while the trailing edge of the removable wing panel carried the ailerons, which extended to the removable tip assembly. All of the control surfaces were conventional in operation, and dynamically and statically balanced. Thanks to the care taken in setting up the flight controls and the area of the flaps, the XA-38 performed well in the air yet could achieve quite slow and short landings.

At the rear of the fuselage was the horizontal tail plane, the ends of which were capped with twin fins and rudders taken from Beechcraft's Model 18. All of the flight control surfaces featured alloy nose sections with the remainder being fabric covered. The undercarriage consisted of two single main wheels and a castoring tail wheel, all of them fully retractable into the nacelles and rear fuselage, respectively. All were hydraulically operated and there was a separate pneumatic blow-down system for use in emergencies. To reduce the complexity of the undercarriage, the doors that covered the bays were operated by rods and linkages.

The Beechcraft XA-38, 43-14406, undertook its maiden flight on 7 May 1944, piloted by company test pilot Verne Carsten. During these initial test flights only mock-up weaponry was installed, although as the flights were proceeding with very little incident in July 1944 it was intended that firing tests of the 75mm cannon be carried out. On 14 August 1945 the first XA-38 was transferred to Eglin Field, Florida, for further intensive testing. Unfortunately for the XA-38, Japan surrendered and so the Grizzly did not proceed any further. The second XA-38, 43-14407, made its first flight in September 1945 and confirmed the performance of the first machine, but there was now no requirement for either aircraft and both were finally grounded and, despite plans at one time to donate one to the USAF Museum, both aircraft were scrapped.

Vultee XA-41

Following on from the XA-38 came the Kaiser Fleetwings XA-39. This was to be powered by a pair of R-2800 radial engine with an armament of four machine guns supplemented by a pair

---

Vultee XA-41

Crew: 1
Length: 48ft 8in (14.83m)
Wingspan: 54ft 0in (16.46m)
Height: 13ft 11in (4.24m)
Empty: 13,400lb (6,080kg)
Loaded: 18,800lb (8,165kg)
Maximum take-off: 24,188lb (10,971kg)
Powerplant: 1 × Pratt & Whitney R-4360 radial engine 3,000hp (2,237kW)

Performance
Maximum speed: 363mph (584km/h)
Combat range: 800 miles (1,290km)
Service ceiling: 29,300ft (8,900m)
Rate of climb: 2,730ft/min (13.9m/s)

Armament
Guns: 4 × 0.50in machine guns
Bombs: 6,400lb (2,900kg) of ordnance
Rockets: 8–12

---

of 37mm cannon. The XA-39 never left the drawing board. A similar fate befell the Curtiss XA-40, a single-seat machine powered by a single R-3350.

After two drawing-board machines, the next attack aircraft managed to go a little further. The Vultee XA-41 had originally been ordered in November 1942 as a dive bomber, but in early 1943 the order was amended to change the role from dive bomber to low-level ground attack; the experience gained by the Army Air Corps in combat had shown the dedicated dive bomber to be ineffective and vulnerable to enemy attack without heavy escort. Combat experience also showed that high-altitude fighters adapted for ground attack were well suited to the role – in particular, the Republic P-47 was an outstanding ground-attack aircraft.

In response, the Vultee engineers decided early in the design process to build the XA-41, known in the company as the Model 90, around the huge Pratt & Whitney R-4360 Wasp Major 28-cylinder radial engine rated at 3,000hp. Originally two prototype aircraft were ordered, but only one was ever completed. Orders for combat aircraft were being reduced as the war turned more in the Allies' favour and as the XA-41 would not have been ready for combat until late 1944 or early 1945, the production run was cancelled, as was the second prototype.

The Vultee XA-41 was originally ordered as a dive bomber, but when combat reports led the USAAC to believe that dive bombers were vulnerable to enemy fighters the contract was amended to change the role to low-level ground attack. While the XA-41 was a potent aircraft, the design lagged behind improving aircraft technology and never entered production. via NARA/Dennis R. Jenkins

The first XA-41, 43-35124, undertook its maiden flight on 11 February 1944, and revealed a good performance. With the cancellation of the production programme the aircraft was used as an engine test bed for the large Pratt & Whitney radial. At the conclusion of Army testing the XA-41 was evaluated by the US Navy, later being passed to Pratt & Whitney for various engine test programmes.

mounted at the far aft portion of the fuselage and also served as the horizontal stabilizer. The design had a conventional vertical stabilizer and rudder, but changes in pitch and roll were accomplished with wing-mounted control surfaces: the elevators were on the inboard wing while the ailerons were outboard. The wingtips were also designed as variable-incidence control surfaces.

Convair XA-44

The next two programmes, the Douglas XA-42 and the Curtiss XA-43, had entirely different fates. The former would eventually go on to be developed into an experimental bomber while the latter was a four-jet, two-seat attack aircraft whose funds were later allocated to the XP-87 Blackhawk.

Possibly one of strangest aircraft to appear at the war's end was the Convair XA-44 – this was the original designation for a bomber aircraft with the designation XB-53. Convair engineers made use of research into forward-swept wings captured from Germany in World War Two as the basis for their design, and the aircraft was to have a 30-degree forward-swept wing with an 8-degree dihedral. The wing was

Convair XA-44/XB-53
Crew: 4
Length: 79ft 6in (24.2m)
Wingspan: 80ft 7in (24.6m)
Height: 23ft 8in (7.22m)
Empty weight: 31,760lb (14,400kg)
Loaded weight: 60,000lb (27,000kg)
Max. take-off weight: 60,000lb (27,000kg)
Powerplant: 3 × General Electric J35 turbojets, 4,000lbf (178kN) each
Performance (estimated)
Maximum speed: 580mph (500kt, 930km/h)
Range: 2,000 miles (1,700nm, 3,200km)
Service ceiling: 44,000ft (13,400m)
Armament
12,000lb (5,400kg) bombs or 40 HVAR

The design called for three General Electric J35 turbojets of 4,000lbf (17.8kN) st thrust mounted in the fuselage and company estimates indicated a possible top speed of approximately 580mph (930km/h). Classified as a medium bomber, the XB-53 carried up to 12,000lb (5,400kg) of bombs but could alternatively mount forty High Velocity Aerial Rockets (HVARs) on underwing pylons. Convair diverted funding initially allotted to the XB-46 programme to work on the XA-44/XB-53 project. Two aircraft were ordered, 45-59583 and -59584, but neither was completed before the programme was cancelled. The Convair machine was the last wartime attack design, the designation for attack aircraft not appearing again until the unified designation system was introduced in 1962.

Naval Prototypes

While the US Navy usually used aircraft from the Grumman, Douglas and Chance Vought companies, they did occasionally look at machines from other manufacturers. On 1 January 1938 the service issued a specification for a light, high-performance, carrier-based fighter that was needed to replace the biplane fighters currently in service. Bell, Brewster, Curtiss, Grumman and Vought submitted proposals for the Navy fighter; some were single-engine while others were twin-engine. After considering the proposals, the USN ordered three aircraft, one Bell Model 5 as the XFL-1 Airabonita, one Grumman Model G-34 as the XF5F-1 Skyrocket and one Vought-Sikorsky Model V-166B as the XF4U-1 Corsair, the latter eventually entering service.

The Bell XFL Airabonita was an experimental shipboard interceptor aircraft developed for the US Navy. It was similar to the USAAC P-39 Airacobra, differing mainly in the use of a tailwheel undercarriage. Only one prototype was constructed. via NARA/Dennis R. Jenkins

Bell XFL-1

The contract for one XFL-1 for testing was signed on 8 November 1938. It specified delivery of a single prototype machine within 300 days to Naval Air Station Anacostia, Washington, DC, this giving a projected delivery date of 4 September 1939. This aircraft, in common with the P-39, was to be powered by a liquid-cooled engine installed behind the pilot with an extension shaft driving the propellor.

Since the XFL-1 was a navalized version of the P-39, many modifications were required before it could be used by the USN. Most significantly, a tail-wheel landing gear and tail hook were to be fitted instead of the tricycle landing gear of the

P-39. To accommodate the tail wheel undercarriage, the main landing gear had to be moved further forward with the attachments being located on the front wing spar; this required a new single-piece wing instead of the P-39's arrangement with the outer panels bolted to a centre section. The use of a tail-wheel landing gear and the engine located far aft immediately raised concerns about centre of gravity problems. Consideration was given to moving the wing 3in (75mm) further aft, though this was never in fact done.

The span, chord, dihedral and so the area of the wing were increased to permit a carrier landing speed not in excess of 70mph (110km/h) and to increase stability, while the length of the fuselage was reduced, the flaps were enlarged to reduce the landing speed, and the vertical tail surfaces were modified to maintain longitudinal stability during carrier landings. Unlike contemporary USAAF aircraft, the wings of the XFL-1 contained flotation bags that would be deployed if the aircraft ditched, although these were later deleted.

Other modifications included strengthening of the entire aircraft for the rough and tumble of carrier operations, raising the cockpit to increase visibility and the inclusion of a small window in the belly of the aircraft, just forward of the wing root, to aid in carrier landings. The final USN requirement was that ten small bomb bays, five per wing, be built into the underside of each wing to accommodate 5.2lb (2.4kg) bombs to be dropped over an enemy aircraft formation.

During the aircraft's construction its gross weight increased due to the strengthening required for carrier operations and an increase in engine weight. The Allison engine was delivered on 4 January 1940, four months after the aircraft was scheduled for delivery. Prior to installation the engine and its accessories were weighed, and it was discovered that the long extension propeller shaft and its gearbox weighed 25 per cent above the original planned weight as given by the manufacturer.

On 13 May 1940 the XFL-1, by now named the Airabonita, began taxi tests at Buffalo Airport, New York. During a high-speed taxi test a strong gust of wind caused the aircraft to become airborne and, since the pilot was running out of runway, he chose to complete the take-off and remain in flight. Once airborne at an altitude of a few hundred feet, one of the flotation bag doors opened and the bag fell out, shortly followed by

---

Bell XFL-1

Crew: 1
Length: 29ft 9in (9.07m)
Wingspan: 35ft 0in (10.67m)
Height: 12ft 9in (3.89m)
Empty weight: 5,161lb (2,341kg)
Loaded weight: 6,651lb (3,017kg)
Max. take-off weight: 7,212lb (3,271kg)
Powerplant: 1 × Allison XV-1710-6 V-12 piston engine, 1,150hp (858kW)

Performance
Maximum speed: 307mph (464km/h)
Range: 1,072 miles (1,725km)
Service ceiling: 30,900ft (9,421m)
Rate of climb: 2,630ft/min (13.4m/s)

Armament
Guns:
2 × 0.30in machine guns
1 × 0.50in machine gun or 37mm cannon

---

the other. Further ground testing in May 1940 revealed engine cooling problems that plagued the aircraft through its four-year life. Another problem was inadequate directional stability, a problem that had first been determined by wind-tunnel testing at the University of Michigan. As a result of these tests, Bell later added fillets, dorsal fins and duct modifications to the XFL-1, but none of these cured the stability problems. Bell eventually tried increasing the area of the horizontal and vertical tail surfaces, but to no avail.

After further testing by Bell the aircraft was flown to the Naval Aircraft Factory at NAS Philadelphia, Pennsylvania, on 27 February 1941 for further trials. During carrier qualification tests on 12 May 1941, the landing gear failed and the aircraft was declared to be unsatisfactory for use as a carrier aircraft or for arrested landings. As a result of this failure and the subsequent report, the US Navy signed a contract with Vought for the F4U-1 Corsair on 30 June 1941. In 1942, the XFL-1 was transferred to the Aircraft Armament Unit at NAS Norfolk, Virginia, for anti-aircraft tests. In March 1944 the Airabonita was transferred to NAS Patuxent River, Maryland, being stricken from service on 25 April 1944. After the war, the runways at NAS Patuxent River were extended into Chesapeake Bay to accommodate jet aircraft, and the XFL-1, minus engine and equipment, was used as landfill.

Grumman XF5F-1

The other aircraft in this fighter competition was the Grumman XF5F Skyrocket. This machine was designated Model G-34 by Grumman and was a twin-engine shipboard fighter powered by a pair of Wright Cyclone engines. A single example was ordered by the US Navy on 30 June 1938 and undertook its maiden flight on 1 April 1940. It was obvious from the outset that the closely cowled engines would suffer from cooling problems. Curing this problem required modifications to the cooling ducts, though these were not the only modifications undertaken. Changes were made to the height of the cockpit canopy, the armament was altered from a pair of cannon to four 0.50in machine guns, spinners were added to the propellor assemblies, while the fuselage was extended past the leading edge of the wing. This modification programme was completed by July 1941, although further minor modifications after flight testing saw the aircraft's full flight testing delayed until January 1942. Having finally launched its latest aircraft Grumman further developed the design, leading to the XFF-1, later to become the Tigercat. During development of this new machine the Skyrocket was employed in various trials in support of this programme. Always plagued by undercarriage

problems, the XF5F-1 finally ended its career after a belly landing on 11 December 1944 that resulted in its being written off. Outside of its real role, the Skyrocket also entered the world of fiction as the mount for the 'Blackhawks' in the eponymous military comic, which ran from 1941 to the 1990s.

Grumman XF5F-1

Crew: 1
Length: 28ft 9in (8.76m)
Wingspan: 42ft (12.80m)
Height: 11ft 4in (3.45m)
Wing area: 303.5ft² (28.2m²)
Empty weight: 8,107lb (3,677kg)
Loaded weight: 10,138lb (4,600kg)
Max. take-off weight: 10,892lb (4,940kg)
Powerplant: 2 × Wright XR-1820-40/42 Cyclone 9-cylinder radial air-cooled engine, 1,200hp (895kW) each

Performance
Maximum speed: 383mph at sea level (616km/h)
Range: 1,200 statute miles (1,930km)
Service ceiling: 33,000ft (10,000m)

Armament
Four 0.50in machine guns
Two 75kg bombs

The Grumman XF5F Skyrocket was a twin-engine shipboard fighter interceptor and was a radical advance in shipboard fighters at a time when single-engine fighters were just changing to monoplane from biplanes. The US Navy ordered one prototype in June 1938 but no production orders were forthcoming. via NARA/Dennis R. Jenkins

Boeing XF8B

Boeing also made a small foray into the fighter market – quite a change for a manufacturer better known at the time for its bomber designs. Designated the Model 400, this machine was a large, single-seat, single-engine aircraft that was capable of carrying out a number of roles: interceptor, long-range escort fighter, dive bomber, level bomber and torpedo bomber, it was sometimes referred to as the 'five in one fighter'. Boeing had selected the Pratt & Whitney XR-4360-10 radial engine driving a six-blade contra-rotating propellor assembly. As this was a big aircraft, the large outer wing panels folded up to allow entry into a carrier hangar. To ensure that the thirsty engine had enough fuel, the internal bomb bay could house overload tanks in place of a bomb load while external tanks could be fitted. The proposed fixed armament was either six 0.50in machine guns or six cannon, while the disposable weaponry included up to 6,400lb (2,900kg) of bombs or a 2,000lb (900kg) torpedo.

A contract for three aircraft was issued on 4 May 1943, these being serialled 57984 to 57986. As Boeing were fully committed to building the B-29, the design and construction of the XF8B lagged a little and only one was completed before the war's end. This machine undertook its maiden flight in November 1944 while the remaining two did not fly until after the war. The third prototype

Boeing XF8B

Crew: 1
Length: 43ft 3in (13.1m)
Wingspan: 54ft (16.5m)
Height: 16ft 3in (5.0m)
Empty weight: 13,519lb (6,132kg)
Loaded weight: 20,508lb (9,302kg)
Max. take-off weight: 21,691lb (9,839kg)
Powerplant: 1 × Pratt & Whitney XR-4360-10 28-cylinder four-row radial engine, 3,000hp (2,240kW)

Performance
Maximum speed: 376kt (432mph, 695km/h)
Cruise speed: 165kt (190mph, 306km/h)
Range: 2,435nm (2,800 miles, 4,500km)
Service ceiling: 37,500ft (11,400m)

Armament
6 × 0.50in or 6 × 20mm wing-mounted guns
2,200lb (1415kg) bomb load or 1 × 2,000lb torpedo

underwent evaluation at Eglin Field for possible use by the USAAF. Although the aircraft was designed as a single-seater, a flight engineer's position was installed in the fuselage for the flight testing and evaluation phases. All three aircraft continued test flying with the USAAF until 1946 and with the US Navy until 1947. Although both services delivered positive reports concerning the XF8B-1, changing post-war priorities and the need for Boeing to concentrate upon jet bomber

The Boeing XF8B was developed for operation against the Japanese home islands from aircraft carriers outside of the range of Japanese aircraft. Despite its formidable capabilities, the XF8B-1 was never entered production. via NARA/Dennis R. Jenkins

projects and to kick start its transport aircraft business meant that the death knell sounded for the fighter. As the USAAF had completely pulled out of the project and the US Navy were only prepared to put forward a small contract, Boeing decided to stop the programme.

Vought XF5U

One of the most unusual aircraft developed during the war was the XF5U 'Flying Flapjack' built by Chance Vought Aircraft of Stratford, Connecticut. Designed by Charles H. Zimmerman, the XF5U-1 was designed as a land- or carrier-based fighter that could be used with or without a catapult, although an arrestor hook was required for landing. The wing consisted of two ellipses that were arranged so that the major axis of one coincided with the minor of the other. This comprised the main structure of the airframe with the exception of the pilot's cockpit and the horizontal and vertical tail surfaces.

The greater part of the wing surfaces and internal structure consisted of Metalite, a sand-

Vought XF5U-1
Crew: 1
Length: 28ft 7in (8.73m)
Wingspan: 32ft 6in (9.91m)
Height: 14ft 9in (4.50m)
Empty weight: 13,107lb (5,958kg)
Loaded weight: 16,722lb (7,600kg)
Max. take-off weight: 18,772lb (8,533kg)
Powerplant: 2 × Pratt & Whitney R-2000-7 radial engine, 1,350hp (1,007kW) each
Performance
Maximum speed: 413kt/475mph at 28,000ft (estimated) (765km/h at 8,534m)
Range: 1,064 miles (1,703km)
Service ceiling: 34,492ft (10,516m)
Armament
6 × 0.50 machine guns or
4 × 20mm machine guns or
2 × 1,000lb bombs

wich material providing a particularly strong and lightweight type of construction. Two Metalite 'ailavators' with trim tabs occupied 70 per of the

One of the most unusual aircraft ever constructed for the US Navy was the Vought XF5U-1 Flying Flapjack. Twin engined and almost circular in shape, the aircraft did actually manage to take to the air in its V-173 prototype form. In this view the lower sighting windows to assist the pilot during landing can clearly be seen. via NARA/ Dennis R Jenkins

trailing edge with balance weights on the tips, this providing lateral and longitudinal control. The pilot's cockpit was a complete monocoque shell with a blown plexiglas canopy. The stick and rudder flight controls were manual, except for proportional hydraulic boost to the ailavators. Neither aircraft had armament, although there was provision for six 0.50in machine guns and ammunition boxes.

Two Pratt and Whitney R-2000-7 radial engines with cooling fans and superchargers were mounted upright in the wing. The four-blade, contra-rotating propellers were driven by cross shafts and gearboxes connected to both engines: if one engine failed it could be declutched from the drive system and the aircraft flown with the remaining engine and both propellers operating. Circular air intakes in the wing leading edge provided carburettor, engine and oil cooling air.

The 16ft (4.88m) diameter propellers were unique for the time and were manufactured by Vought. They were hydraulically operated, fast-acting and electro-mechanically governed, and each had four Pregwood blades and load-relieving hubs; these differed from the conventional four-way hub in that the blades were free to flap in pairs about the shaft axis. Low-pitch stop was 15 degrees while high-pitch stop was 70 degrees. The propeller pitch control set the left-hand propeller governor mechanism, which controlled the right-hand propeller governor mechanism electronically; this in turn adjusted the propeller blade angle. Movement of the pitch control lever upward decreased pitch whilst downward increased the pitch. Full forward position governed take-off power while the fully aft position gave enough power for take-off and for flight.

A further unique feature of the XF5U-1 was the stability flap that was located symmetrically about the centreline of the aircraft at the wing trailing edge. The 15sq ft (1.4sq m) hinged surface required no pilot control, but automatically provided for change in trim with the change in attitude: the air loads upon the flap adjusted the deflection against a spring-loaded strut. The stability flap was linked to the tail wheel to ensure locking in the 'up' position when the tail wheel was extended.

The letter of intent for the VS-315, as the XF5U-1 was known to Vought, was issued on 17 September 1942 by the US Navy. The first

XF5U-1, 33958, was used for static tests and proof loading. The second aircraft, 33959, was used for experimental flight testing although it was never actually flown because many hours of engine runs revealed excessive mechanical vibration between the engine propeller shafting, gearboxes and airframe structure. The aircraft was taxi tested in February 1947 at Stratford, but vibration levels were considered excessive. The aircraft was being readied for shipment by sea through the Panama Canal to Edwards AFB, California, when the contract was cancelled in March 1947.

Consolidated XP4Y

Flying boats played an important part in the US Navy's patrol strategy, so numerous designs were put forward to cover the service's needs. Already known as a provider of flying boats and amphibians, Consolidated Aircraft began the design of the XP4Y Corregidor in 1938 at the behest of the US Navy. As this twin-engine machine was going to be large, Consolidated also undertook development work for a civilian version. The aircraft was of all-metal construction and featured the Davis wing that would later appear on the B-24 Liberator bomber. At the rear of the upswept fuselage was the tail unit with twin fins and rudders. The high-mounted wing featured retractable floats

---

Consolidated XP4Y-1

Crew: 2–6
Length: 74ft 1in (22.58m)
Wingspan: 110ft 0in (33.53m)
Height: 25ft 2in (7.67m)
Gross weight: 48,000lb (21,772kg)
Powerplant: 2 × Wright R-3350-8 Cyclone 18 twin-row radial piston engine, 2,300hp (1,715kW) each

Performance
Maximum speed: 247mph (398km/h)
Cruise speed: 136mph (219km/h)
Range: 3,280 miles (5,279km)
Service ceiling: 21,400ft (6,520m)
Rate of climb: 1,230ft/min (6,25m/s)

Armament
1 × 37mm cannon in bow turret (proposed)
2 × 0.5in machine-guns dorsal and tail (proposed)
4,000lb (1,814kg) of external bombs or depth charges (proposed)

under the wings, while mounted on the leading edges were Wright Duplex Cyclone engines. The civilian version had accommodation for fifty-two seated passengers or twenty-eight in sleeper cells.

The single prototype undertook its maiden flight on 5 May 1939 and was reported as almost trouble-free, a rare occurrence for a prototype. The aircraft had completed its flight testing by the time of the Japanese attack on Pearl Harbor in December 1941 that brought America into the war. Soon after this event the US Navy purchased the Model 31 as the XP4Y-1, returning it to Consolidated for the installation of military equipment including nose, tail and dorsal turrets, and mountings for 4,000lb (1,800kg) of external stores. In October 1942 an order for 200 production machines was placed, but this was later cancelled as the proposed engines were desperately needed for the Boeing B-29 and so the factory in New Orleans that was to have built the Corregidor was turned over to building the Catalina flying boat.

Consolidated XPB3Y

Consolidated designed a further flying boat, called the Model 30 in-house. A four-engined machine, the XPB3Y began development in 1940 and required the company to undertake a full range of naval missions that included the possible bombing of Germany and patrols that could reach Antarctica. In the event, this ambitious project never left the drawing board.

Boeing XPBB

Although Consolidated and Martin were the primary providers of flying boats to the US Navy, Boeing also put forward a single design, a twin-engine patrol flying boat designated the XPBB Sea Ranger. After it made a successful first flight on 9 July 1941 an order for fifty-seven machines was placed by the US Navy in 1942, with manufacture to take place at the Government factory at Renton. In a complicated deal, however, the flying boat was cancelled so

The sole Consolidated XP4Y Corregidor, still sporting its civil registration NX21731. Although flight trials were successful, the events at Pearl Harbor saw the programme cancelled , the production capacity thus released being used to build the Catalina.
via NARA/ Dennis R Jenkins

The Boeing XPBB Sea Ranger was a prototype twin-engine flying boat patrol bomber. While an initial production order was awarded to Boeing in 1941, it was later cancelled so that the factory could be used to build the B-29 Superfortress.
via NARA/Dennis R. Jenkins

Boeing XPBB
Crew: 10
Length: 94ft 9in (28.89m)
Wingspan: 139ft 8½in (42.59m)
Height: 34ft 2in (10.42m)
Empty weight: 41,531lb (18,878kg)
Loaded weight: 62,006lb (28,185kg)
Max. take-off weight: 101,130lb (45,968kg)
Powerplant: 2 × Wright R-3350-8 radial engines, 2,300hp (1,716kW) each

that the facility could be used to manufacture the B-29 Superfortress, while in return the US Navy received large quantities of the B-25 Mitchell for use by the US Marine Corps in the Pacific theatre.

Consolidated XR2Y-1

While transport aircraft were not of great consequence to the US Navy, they occasionally expressed an interest in emerging types to supplement their fleet of Douglas C-47s. One

---

Consolidated XR2Y-1

Crew: 4
Capacity: 48 passengers
Payload: 12,000lb (5,500kg) of cargo
Length: 90ft 0in (27.45m)
Wingspan: 110ft 0in (33.55m)
Loaded weight: 56,000lb (25,000kg)
Max. take-off weight: 64,000lb (29,000kg)
Powerplant: 4 × Pratt & Whitney R-1830-94 radial engines,
1,200hp (900kW) each

Performance
Cruise speed: 240mph (210kt, 380km/h)
Range: 4,000 miles (3,500nm, 6,400km) at 200mph (322km/h)

---

airframe that was sponsored by the navy was the Consolidated Model 39; this used major items from the B-24 Liberator including the Davis wing and the tricycle undercarriage, while the fin and rudder were borrowed from the PB4Y Privateer. The major change was the manufacture of a completely new fuselage complete with windows. Nicknamed the Liberator Liner, the XR2Y-1 was used by the Navy for hauling both freight and passengers, but although the service appreciated its capability they did not order any more. Eventually the aircraft was returned to the manufacturers, who later sold it on to American Airlines for freight use.

Ryan XF2R

As the war was coming to a close the need for new aircraft types began to wane, but the Navy

---

Ryan XF2R

Crew: 1
Length: 36ft 0in (10.97m)
Wingspan: 42ft 0in (12.80m)
Height: 14ft 0in (4.27m)
Loaded weight: 11,000lb (4,990kg)
Powerplant:
1 × General Electric J31 turbojet, 1,600lbf (7.1kN)
1 × General Electric T31 turboprop, 1,760hp (1,310kW)

Performance
Maximum speed: 497mph (432kt, 800km/h) at sea level
Service ceiling: 39,100ft (11,900m)

---

still encouraged the various manufacturers to put forward designs for new and innovative aircraft. One of these was the Ryan XF2R Dark Shark, which combined a turboprop and turbojet in one airframe. This machine was based on the same company's FR Fireball, although the piston engine for the former was replaced by a General Electric T-31 turboprop driving a four-blade Hamilton Standard propellor. Although the turboprop improved the Dark Shark's performance over the earlier FR, the US Navy had already lost interest in mixed-power fighters and switched its attention to all-jet machines. Fortunately for Ryan, the USAF were investigating the Convair XP-81 and asked the company to modify the XF2R to accept a Westinghouse jet engine instead of the previously installed General Electric J31, this requiring that the original wing leading edge intakes be replaced by intakes mounted on the forward fuselage. These modifications resulted in the aircraft being redesignated as the XF2R-2. Although in both guises the aircraft delivered an adequate performance, the growing range of jet-powered designs overshadowed the combination aircraft.

Curtiss Designs

The final batch of prototypes ordered by the US Navy came from Curtiss, the first being

---

Curtiss XF14C

Crew: 1
Length: 37.75ft (11.5m)
Wingspan: 46.0ft (14.0m)
Height: 12.33ft (3.8m)
Empty weight: 10,582lb (4,800kg)
Loaded weight: 13,405lb (6,080kg)
Max. take-off weight: 14,582lb (6,614kg)
Powerplant: 1 × Wright XR-3350-16 radial eighteen-cylinder
twin-row air-cooled engine, 2,300hp (1,716kW)

Performance
Maximum speed: 317mph at sea level, 424mph at 32,000ft
(510km/h at sea level, 682km/h at 9,800m)
Range: 1,355 statute miles at 162mph (2,181km at 260km/h)
Service ceiling: 39,500ft (12,000m)
Rate of climb: 2,700ft/min (13.72m/s)

Armament
4 × wing-mounted 20mm cannon

Curtiss XF15C

Crew: 1
Length: 44ft 0in (13.41m)
Wingspan: 48ft 0in (14.63m)
Height: 15ft 3in (4.65m)
Empty weight: 12,648lb (5,739kg)
Gross weight: 16,630lb (7,543kg)
Powerplant: 1 × Pratt & Whitney R-2800-34W 18-cylinder two row radial, 2100hp (1566kW), 1 × Allis-Chalmers J36 turbojet, 2,700lbf (12.01kN) thrust

Performance

Maximum speed: 469mph (755km/h)
Range: 1,385 miles (2,228km)
Rate of climb: 5,020ft/min (25.5m/s)

Armament

4 × wing-mounted 20mm cannon

---

the XF14C requested in 1941. In a change from previous practice, the service requested that a liquid-cooled Lycoming XH-2470 be used instead of the normally preferred air-cooled engine. On 30 June 1941 a contract was awarded to Curtiss Wright for a single XF14C-1. Even as the design was progressing the Navy requested that Curtiss find a way of improving the aircraft's performance. As the Lycoming engine was unable to meet its output requirements, it was decided to modify the aircraft to accept the Wright R-3350 Duplex Cyclone air-cooled engine driving a contra-rotating propeller assembly. In its new form the aircraft was designated XF14C-2.

The XF14C-2 was developed in parallel with the XF14C-3, which was intended for operations up to 40,000ft (12,200m), this requiring the installation of a pressurized cockpit. Eventually only the -2 was completed, making its maiden flight in July 1944, and the performance was less than expected. The performance deficit and problems with the engine eventually resulted in the cancellation of this project.

Although the first Curtiss offering had fallen through, the US Navy approached the company again to design and build a single mixed-power prototype. The order was placed on 7 April 1944,

the proposed engines being a Pratt & Whitney piston engine plus an Allis Chalmers J36 turbojet in the rear fuselage. The aircraft was ready for its first flight on 27 February 1945, though the turbojet was not installed at this time. The turbojet was installed in April and the XF15C undertook a series of flights over the next few weeks, but its career was terminated during the following month when the aircraft crashed on approach. Two other prototypes flew in late 1945 but by October 1946 the US Navy had lost interest in the mixed-plant aircraft and the project was cancelled.

The final design for the US Navy produced by Curtiss was a pure attack aircraft designated the XBTC. Known as the Model 96, the aircraft was entered in a competition against other contenders in 1943. Although the aircraft was described as a first-class performer with good weapons-carrying capability it lost out to the Douglas Skyraider and the Martin Mauler. A further version of this aircraft, known as the Model 98 or XBT2C-1, featured a reduced armament, two crew and a radar pod under the wing. Although nine of the ten aircraft ordered were eventually built they spent their entire time on trials work. This aircraft was the last Curtiss type built for the US Navy.

Curtiss XBT2C-1

Crew: 1–2
Length: 39ft 2in (11.94m)
Wingspan: 47ft 7in (14.5m)
Height: 12ft 1in (3.68m)
Empty weight: 12,268lb (5,565kg)
Max. take-off weight: 19,000lb (8,618kg)
Powerplant: 1 × Wright R-3350 Cyclone radial engine, 2,500hp (1,864kW)

Performance

Maximum speed: 330mph (531km/h)
Range: 1,310 miles (2,108km)
Service ceiling: 26,300ft (8,015m)

Armament

Guns: 4 × 20mm cannon (wing)
Bombs: 2,000lb (907kg) or one torpedo

The Curtiss XF14C was designed in response to a request by the US Navy to produce a new shipboard high-performance fighter. Only the XF14C-2 prototype was completed, and poor performance and delays with the availability of the XR-3350-16 engine led to cancellation of the aircraft. via NARA/Dennis R. Jenkins

CHAPTER FIVE

Bomber Development During World War Two

Although much of the American prototype effort had been expended on developing a range of fighters, the USAAC hierarchy was well aware that there was a need for a strong bomber force as well. Prototype and experimental bomber development covered two distinct paths: the first looked at various aircraft for the tactical bomber role while the other concentrated upon the strategic option. The tactical bomber was normally a twin-engine machine and underwent a genesis that eventually led to the Martin B-26 Marauder and North American B-25 Mitchell. Getting to that point required the efforts of many manufacturers.

North American XB-21

The first of these was the XB-21 – North American Aviation's first venture into the bomber field. It was a twin-engine, six-seat, mid-wing monoplane medium bomber powered by a pair of turbo-charged Pratt & Whitney R-2180-1 Twin Hornet radial engines rated at 1,200hp and armed with five 0.30in machine guns for defensive purposes. One gun each was carried in the power turrets installed in the nose and in the rear dorsal positions, one fired from a ventral hatch and the others from left and right waist positions. The XB-21 could carry two 1,100lb bombs over

The North American XB-21, or Model NA-21, was a prototype bomber aircraft evaluated by the USAAC in 1937. However, it was not ordered into production as the Douglas B-18 Bolo was available for around half the price. via NARA/Dennis R. Jenkins

North American XB-21

Crew: 6–8
Length: 61ft 9in (18.8m)
Wingspan: 95ft 0in (29.0m)
Height: 14ft 9in (4.5m)
Empty weight: 19,082lb (8,674kg)
Loaded weight: 27,253lb (12,388kg)
Max. take-off weight: 40,000lb (18,000kg)
Powerplant: 2 × Pratt & Whitney R-2180-1 radial engines,
1,200hp (900kW) each

Performance
Maximum speed: 220mph (190kt, 350km/h) at 10,000ft
(3,000m)
Cruise speed: 190mph (165kt, 310km/h)
Range: 1,960 miles (1,700nm, 3,140km)
Service ceiling: 25,000ft (7,600m)

Armament
Guns: 5 × 0.30in machine guns
Bombs: 8,800lb (4,000kg)

Douglas XB-22

Crew: 6
Length: 57ft 10in (17.6m)
Wingspan: 89ft 6in (27.3m)
Height: 15ft 2in (4.6m)
Empty weight: 16,321lb (7,400kg)
Loaded weight: 22,123lb (10,030kg)
Max. take-off weight: 27,500lb (12,600kg)
Powerplant: 2 × Wright R-2600-1 radial engines, 1,600hp
(1,200kW) each

Armament
Guns: 3 × 0.30in machine guns
Bombs: 4,500lb (2,200kg)

1,960 miles (3,150km) or eight over a 660-mile
(1,060km) range.

The aircraft was given the company designation NA-21 and design work on the project was begun in January 1936. The prototype made its maiden flight on 22 December 1936. Although the aircraft performed adequately there were some defects noted by the flight-test crew; after rectification of these it was accepted by the Air Force as the XB-21 with the serial number 38-485.

The XB-21 found itself in competition with the Douglas B-18A Bolo for production orders. The purchase price was the determining factor as both aircraft had roughly similar performances. However, North American was asking for $122,600 per aircraft while Douglas was prepared to deliver each machine at a cost of $63,977. Taking this into consideration Douglas got the order with a contract for 177 B-18As, this being issued in June 1937.

Douglas XB-22

Although the Douglas B-18A Bolo had proved to be an adequate stop-gap in the medium bomber role, it was rapidly becoming obsolete. In response Douglas Aviation proposed that Wright R-2600-1 radials rated at 1,600hp be fitted to a standard B-18A in place of the 1,000hp R-1820s

previously used, the result being redesignated the XB-22. Despite the substantial increase in power offered by the larger engines, the performance of the XB-22 still fell short of USAAC requirements, therefore the project was cancelled before any aircraft were built.

Martin XB-27

Many of the bomber projects of the war years concentrated upon improving those aircraft already in service. The first of these numerically was the Martin XB-27, designated by the company as the Model 182, which was to have

Martin XB-27

Crew: 7
Length: 60ft 9in (18.5m)
Wingspan: 84ft 0in (25.6m)
Height: 20ft 0in (6.10m)
Loaded weight: 33,000lb (15,000kg)
Powerplant: 2 × Pratt & Whitney R-2800-9 radial engines,
2,000hp (1,500kW) each

Performance (estimated)
Maximum speed: 280mph (450km/h)
Range: 2,900 miles (4,600km)
Service ceiling: 33,500ft (10,200m)

Armament
Guns:
3 × 0.30in machine gun
1 × 0.50in machine gun
Bombs: 4,000lb (1,800kg)

been a high-altitude version of the existing B-26 Marauder. It was to have been powered by a pair of turbocharged Pratt & Whitney R-2800-9 air-cooled radial engines rated at 2,000hp and was fitted with a pressurized cockpit. The crew was to have consisted of seven while the estimated maximum speed was 280mph (450km/h). Although on paper this looked like a good aircraft, the USAAF finally realized that its inventory was already sufficiently equipped to cover its missions, so this remained a paper design only.

North American XB-28

North American Aviation put forward a high-altitude development of its B-25 Mitchell twin-engine medium bomber, which was already in widespread USAAF service. This was the XB-28 Dragon, given the company designation NA-63; two prototypes were ordered on 13 February 1940 by the USAAF.

The XB-28 aircraft was very similar to the B-25 in overall configuration although it had a single vertical fin instead of the twin-fin installation fitted to the B-25. It had considerably more power

> **North American XB-28**
>
> Crew: 5
> Length: 56ft 5in (17.20m)
> Wingspan: 72ft 7in (22.12m)
> Height: 14ft 0in (4.27m)
> Empty weight: 25,575lb (11,600kg)
> Loaded weight: 35,740lb (16,210kg)
> Max. take-off weight: 37,200lb (16,874kg)
> Powerplant: 2 × Pratt & Whitney R-2800-27 turbosupercharged radial engines, 2,000hp (1,500kW) each
>
> **Performance**
> Maximum speed: 372mph (599km/h) at 25,000ft (7,600m)
> Cruise speed: 255mph (410km/h)
> Range: 2,040 miles (3,280km)
> Service ceiling: 33,500ft (10,213m)
>
> **Armament**
> Guns: 6 × 0.50in machine guns in remote-sighted turrets
> Bombs: 4,000lb (1,800kg)

than the B-25 from its pair of turbocharged Pratt & Whitney R-2800 engines rated at 2,000hp. The aircraft carried a crew of five in a pressurized cabin and could carry up to 4,000lb (1,800kg)

The B-25 was based on the earlier XB-21 from the mid 1930s. Experience gained in developing that aircraft was eventually used by North American in designing the Model 40. One NA-40 was built, this being used to trial the Wright R-2600 radial engine that would later become standard on the later B-25. via NARA/Dennis R. Jenkins

The **XB-26H** had its original tricycle undercarriage replaced by a set of tandem main wheels that retracted into the fuselage. In addition, a set of outrigger legs were added for lateral balance while the fuselage had to be externally stiffened to take the additional landing loads of this tandem undercarriage. via NARA/Dennis R. Jenkins

The **North American XB-28** was an aircraft proposal by North American Aviation to fill a perceived need by the USAAF for a high-altitude medium bomber. However, it never entered production as the Martin B-26 proved more than capable of covering the service's requirements. via NARA/Dennis R. Jenkins

of bombs. The defensive armament consisted of remotely controlled upper, lower and tail turrets, each of which contained two 0.50in machine guns. Gunners inside the pressurized fuselage controlled the turrets using periscope sights located in stations behind the pilot's seats.

The first XB-28, serialled 40-3056, flew for the first time on 26 April 1942. The second prototype, 40-3058, was completed as the XB-28A reconnaissance version with R-2800-27 engines. Although the high-altitude performance of the XB-28 greatly exceeded that of the previous B-25, most medium bombing missions undertaken during the war were carried out from relatively low altitudes: high-altitude bombing was too susceptible to errors caused by wind, and also affected by the cloud cover that was prominent in the Pacific Theatre of Operations. With this in mind USAAF decided not to interrupt Mitchell production for an untried type, and so the XB-28 project was cancelled after only two examples had been built.

Martin XB-33

The Glenn L. Martin Company's next effort was the Martin XB-33, company designation Model 190, which was conceived as a high-altitude version of the B-26 Marauder. It featured a pressurized crew compartment and a twin fin and rudder tail assembly. The proposed armament was to have been six to eight 0.50in machine guns and a 4,000lb (1,800kg) maximum bomb load.

The Martin engineers originally designed the aircraft with two Wright R-3350 radial engines, but it was soon decided to radically alter the original design by adding two more engines, the entire project being scaled up to the approximate size of the Boeing B-29. The USAAF was impressed with the new design and two prototypes were ordered, 41-28407 and 41-28408, these being designated the XB-33A. It was intended that the XB-33A would be powered by four Wright R-2600-15 engines instead of the more powerful R-3350 that was in great demand for B-29 manufacture. An order for 400 production B-33A 'Super Marauders' was

Martin XB-33	
Crew: 7	
Length: 79ft 10in (24.3m)	
Wingspan: 134ft (40.8m)	
Height: 24ft (7.32m)	
Empty weight: 85,000lb (39,000kg)	
Loaded weight: 95,000lb (43,000kg)	
Powerplant: 4 × Wright R-2600-15 radial engines, 1,800hp (1,300kW) each	
Performance (estimated)	
Maximum speed: 345mph (300kt, 555km/h)	
Cruise speed: 242mph (210kt, 389km/h)	
Range: 2,000 miles (1,700nm, 3,000km)	
Service ceiling: 39,000ft (12,000m)	
Armament	
Guns: 8 × 0.50in machine guns	
Bombs: 10,000lb (4,500kg)	

Competitors to the B-29

The USAAF also kept a close eye on possible heavy bomber development during the war,

The Martin B-33 was designed by the Glenn L. Martin Company and was a high-altitude version of the B-26 Marauder.
via NARA/Dennis R. Jenkins

placed by the Army although it was cancelled before the prototypes were completed; instead of building B-33As, Martin was awarded a contract to assemble 400 B-29s at its Omaha, Nebraska plant.

although for most of this period the service was well served by the aircraft already on inventory: the Boeing B-17 and B-29 and the often-overlooked Consolidated B-24 Liberator. The competition that gave rise to the outstanding Boeing

B-29 Superfortress was initiated by the outbreak of war in Europe. The head of the US Army Air Corps, General Henry H. Arnold, had become troubled by the growing war clouds over Europe and the growing menace of Japan's posturing in the Far East.

In response the general established a special investigative committee, chaired by Brigadier General W.G. Kilner, to make informed recommendations for the long-term bomber needs for the US Army Air Corps. Also involved was the famous aviator Charles Lindbergh, who became a member of the committee; Lindbergh had recently toured German aircraft factories and Luftwaffe bases and had become convinced that Germany was well ahead of its potential European adversaries in the development of both bombers and fighters. In their initial report, delivered in June 1939, the Kilner committee recommended that several new long-range medium and heavy bombers be developed for possible use in Europe and the Far East.

Hastened by a new urgency caused by the outbreak of war in Europe on 1 September 1939, General Arnold requested authorization on 10 November to issue contracts to the major aircraft companies for studies of a Very Long Range (VLR) bomber that was capable of carrying any future war well beyond American shores. Approval for this programme was granted on 2 December and USAAC engineering officers under Captain Donald L. Putt of the Air Material Command at Wright Field began to prepare the official specification.

In January 1940 the USAAC issued the requirements for a super bomber with a speed of 400mph (640km/h), a range of 5,333 miles (8,850km) plus a bomb load of 2,000lb (900kg) that could be carried and dropped at the mid-point of the requested range. The official specification was revised in April to incorporate the lessons learned during the early days of the European war. The requested changes now included increased defensive armament, increased protective armour and self-sealing fuel tanks. This revision became the basis for Request for Data R-40B and Specification XC-218. On 29 January 1940 the War Department formally issued Data R-40B, this being circulated to Boeing, Consolidated, Douglas and Lockheed. On 27 June 1940 the USAAC issued contracts for preliminary engineering data for the new super bomber to the four manufacturers, these

---

Lockheed XB-30

Crew: 12
Length: 104ft 8in (31.91m)
Wingspan: 123ft 0in (37.50m)
Height: 23ft 9in (7.25m)
Empty weight: 51,616lb (23,462kg)
Loaded weight: 85,844lb (39,020kg)
Max. take-off weight: 93,808lb (42,640kg)
Powerplant: 4 × Wright R-3350-13, 2,200hp (1,600kW) each

Performance
Maximum speed: 382mph (615km/h)
Range: 5,333 miles (8,045km)
Service ceiling: 17,832ft (5,440m)

Armament
Guns:
8 × 0.50in machine guns in four fuselage turrets
2 × 0.50in machine guns
1 × 20mm cannon in tail barbette
Bombs: 3,300lb

---

being designated in order of preference as Boeing XB-29, Lockheed XB-30, Douglas XB-31 and Consolidated XB-32.

The Lockheed XB-30 proposal envisaged a bomber powered by four Wright R-3350-13 air-cooled radials rated at 2,200hp. It was to have carried a crew of twelve in pressurized compartments. The wingspan had been 123ft (37.5m) with a length of 104ft 8in (31.9m). As Boeing had already completed much of the B-29 draughting and prototype mock-ups it was obvious that Lockheed were at a technical and competitive disadvantage, so the company withdrew its XB-30 proposal from the competition before any detailed designs could be completed. However, the work that Lockheed performed on the abortive XB-30 did not go to waste, since it was later put to use on the development of the C-69 Constellation transport.

Another project that never reached fruition was the Douglas XB-31, company designation Model 423; this was larger and heavier than the other three competitors in the Data R-40B programme. It was to have been powered by four Pratt & Whitney R-4360 28-cylinder air-cooled radials rated at 3,000hp, each driving a three-blade propeller unit. Wingspan was to have been 207ft (63.1m) with a wing area of 3,300sq ft (306.58sq m) while the length of the fuselage was to have been 117ft 3in (35.74m). The rear of the aircraft was dominated by an exceptionally

---

Douglas XB-31

Crew: 8
Length: 117ft 3in (35.7m)
Wingspan: 207ft 0in (63.1m)
Height: 42ft 7in (12.99m)
Empty weight: 109,200lb (49,530kg)
Loaded weight: 134,200lb (60,870kg)
Max. take-off weight: 198,000lb (90,000kg)
Powerplant: 4 × Wright R-3350-13 Cyclone radials, 2,200hp (1,641kW) each
Powerplant after later redesign: 4 × Pratt & Whitney R-4360 Wasp Major radials, 3,000hp (2,238kW) each

Performance (estimated)
Maximum speed: 357mph (575km/h)
Range: 3,000 miles (4,830km)
Service ceiling: 35,000ft (10,675m)

Armament
Guns:
4 × 0.50in machine guns in remote ventral and dorsal turrets
2 × 37mm cannon in tail
Bombs: 25,000lb (11,000kg) in two ventral bomb bays

---

tall fin and rudder. Weights were expected to be 109,200lb (49,530kg) empty and 198,000lb (90,000kg) maximum. The pilot and co-pilot were seated under separate 'double bubble' canopies that were similar to those later fitted to the C-74 Globemaster I transport and the XB-42 and XP-43 experimental bombers; the six other crew members were accommodated at separate stations throughout the fuselage. Defensive armament was to have consisted of twin 0.50in machine guns in remotely controlled dorsal and ventral turrets, plus a pair of 37mm cannon carried in the tail. A maximum bombload of 25,000lb (11,000kg) was to have been housed in two fuselage bays.

Although this design showed much promise, the Boeing B-29 had the edge in the competition since work on the Boeing design was much further advanced. On 17 May 1941 the USAAF announced that an initial order was placed for 250 B-29s. This order was confirmed in September 1941. The result was that the Douglas XB-31 project was formally cancelled in late 1941 before any metal was cut.

Strangely enough the last design, the Consolidated XB-32, was allowed to continue as a back up to the Boeing B-29. Eventually the B-32 Dominator entered limited air force service and would have made a good bomber, had enough

time been given to the manufacturers to iron out its various problems.

Lockheed XB-38

Having sorted out the very-long-range, bomber the USAAC, later USAAF, continued to encourage its favoured manufacturers to develop their already in-service designs. One of the first such projects was the XB-38: a modification undertaken by the Vega Airplane Division of Lockheed Lockheed Vega – who were building B-17s under license – on the ninth Boeing B-17E, 41-2401. Vega proposed in March 1942 that a B-17 airframe be converted to become an engine test bed by replacing the standard Wright R-1820 radial engines with Allison V-1710 engines. In July the USAAC approved the project AC-28120 for development. In addition to the new engines, the aircraft featured an increased fuel capacity and fully feathering propellers. The XB-38 project was undertaken in order to improve the overall performance of the basic B-17 and to provide an alternatively powered version in case the Wright R-1820 radial engine became scarce. Vega received the B-17E and intended to use it as a pattern for an all-new design. Serial number 42-73515 was reserved for this design, but due to the urgency of the project, the B-17E was used and the new design was never completed.

The modifications to the B-17E model took less than a year to complete, the aircraft making its first flight on 19 May 1943. Initial performance tests showed that the aircraft was slightly faster than the standard production B-17E. Although this slight increase in performance was welcome, the XB-38 was grounded after a few flights because of a serious problems with leaking engine exhaust manifold joints. After this problem was rectified the flight test programme continued until 16 June 1943 and the XB-38's ninth test flight. On this flight, the No. 3 engine caught fire in flight. The test pilots were unable to suppress the fire and were forced to bail out, but both parachutes malfunctioned, killing one pilot and seriously injuring the other. The resulting crash near Tipton, California, completely destroyed the XB-38. All future plans for the XB-38 were later dropped because the V-1710 engines were needed for higher-priority projects and some concerns were raised over the survivability of such an

The XB-38 project was intended to improve on the overall performance of the basic B-17 and to provide a fall-back in case the Wright R-1820 radial engine became scarce. Although one aircraft was completed by Lockheed Vega, continuing engine problems saw the programme abandoned. via NARA/Dennis R. Jenkins

aircraft in the hostile environment of a bomber stream.

Lockheed YB-40

Lockheed Vega put forward another development of the B-17 to the USAAF: the YB-40 bomber escort. This was produced by converting existing B-17Fs in an attempt to provide better defence for the B-17 daylight bomber force, which was suffering appalling losses when it ventured into areas beyond the range of contemporary escort fighters – at this time the Lockheed P-38 and Republic P-47. The first XB-40 prototype was rolled out by Vega in November 1942; it was a standard Boeing-built B-17F, 41-24341, modified to escort configuration.

A dorsal turret mounting a pair of 0.50in machine guns was put in the radio compartment position while the chin turret underneath the nose was fitted with an extra pair of 0.50in machine guns and at each waist position twin, instead of the usual single, gun mounts were fitted. The regular upper, ventral and tail turrets were retained, bringing the total gun armament to fourteen 0.50in machine guns. Additional protective armour was fitted for improved crew

protection and the bomb bays were fixed in the closed position, the resulting extra space being used to carry additional ammunition for the guns. The normal ammunition load was 11,135 rounds; this could be increased to 17,265 rounds if the fuel load was reduced.

A further twenty Vega-built B-17Fs were

Lockheed YB-40

Crew: 10
Length: 74ft 4in (22.7m)
Wingspan: 103ft 10in (31.6m)
Height: 19ft 1in (5.8m)
Empty weight: 54,900lb (24,900kg)
Loaded weight: 72,134lb (32,720kg)
Max. take-off weight: 74,000lb (34,000kg)
Powerplant: 4 × Wright R-1820-65 turbosupercharged radial engines, 1,200hp (895kW) each

Performance
Maximum speed: 292mph (470km/h)
Cruise speed: 196mph (315km/h)
Range: 2,260 miles (3,640km)
Service ceiling: 29,200ft (8,900m)

Armament
Guns: 14 × 0.50in machine guns. Typically used 14–16

converted to YB-40 configuration while another four became TB-40 trainers. While the aircraft were given the Vega model number of V-139-3, they were actually modified by Douglas at Tulsa, Oklahoma, using Vega-built B-17F airframes as the basis. A variety of different armament configurations were tried before the configuration described above was adopted as standard. Some YB-40s were fitted with four-gun nose and tail turrets as part of the Rand project. Some carried cannon up to 40mm in calibre while others carried up to as many as thirty guns of various calibres in multiple hand-held positions in the waist, as well as in additional power turrets above and below the fuselage.

The YB-40s were sent to equip the 327th Bombardment Squadron, part of the 92nd Bombardment Group (Heavy) based at Alconbury. The first operational YB-40 sortie took place on 29 May 1943 against St Nazaire, during which one of the YB-40's was shot down. On 22 June eleven YB-40s were despatched as escorts to protect a raid on the rubber plant at Huls during which another was lost to anti-aircraft fire. Four days later the bomber stream attacking the airfield at Villacoublay was attacked, during which the five YB-40s claimed two kills. As the YB-40s continued undertaking missions their serviceability began to drop, so as the trials progressed the numbers available continually fell.

On 24 July during the 8th Army Air Force 'blitz' week, a pair of YB-40s was despatched of which one was hit by a fighter over the target.

This attack wounded the pilot who lost control of his functions, leaving the co-pilot with the difficult task of flying the aircraft with one hand while with the other restraining the pilot, who seemed intent on crashing the aircraft. Eventually as the aircraft left the target another crew member came onto the flight deck to help. For his actions the co-pilot was awarded the Medal of Honor. The final mission undertaken by the YB-40s was on 29 July 1943 against targets in Kiel area. Five kills and two probables were claimed during these missions, with the loss of two YB-40s.

From the outset it was found that the effect of the additional drag of the turrets and the extra weight of the guns, armour and additional ammunition reduced the speed of the YB-40 to a point where it could not maintain formation with the standard B-17s on the way home from the target once they had released their bombs. The YB-40 could protect itself fairly well, but not the bombers it was supposed to defend. Consequently, it was recognized that the YB-40 project was an operational failure, and the surviving YB-40s were converted back to standard B-17F configuration or used as gunnery trainers in the United States. However, the YB-40 did trial one important modification that later became standard, this being the chin turret originally introduced on the YB-40 that was adopted as standard for the late-build B-17Fs and the B-17G series. Late in the war many of these turrets were removed as their firepower was no longer needed, the Luftwaffe fighter threat having almost disappeared.

The YB-40 Flying Fortress was a modification of the B-17 Flying Fortress that was converted to act as a heavily armed escort for other bombers. While able to keep up en route to the target, on the way back to base the lightly loaded bombers left the YB-40 behind. via NARA/Dennis R. Jenkins

The 'Project Reed' aircraft was another attempt to produce a bomber escort. Like the YB-40, the Reed aircraft was too heavy on the return journey to keep up with the lightly loaded B-17s. via NARA/Dennis R. Jenkins

Boeing XB-39

Boeing built another conversion, this time of the B-29 Superfortress. The XB-39, 'Spirit of Lincoln', was a modification of the first YB-29, 41-36954. As with the XB-38, the standard air-cooled radial engines of the production aircraft were replaced by liquid-cooled 'Vee' engines; in this case the original Wright R-3350-21 Cyclone being replaced by the Allison V-3420-11. The V-3420 was essentially two V-1710 engines spliced together with a single crankcase and the two crankshafts geared together.

The XB-39 project was basically a proof-of-concept project to demonstrate performance with liquid-cooled engines installed; it was also another insurance against shortages of the production engine. Only one XB-39 was built, this being delivered the US Army Air Force in early 1944 for testing. Most of the problems with the standard B-29 production version were fixed by mid-1944, so no orders for the XB-39 were placed.

Boeing XB-50

A further version of the Boeing B-29 was requested and tested late in the war. Although the Wright-powered B-29 had always been somewhat under-powered for its ever-increasing weight, it became clear that the aircraft was capable of absorbing substantially more engine power if it were available. To trial this a single B-29A, 42-93845, was bailed to Pratt & Whitney for conversion as a test bed for the new 28-cylinder Pratt & Whitney R-4360 Wasp Major air-cooled radial engine, rated at 3,500hp. The reworked aircraft was redesignated the XB-44; it was easily recognized by the new engine installation, in which the oil cooler intake was mounted further back on the lower part of the nacelle. To compensate for the increased engine power a larger fin and rudder were fitted.

An initial order for 200 production examples under the designation B-29D was placed in July 1945, although this was quickly reduced to only fifty examples after V-J Day. In December 1945 the designation of the B-29D was changed to B-50A. This was a ruse to win appropriations for an aircraft that appeared – by its original designation – to be merely a new version of an existing model; orders for B-29s were being cancelled with the war's end while many newly built examples were being flown straight into storage from the factory. Officially the reason for the new B-50 designation was that the changes introduced in the B-29D were so major that it was at heart a completely new aircraft. This explanation worked, and the B-50 continued to become an important component of the post-war Air Force.

The XB-44 was a modification of a Boeing B-29A undertaken by Pratt & Whitney to adapt the aircraft for R-4360 supercharged radial engines. The larger and more powerful engines required a complete redesign of the engine nacelles that featured a distinctive scoop air inlet on the underside. Eventually this machine led to the Boeing B-50. via NARA/Dennis R. Jenkins

Consolidated XB-41

The XB-41 was developed as a long-range bomber escort version of the B-24D Liberator, designed to fill a similar requirement to that of the Boeing YB-40. The only XB-41 built was a conversion of a B-24D-CO, 41-11822. The conversion was carried out at Consolidated's Fort Worth plant and delivered to Eglin Field, Florida, on 29 January 1943 for service testing.

Additional guns were installed over and above the normal setup, bringing the total available armament to fourteen 0.50in machine guns. A

second Martin A-3 power turret was added to the dorsal fuselage just aft of the wing trailing edge. A Bendix remotely controlled turret was installed in the chin position beneath the nose and the nose glazing was modified to give the operator of the Bendix turret a clear field of view. The nose cheek guns normally seen on the later B-24D were not fitted, while a pair of power-boosted 0.50in machine guns were installed at each waist position to replace the single flexible mounts originally fitted. The original Martin A-3 power turret behind the cockpit was modified so that it could be raised during flight to increase its field

The Consolidated XB-41 Liberator was converted from a standard B-24D for the long-range escort role. The aircraft received limited testing before stability problems resulted in the programme being cancelled. via NARA/Dennis R. Jenkins

Consolidated XB-41

Crew: 9
Length: 66ft 4in (20.22m)
Wingspan: 110ft 0in (33.54m)
Height: 17ft 11in (5.46m)
Max. take-off weight: 63,000lb (28,576kg)
Powerplant: 4 × Pratt & Whitney R-1830-43 radial engines,
1,250hp (934kW) each

Performance
Maximum speed: 289mph (465km/h)
Range: 3,100 miles (4,989km)
Service ceiling: 28,500ft (8,689m)

Armament
Guns: 14 × 0.50in machine guns

of fire and then lowered to decrease aerodynamic drag when not in use. A total of 12,420 rounds of ammunition was carried, including 4,000 reserve rounds carried in a container installed in the forward bomb bay. The additional weight of armour, guns and ammunition brought the gross weight up to 63,000lb (28,600kg), at least 6,000lb (2,700kg) heavier than a standard B-24D.

Flight tests were carried out at Eglin Field during the early winter of 1943. These flights indicated centre of gravity problems that made the aircraft unstable in flight, and the climb rate and service ceiling were reduced due to the additional weight. The port waist-gun position had originally been covered by a plexiglas bubble when delivered, but this was found to cause severe optical distortion and was removed. As a result of these problems the USAAF decided on 21 March 1943 that the XB-41 was operationally unsuitable, and the original plan for thirteen service-test YB-41 Liberator conversions was cancelled.

Although the USAAF had pulled out of the XB-41 programme Consolidated continued to develop the XB-41 prototype, equipping the aircraft with wide-blade propellers and also putting it through a weight-reduction programme during which some of the armour plating was removed. On 28 July 1943 the XB-41 was returned to Eglin Field for further flight tests. These flights revealed that the stability problem had been cured, but the aircraft was still plagued with poor manoeuvrability. While Consolidated worked to bring the XB-41 up to an operational standard

the Boeing YB-40 had entered combat service in Europe and the initial results revealed that the very concept of the escort gunship was fundamentally flawed. As a result of the negative experience with the YB-40 further work on the XB-41 was cancelled. The only XB-41 was later redesignated as the TB-24D and was used as an instructional airframe for engineering and maintenance training.

Other B-24 Developments

The Liberator was subject to several other modification programmes. The first of these was the Consolidated XB-24F, a modification of a standard B-24D, 41-11678, to test thermal de-icers. The standard de-icer of the early 1940s was a rubber 'boot' covering the wing leading edge that could by inflated in flight: the expansion of the inflated de-icer would crack the ice into pieces that then broke off. Thermal de-icers circulate hot air – drawn from the engine exhaust – through the leading edges of the wings and tail surfaces to prevent ice build-up. The XB-24F was sent to the NACA test facility at Moffett Field where the system was tested; during its time at Moffet the aircraft carried the nickname 'The Flying Icing Wind Tunnel' plus artwork on the nose. Although the trials were successful, no further aircraft were converted. However, the pioneering work carried out using the aircraft converted to use new types of de-icing bore fruit in post-war aviation. After its time at Moffett Field the XB-24F was retired in 1947 for reclamation.

The next Liberator experimental version was the XB-24K. This was modified from a standard B-24D by replacing the original twin vertical stabilizer empennage with a more conventional single-tail arrangement. Ford, a Consolidated contractor, was contracted to undertake the work by splicing a B-23 empennage section onto the B-24. The completed aircraft first flew in March 1943. The single-tail project was of interest to both the US Army Air Force and the Navy, and led directly to the development of the Navy's PB4Y Privateer series of patrol and anti-submarine aircraft.

The single-tail Liberator was more stable and handled better than the twin-tailed original. Following on from the XB-24K came the

The XB-24F was a single B-24D, 41-11678, that was fitted with an experimental thermal anti-icing system for tests by NACA at Moffett Field, California where it sported the nickname 'The Flying Icing Wind Tunnel'. via NASA/Dennis R. Jenkins

B-24N. This design was based on the B-24J and used data from the XB-24K tests to facilitate the extensive design changes necessary for a single tail. The B-24N also had improved tail and nose turrets installed to improve defensive capabilities. Aerodynamic and weight reduction improvements gave the B-24N very good estimated performance. The Army Air Force ordered 5,168 N models and the prototype began its flight test programme in late 1944. A single XB-24N, 44-48753, was constructed, plus seven YB-24N pre-production aircraft, serialled 44-52053 to 44-52059. However, the end of the war saw the entire Liberator programme cancelled. As for the XB-24K, it was sent for scrapping in November 1945.

The final two models of Liberator assigned to experimental trials were the XB-24P and the XB-24Q. The XB-24P-CO was a San Diego-built standard B-24D, 42-40344, modified by Sperry Gyroscope Co. in July 1945 for airborne fire-control system research. After trials at Wright Field the aircraft was sent for scrapping in June 1945. The following aircraft, the XB-24Q, was

The YB-24Ns were ordered as the pre-production test aircraft for a planned production run of 5,168 B-24Ns. Seven were built before all B-24 production stopped in May 1945 as the war drew to an end. via NARA/Dennis R. Jenkins

The **XB-24K** was modified from a B-24D by replacing the original twin vertical stabilizer empennage with a conventional single tail. This aircraft led directly to the development of the **PB4Y Privateer** aircraft for the **US Navy**. via NARA/Dennis R. Jenkins

The **XB-24N** was the prototype aircraft for the production version of the **B-24N**. via NARA/Dennis R. Jenkins

originally built as a B-24F, 44-49916, before being bailed to Emerson Electric for trials purposes. Eventually acquired by General Electric, the XB-24Q was used for trials of the tail turret for the forthcoming Boeing B-47 Stratojet. At the conclusion of these trials the airframe was used for testing various jet engines carried in the rear fuselage. Due to its trials work the XB-24Q was one of the last Liberators flying, not being sent for scrap until August 1948.

Northrop N1-M

Possibly one of the most innovative aircraft to appear towards the end of World War Two began its development before the war and did not come to complete fruition until the twentieth century was almost spent. Behind this innovation was Jack Northrop, who had started his career as secretary and designer at Lockheed Burbank near Los Angeles in 1928. Northrop had a dream of

The Northrop N-1M was an
early flying-wing aircraft and
was the first true flying wing
produced in America. It first
flew in July 1941 at Baker Dry
Lake in California. Although
it was unstable and under
powered, the N-1M paved the
way for Northrop's later flying
wings. via NARA/
Dennis R. Jenkins

designing aircraft without what he saw as extra-
neous extras, these including the rear fuselage
and empennage that was common at the time.
To follow his dream Northrop resigned from
Lockheed and with Ken Jay he formed the Avion
Corporation in a building next to the Lockheed
Corporation premises.

It was obvious that much of the Avion
Corporation's first design had already been
worked out, as their first product, known as the
Wing and serialled X-216H, was ready for its
maiden flight in 1929. While it sported a small
conventional twin-boom tail, X-216H featured
a major constructional innovation: instead of
the wood usually used at the time, Northrop had
decided to use Duralumin throughout. Both the
structure and the skin were made of metal, all
being held together by flush riveting. The engine
was a four-cylinder Menasco Pirate 90hp engine
driving a two-blade pusher propeller connected
to the engine via a long drive shaft. The aircraft
had two cockpits, one each side of the propellor
shaft, though the right-hand cockpit was normally faired over. The undercarriage was of the
reverse tricycle type, the nose leg being carried
in the tailwheel position. The main wheels were
to the front while the single wheel was carried aft
and was steerable.

The pilot hired to fly X-216H was Eddie
Bellande, a freelance pilot who had already
undertaken the maiden flight of the Lockheed
Vega; the practice of small corporations hiring
freelance test pilots was not unusual prior to
1939 as most did not have the funds or work

to employ them full-time. The aircraft took off
from Burbank Field and landed at Muroc, later to
become better-known as Edwards Air Force Base.
The pilot's report indicated that the little wing
flew without any perceptible vices. After its first
test flight the long drive shaft was removed, the
propellor being mounted in the tractor position.

After his first tentative steps with the flying
wing Jack Northrop was forced to concentrate
on the production of more conventional types
from 1932, acting as a subcontractor for Douglas
Aircraft of El Segundo, and in 1938 Northrop's
company was consumed by Douglas. The following year Northrop resigned from Douglas and
formed another Northrop Aircraft Corporation
at Hawthorne, Los Angeles.

During the period between leaving Douglas and
forming his own company Northrop had carried
out intensive studies of tailless aircraft and all-
wing machines. It was obvious to Northrop that

Northrop N-1M

Crew: 1
Length: 17ft 11in (5.46m)
Wingspan: 38ft 8in (11.80m)
Height: 4ft 11in (1.50m)
Loaded weight: 3,900lb (1,769kg)
Powerplant: 2 × Lycoming O-145, 65hp (50kW) each

Performance
Maximum speed: 200mph (322km/h)
Range: 300 miles (483km)
Service ceiling 4,000ft (1,219m)

there were some fundamental problems with an all-wing aircraft, these centring around stability problems and, in turn, centre of gravity shifts as fuel was consumed and instability after engine failure. Northrop made extensive use of a wind tunnel to study the behaviour of various wing shapes before committing himself to cutting metal.

To prove all that he had learned, Northrop and his team began to construct the N-1M (Northrop Model 1) mock-up – in fact a flying machine. This was a pure flying wing whose only visible 'lumps and bumps' were the canopy over the pilot on the aircraft's centreline and the fairings over the propellor shaft extensions that led from the 65hp Lycoming 0-145 to the pusher propellors. The wingtips were canted downwards by 35 degrees to help with the stability while the control surfaces, which combined the function of ailerons and elevators in one surface, were dispersed along the trailing edge. The aircraft was carried on a fully retractable tricycle undercarriage. Painted in overall yellow and registered NX28311, the aircraft undertook its maiden flight from a location close by Muroc Lake on 3 July 1940. The pilot was the flamboyant Vance Breese, later to pilot the prototype P-51 Mustang. The initial flight saw the pilot holding the aircraft at no more than 20ft above the desert, although as he gained in confidence it was found that the N-1M handled as well as, if not better than, conventional designs.

At the conclusion of these flights the N-1M had its original engines replaced by the more powerful Franklin, rated at 120hp. The chance was also taken to replace the cranked-down outer wing panels with straight-edged examples. Fitting these outer wing panels allowed Northrop to add another innovation: a 'deceleron', which allowed the outer flight control surface to split in two and present two surfaces to the airflow. This invention later found employment in the Fairchild A-10 Thunderbolt and the B-2 flying-wing bomber.

Northrop N-9M

Having proven the concept of the flying wing, Northrop looked around for a market for his new aircraft; this being 1941, the only use for such a machine was as a bomber. The USAAF requested Northrop not to disclose the existence of his aircraft as the flying-wing concept was an ideal carrier for a significant bomb load. To reinforce their interest the USAAF issued a contract in 1941 for four scale models that would evaluate aerodynamic, stability, control and structural behaviours. This new flying wing, one-third the size of the proposed B-35 bomber, was designated the N-9M and like the N-1M was a pure flying wing, its outline only broken by the canopy and the fairings for the propellor shafts.

The first three machines were powered by a pair of Menasco Buccaneer engines rated at 275hp each while the fourth was powered by a pair of 300hp Franklin O-540s and was designated the N-9MB. The flight control system was controlled by a single control column that was connected to the elevons for pitch and roll control while the rudder pedals were connected to the tip-mounted decelerons to manage turns and asymmetric control. The colour schemes applied to these machines were overall yellow for the first two aircraft, blue uppers and yellow below for the third, and yellow uppers and blue underneath for the fourth. Originally some form of assisted escape system had been proposed, but it was eventually agreed that the pilot's seat would be fixed: to escape, the drill was to close the throttles, brake the propellors, jettison the canopy and bale out manually.

The first N-9M undertook its maiden flight on 27 December 1942 from Northrop Field, Hawthorne, the pilot being John Myers. During the initial sequence of flights the aircraft performed as expected, but on the forty-ninth flight, during March 1942, the aircraft crashed near Rosamund Dry Lake. The pilot, Max Constant, had been investigating the stall behaviour at

---

Northrop N-9M

Crew: 1
Length: 17.79ft (5.4m)
Wingspan: 60ft 0in (18.3m)
Height: 6.58ft 0in (2.00m)
Wing area: 490ft² (45.5m²)
Empty: 5,893lb (2,670kg)
Loaded: 6,326lb (2,870kg); 6,818lb (3,092kg) N-9MB
Powerplant: 2 × Menasco C6S-4, 275hp(205kW) each
Powerplant: (N-9MB) 2 × Franklin XO-540-7, 260hp (194kW) each

Performance
Maximum speed: 258mph (415km/h)
Range: 500 miles (805km)
Service ceiling: 21,500ft (6,555m)

The Northrop N-9M was a one-third scale development aircraft for the Northrop YB-35 flying-wing bomber. The N-9M crashed near Muroc Army Air Base in May 1943, killing the pilot, Max Constant. via NARA/ Dennis R. Jenkins

full-aft centre of gravity and it would appear that the control wheel had been fully back and the pilot had not been able to overcome the resultant g-forces. Flight trials using another N-9M proved that the aircraft was flying well within acceptable stall limits, but in order to counter any reoccurrence of Constant's accident, a powerful hydraulic ram was fitted that would push the control column forward in an emergency. Although the loss of the first aircraft was regrettable the other three continued to provide data for the proposed bomber, and also showed that the handling of such a wing shape was exceptional, especially in the turn.

Northrop XB-35

Northrop also took part in a fighter contest that resulted in the XP-79, another flying-wing project. Although the XP-79 was a diversion it did provide more data towards developing the flying-wing bomber. Throughout the war period Northop continued to develop the XB-35 flying-wing bomber, having been awarded a contract in November 1941 to manufacture two prototypes. On 3 July 1945 the first basic airframe was rolled out of the No. 3 Plant at Hawthorne and taxi testing began in April 1946. It was during these ground tests that problems were revealed concerning the propeller governors and gearboxes. These faults were soon rectified and the first aircraft was ready for its maiden flight from Northrop Field on 25 June 1946. The crew on this occasion was pilot Max Stanley, co-pilot Fred Bretcher and Orva

Douglas. After a clean take-off the XB-35 then made a successful landing at Muroc Dry Lake where the flight testing was undertaken.

The XB-35 could carry a bomb load of 10,000lb (4,500kg) over a range of 5,000 miles (8,000km) with a 15 per cent diversionary fuel load. The engines were four Pratt & Whitney R-4350-17 engines rated at 3,000hp, each driving an eight-blade contra-rotating propellor assembly. Within the wing, along the centreline, were pressurized compartments that could house a crew of between twelve and fifteen. The bombardier was housed behind transparent panels in the leading edge, just to the right of the central apex. Just aft of the bombardier was the tandem cockpit that housed the two pilots under a fighter-type canopy. Had there been a full production version of the B-35 it would have been equipped with seven power turrets: three on the centreline and four mounted above and below the wings. The intended armament was either twenty 0.50in machine guns or 20mm cannons.

Like the N-9M, the XB-35 had flight controls dispersed along the entire trailing edge. This setup consisted of the split-surface ailerons, known as decelerons, in the outboard position, inboard of which were the elevons. Between the engines were further split flaps that could be deployed upon landing. The leading edges of the outer wing panels had slots that remained retracted until the aircraft was close to the stall. All the flight controls were hydraulically powered, although the pilots commented that the XB-35 handled the same as any other large aircraft they had flown. To retain control in the event of a control system

The XB-35 was the first Northrop flying-wing bomber design. The initial contract for a single aircraft was awarded in November 1941 and amended to include another in January 1942. This view shows the location of the wing turret bulges.
via NARA/Dennis R. Jenkins

failure each surface was fitted with dual control power units, and in the event of a complete hydraulic failure the aircraft was fitted with an electric-powered pump. To ensure that the pilots did not overstress the airframe the flight control surfaces were fitted with force feedback in the control system runs.

The XB-35 was significantly delayed due to problems with the pusher propellers; it was not the only aircraft under development that was suffering from this fault as the Convair B-36 was also suffering from stripped gear teeth in the gearboxes, engine fires, uncontrolled runaways and uncommanded pitch reversals. Curing all of these faults took some eighteen months.

Its engine and propeller problems finally cured, the first XB-35, 42-13603, undertook its maiden flight on 25 June 1946 with Max Stanley as pilot and Dale Schroeder as flight engineer. The entire flight lasted no more than forty-five minutes as the aircraft was flown from Hawthorne to Muroc Dry Lake, which was the intended base of flight operations. From the outset the flight-test programme ran into difficulties as the propeller and gearbox assemblies began to malfunction again. These problems finally grounded the aircraft on 11 September after nineteen flights had been completed. The second XB-35, 42-38323, made its maiden flight on 26 June 1947, although it completed only eight flights before it was grounded for major rectification. The main item that was causing all the problems were the contra-rotating propeller assemblies and their gearboxes, and both prototypes were grounded so that these troublesome items could be replaced by single four-blade units. Once these had been replaced, both aircraft resumed flight testing in February 1948.

Seven more flights were made by the first prototype between 12 February and 1 April 1948. Although the aircraft behaved as expected, the new propellers induced excessive vibration problems, which meant that the aircraft was flown with reduced performance. While the engines and propellers were working satisfactorily, the intricate exhaust system fitted to the R-4360 engines was a maintenance nightmare and the cooling fans in the system were causing excessive wear in the engines. As it was becoming obvious that the piston-engine XB-35 was becoming outmoded they were finally grounded by the end of 1948, both being struck off charge in August 1949 for scrapping.

Following the two XB-35s down the production line were the first two YB-35s and a further four aircraft that were close to production standard. The first YB-35, 42-102366, undertook its first flight on 15 May 1948, this being the only airframe to be fitted with defensive armament. From the outset the first YB-35 was fitted with standard propeller assemblies and was the only one of the thirteen ordered to actually fly. Although the YB-35 performed as expected, the jet age had now dawned and piston power was regarded as too slow to compete. In order to recoup some of the money already expended, the air force decided to authorize the conversion of some of the B-35 aircraft to jet power.

Douglas XB-42

The final propellor-driven aircraft of the era was the Douglas XB-42. This project began life as a private venture by the manufacturer as no original official requirement existed. In early 1943 the

The XB-35 was powered by four Pratt & Whitney R-4360 turbocharged radial engines driving dual contra-rotating three-blade propellers, as shown in this under-view of the aircraft. via NARA/Dennis R. Jenkins

Douglas designer Ed Burton began a company-funded study to determine the possibility of designing a twin-engine bomber with a maximum speed in excess of 400mph (640km/h) and capable of carrying a bomb load of 2,000lb (900kg) to targets within a 2,000-mile (3,200km) radius. The design team came up with the idea of mounting the engines entirely within the fuselage, leaving the wing completely clean. Once the design had been firmed up the company felt confident enough to send an unsolicited proposal to the USAAF in May 1943. The proposal attracted the attention of the Bombardment Branch of the Engineering Division of the Air Technical Service Command,

and on 25 June 1943 a contract was issued for two flying prototypes and one static-test airframe. The resultant aircraft was considered as an attack aircraft by the Bombardment Branch and so assigned the designation XA-42.

As with many such projects the USAAF began to consider the Douglas proposal as a possible high-speed bomber that could match the range of the B-29 at only a fraction of the cost. On 26 November 1943 the USAAF changed the designation of the Douglas design to XB-42. Progress on the XA-42/XB-42 was quite rapid under the supervision of Ed Burton and Carlos C. Wood, the Chief of the Preliminary Design Division, and the mock-up was inspected by the Air Technical officials and approved in September 1943.

The aircraft that was finally rolled out was powered by a pair of Allison V-1710-125 liquid-cooled V-12 engines rated at 1,325hp, which were installed completely inside the fuselage immediately aft of the pilot's cabin. Air for the cooling radiators was provided by narrow slots let into the leading edges of the inner mainplanes. The centreline of each engine was approximately 20 degrees to the vertical while the engines were toed in by a few degrees to the vertical. The power was transmitted via five lengths of shafting to a contra-rotating propeller assembly that was installed in the extreme tail cone. Each of the three-bladed contra-rotating propellers was driven by its own engine: the left engine drove the forward propeller and the right engine the aft propellor. A lower fin and rudder was fitted underneath the tail to prevent the propellers from

---

Northrop XB-35

Crew: 9
Length: 53ft 1in (16.2m)
Wingspan: 172ft (52.2m)
Height: 20ft 3in (6.2m)
Empty weight: 89,300lb (40,590kg)
Loaded weight: 180,000lb (82,000kg)
Max. take-off weight: 209,000lb (95,000kg)
Powerplant: 2 × Pratt & Whitney R-4360-17 and 2 × R-4360-21 radial engines, 3,000hp (2,200kW) each

Performance
Maximum speed: 393mph (632km/h)
Range: 8,150 miles (13,100km)

Armament
Guns: 20 × 0.50in machine guns
Bombs: 51,070lb (23,210kg)

Douglas XB-42 Mixmaster

Length: 53ft 8in (16.4m)
Wingspan: 70ft 6in (21.5m)
Height: 18ft 10in (5.7m)
Empty weight: 20,888lb (9,475kg)
Loaded weight: 33,200lb (15,060kg)
Max. take-off weight: 35,702lb (16,194kg)
Powerplant: 2 × Allison V-1710-125 V12 engines, 1,800hp (1,300kW) each

Performance
Maximum speed: 410mph (660km/h)
Combat range: 1,800 miles (2,900km)
Service ceiling: 29,400ft (8,960m)

Armament
Guns: 4 × 0.50in machine guns
Bombs: 8,000lb (3,600kg)

striking the ground during nose-high take-offs and landings.

The tricycle undercarriage that supported the aircraft had main members that retracted aft into large wells in the fuselage sides, while the nose undercarriage leg retracted aft into the fuselage and was covered with a pair of doors. The clean, laminar-flow wing was mounted at middle fuselage level; it had double slotted flaps on the inboard trailing edge while the ailerons were carried on the outboard trailing edge. A remotely controlled General Electric turret with a pair of 0.50in machine guns was installed in the trailing edge

of the wing between the ailerons and flaps. The guns were normally housed inside the wing underneath snap-action doors, and when extended into the firing position they covered an area extending 25 degrees to either side, 30 degrees above and 15 degrees below. They were controlled remotely by the co-pilot who had a sighting station at the rear of his cockpit. The crew consisted of three: a pilot and co-pilot/gunner in a side-by-side cockpit with small separate canopies, and the navigator/bomb-aimer in the glazed nose section.

The first XB-42, 43-50224, was completed in May 1944 and rolled out for ground trials immediately. The XB-42 undertook its maiden flight for the first time on 6 May 1944 with test pilot Bob Brush at the controls. As a safety and security measure this initial flight was carried out entirely over Palm Springs Army Air Base. The performance of the XB-42 was rated as outstanding: speed was within a single percentage point of that predicted while the range and rate of climb exceeded expectations. The XB-42 was as fast as the de Havilland Mosquito B.XVI but carried a greater load: its maximum bombload was 8,000lb (3,600kg) versus 4,000lb (1,800kg) over short ranges or a bombload of 3,750lb (1,700kg) versus 1,000lb (450kg) over a range of 1,850 miles (3,000km). Also, the XB-42 carried a defensive armament of four 0.50in machine guns in two remotely controlled turrets while the Mosquito flew without defensive armament.

There were a few problems, as the twin canopies of the XB-42 were found to interfere with pilot/

The Douglas XB-42 Mixmaster was an unconventional experimental bomber aircraft designed for high-speed flight. The two engines were mounted inside the fuselage and drove a pair of contra-rotating propellers at the tail.
via NARA/Dennis R. Jenkins

The XB-42 was later used as a test bed for the Westinghouse 19XB-2A turbojet. It survived the trials to end up in the Smithsonian. via NARA/Dennis R. Jenkins

co-pilot communication, while the aircraft suffered from yaw, excessive propeller vibration especially when the bomb bay doors were open, poor harmonization of the control forces, and inefficient leading edge cooling ducts.

The second XB-42 prototype, 43-50225, flew on 1 August 1944 and was powered by more powerful V-1710-129 engines. Not long after its first flight the original twin canopies were replaced with a single canopy that was proposed for the production versions of the aircraft. In early December 1945 it was flown from Long Beach, California, to Bolling Field near Washington, DC, at an average speed of 433.6mph (697.7km/h) where it undertook a series of flight trials. However, on 16 December the aircraft crashed near Bolling Field and was completely destroyed; fortunately the crew managed to parachute to safety. While the XB-42 had delivered on its promises the USAAF had decided not to put it into production as the end of the war had made it possible to wait for more advanced, higher-performance jet-powered bombers that were already on the drawing boards of the various aircraft manufacturers.

The surviving XB-42 was allocated to various test purposes. One of the modifications undertaken on the surviving XB-42 was the replacement of the original V-1710-125 engines by a pair of Allison-133 engines rated at 1,375hp. In addition, a pair of Westinghouse 19XB-2A axial-flow turbojets rated at 1,600lb (7.1kN) were installed underneath the wings. After these changes the aircraft was redesignated as the XB-42A and

flew for the first time in its new guise at Muroc Dry Lake, California on 27 May 1947. A total of twenty-two flights with the XB-42A were undertaken by the Douglas flight-test crews, accounting for a total of seventeen hours in the air. A maximum speed of 488mph (785km/h) was achieved during these flight tests. On 15 August 1947 the XB-42A made a hard landing in the tail-down position, damaging the lower vertical stabilizer and lower rudder. After this incident the aircraft was returned to Santa Monica late in 1947 for modifications to the jet nacelles. The remainder of the XB-42 modification programme was cancelled in August 1948, after which the XB-42A was struck off charge on 30 June 1949. Instead of being scrapped it was turned over to the National Air and Space Museum and kept at the museum's storage facility in Park Ridge, Illinois. In April 1959, the fuselage of the XB-42A was moved to the Paul Garber restoration facility in Maryland, although the wings have apparently been lost somewhere along the line.

Throughout World War Two both fighter and bomber manufacturers not only delivered the machines needed to fight the war, but were able to develop numerous experimental prototypes to develop both types of aircraft even further, especially when the intelligence gathered from a fallen Germany was absorbed. Although some were unusual in shape, the following decades saw even more bizarre aircraft emerge as aerodynamic and powerplant challenges were conquered.

Index